**THE STANLEY THORNES**
**TEACHING PRIMARY ENGLISH SERIES**

SERIES EDITOR
**JENI RILEY**

# Teaching
# Writing

JUN 2022

ΓHDRAWN

## at Key Stage 1
## and Before

**ANN BROWNE**

**STANLEY THORNES (PUBLISHERS) LTD**

First published in 1999 by
Stanley Thornes (Publishers) Ltd
Ellenborough House
Wellington Street
Cheltenham
GL50 1YW
UK

ISBN 0 7487 4041 4

99 00 01 02 03 / 10 9 8 7 6 5 4 3 2 1


Typeset by
The Florence Group, Stoodleigh, Devon
Northern Phototypesetting Co Ltd., Bolton

Printed and bound in Great Britain by
Martins the Printers Ltd., Berwick upon Tweed

# Contents

# The Teaching Primary English series

The importance of literacy for individuals and society cannot be overstated. This series of six complementary volumes supports the Government's initiatives to raise standards in reading and writing. At the individual level, literacy determines personal growth, quality of life, self-image and the ability to function in the world. Being literate opens up opportunities, in an increasingly information-rich world, to access knowledge, to make choices and to achieve self-fulfilment. At national level, the smooth functioning and economic prosperity of a society depends upon a well-educated, flexible and highly skilled workforce.

> Literacy is fundamental to thinking, to formal education, and to life-long learning. The link between high levels of literacy and academic success occurs, initially, through allowing individuals access to the curriculum, and secondly, through enabling them to achieve success educationally (McGaw, Long, Morgan and Rosier, 1989).

## THE NEED FOR HIGHER LEVELS OF LITERACY

Schools continually strive to maintain literacy standards, but with higher and higher levels of literacy required by modern society, more is demanded of them. Reading and writing have become even more crucial with the increased use of information and communications technology, although the production and form of texts are changing with the advent of fax, e-mail and the Internet. More has to be done to enable teachers to meet the greater demands placed upon them.

## THE IMPORTANCE OF PRIMARY EDUCATION IN IMPROVING STANDARDS OF LITERACY

Primary schools and, in particular, the early years of education, are key to the success of any literacy drive. There is a body of research evidence that supports the claim that the foundations of literacy are laid in the first two years of school. I have argued elsewhere that a positive early start to school benefits pupils for the whole of their school careers (Riley, 1996). Furthermore, researchers in Australia suggest that efforts to correct literacy difficulties after the third grade (year) are largely unsuccessful:

> Students who fail to make progress in literacy during the first two years of school rarely catch up with their peers and are at risk of becoming low achievers who are alienated with school and drop out at the earliest opportunity.

> (Kennedy, Birman and Demaline, 1986)

Conversely, there is empirical evidence that supports the view that it is possible for all children, except a very small percentage, to be successfully taught to read and write (Piluski, 1994). This encouraging evidence comes from the evaluations of the effectiveness of whole-school programmes such as *Success for All* (Slavin *et al.*, 1996) and an intervention programme, *Reading Recovery* (Hurry, 1995).

## HOW ARE LITERACY STANDARDS TO BE RAISED?

It is clear from the American and Australian experience that class teachers cannot raise literacy standards alone and simply by working harder (Crevola and Hill, 1998). However, dramatic improvements can be achieved with comprehensive programmes that embrace 'system and school-wide commitment and co-ordination' (ibid.).

As Crevola and Hill (1998) suggest, the principles that underpin comprehensive initiatives to raise standards of literacy are that:

- there needs to be an attitude shift. High expectations and a belief that all children can be successful are the essential first step
- there is a need for a detailed, systematic and on-going record of progress to be kept on every pupil. This information guides decision-making regarding identification of, and intervention relating to, children 'at risk' and monitoring the teaching and learning of all
- teaching needs to be targeted at raising standards of literacy. Such a requirement demands teachers who are well trained and who understand the literacy process; additional in-service opportunities are needed to support class teachers in their development of new modes of pedagogy and co-ordinating the programme across the school
- intervention programmes need to be available for the children who, despite effective teaching, fail to make progress
- strong links need to be in place between schools and their pupils' homes and communities.

Concern was identified by the Labour Party's Literacy Task Force in 1996, and the National Literacy Strategy, with the above characteristics, was planned and introduced in the United Kingdom in September 1998. As well as the introduction of this programme, initial teacher education received increasingly prescriptive directives on how the country's primary teachers should be trained (DfEE Circulars 10/97 and 4/98).

## THE SERIES

### The underlying principle

> ... that almost all children will become literate more easily and fully if they are given systematic help which is based on a good understanding of the nature of the enterprise but which never fails to respect them as individual learners.

> (Donaldson, 1993, p. 57)

This series of six complementary and interconnecting volumes reaffirms a wide and balanced ideological base for teaching language and literacy in primary schools and one that builds on existing successful provision. Such a view of the teaching and learning of English is informed by research evidence and established educational principles. The books aim to provide primary teacher educators, primary teachers and students with the knowledge, understanding and skills that are required to teach English effectively and imaginatively in primary classrooms. The intention is also to view reading in a wide frame of reference. The series dovetails reading with writing into literacy and sees them as integral with and inseparable from speaking and listening.

### Previous influences on the teaching of English

Concern about literacy standards in primary schools has been the driving force for the government initiatives referred to earlier. The teaching of English has been the source of much debate, and the recipient of fruitful and abundant research. Important initiatives such as the National Curriculum, the National Writing Project, the National Oracy Project and the LINC (Language in the National Curriculum) Project have contributed to the advancement of thinking to its present position regarding the teaching and learning of speaking and listening, reading and writing. There is a great deal to be understood by primary teachers to enable them to teach English well; and the support of literacy particularly in the early years of school requires great skill and a rich knowledge base of the theory which informs understanding and underpins practice.

## The DfEE Circulars and the National Literacy Strategy

This series readily acknowledges the need for DfEE Circulars 10/97 and 4/98 and the value of the introduction of the National Literacy Strategy. For the first time in history all teacher education institutions will be designing courses of initial teacher education that have the same starting points for English, mathematics and science. All students will be taught how to teach the core subjects of the National Curriculum from the same viewpoints with the same emphases and using the same content. No longer is there room for personal preferences, ideologies or flights of fancy. The National Literacy Strategy provides in considerable detail the content to be covered by teachers at different stages of primary education, stipulating when and how it is to be addressed. This unification and prescription of the English curriculum and how it is to be taught will have an immense effect on primary teachers and their professional functioning. Whilst some will mourn the loss of the greater autonomy of the past, many will find the framework and the structure supportive and enabling. Pupils remaining in the same school, or moving from school to school, will benefit from the consistency of approach, and the clearly thought-out progression of teaching.

The above introduction might seem to render unnecessary a series of books on the teaching and learning of language and literacy. The authors would like to argue exactly the reverse; we consider that these government initiatives require a series of volumes to expand on the documents, to explain them from a theoretical standpoint and to provide an academic rationale for the practice suggested. I have suggested elsewhere (Riley, 1996) that teachers have to be extraordinarily knowledgeable about the processes involved if they are to enable their pupils to become effective users of spoken and written language.

Teachers are not technicians, they are professionals making complex and finely tuned judgements that inform their teaching. Primary teachers cannot be given the equivalent of a painting-by-numbers kit and told to teach it. This is as unthinkable as a surgeon being given a step-by-step guide on how to conduct a heart operation. Both require a thorough and deep understanding of what is involved, the processes at work and sound direction regarding proven successful practice. These volumes aim to flesh out the theoretical references that underpin the thinking, to fill in the gaps in the explanations so that teachers are better able to implement the National Literacy Strategy with confidence and genuine understanding.

## PSYCHOLOGICAL PROCESSES AT WORK WHEN READING

The view of literacy held by this series is one based firmly on the evidence of psychological research.

The starting point for these volumes is that literacy is an inter-related process and needs to be taught in a balanced way: that is a way that takes into account the different aspects of the processing. This perspective is the one adopted by the government initiatives. Teachers, we believe, in order to teach reading effectively, need to have an understanding of the processing which takes place in order for an individual to be able to read.

Any methods of teaching reading that aim to be comprehensive need to look for an explanation of the literacy process that accounts for its complexity. Figure I.1 demonstrates the inter-relatedness of the different processes involved.

**Figure I.1**
*The inter-relatedness of the reading process*

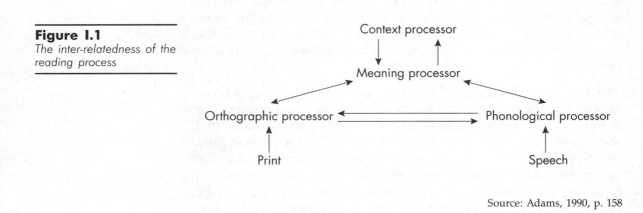

Source: Adams, 1990, p. 158

This diagram shows how the two main strategies of reading work together to help the reader make sense of the text. The two strategies are the so-called 'top-down' processing and the 'bottom-up' processing of text.

### Top-down processing skills

It can be seen from the Adams diagram that at the centre of the act of reading lies meaning-making, which fulfils the whole purpose of the activity. The context of the grammar and the meaning allows the reader to be supported in the task of decoding by being primed to expect what words might come next. The use of context is described as top-down processing and is in turn supported by the child's knowledge of the world, the story as a whole, the cover, the illustrations and the format of the book.

## Bottom-up processing skills: sound awareness and print awareness

In order to read text, readers have to realise that there is a connection between the sounds that are spoken and the written marks on the page. Very crudely and simply this is the understanding that there is a written code (the alphabet) that represents the sounds of speech. There are various stages of progress as readers work towards this understanding.

On the way to learning to read, the child has to be able to hear and distinguish between the different words and then to discriminate between the constituent sounds in words (phonemic segmentation). These are then decoded from the letters and groups of letters on the printed page. The child who has this ability is said to understand grapheme–phoneme (letter–sound) correspondence. This aspect of reading is shown clearly in Figure I.1. An appreciation of the visual aspects of print (orthographic processing) and the identification of the aural sounds of spoken language (phonological processing) develops side by side, and the inter-relationship ensures that each complements the other. This processing is referred to as bottom-up or decoding skills.

Both top-down and bottom-up processing strategies have to be functioning if children are to learn to read successfully and speedily. Teachers need to know how to teach reading so that the whole processing system is developed and can operate effectively. This is the important principle that underpins the series and the two books on the teaching of reading in particular (*Teaching Reading at Key Stage 1 and Before* and *Teaching Reading at Key Stage 2*).

The authors of the volumes reaffirm their belief that:

> Means must be found to ensure that all children's first experiences of reading and writing are purposeful and enjoyable. Only in this way will they be drawn into applying their meaning-making strategies to the task of making sense of written language. Only in this way will they learn to exploit the full symbolic potential of language and so become fully literate.

> (Wells, 1987, p. 162)

Jeni Riley, Series Editor
January 1999

**References**

Adams, M. J. (1990) *Beginning to Read: Thinking and Learning about Print*, MIT Press, Cambridge, Massachusetts

Crevola, C. A. and Hill, P. W. (1998) 'Evaluation of a whole-school approach to prevention and intervention in early literacy', *Journal of Education for Students Placed at Risk*, 3 (2), 133–57

DfEE (1997) Circular 10/97 and DfEE (1998) Circular 4/98, *Teaching: High Status, High Standards*, DfEE, London

Donaldson, M. (1989) 'Sense and sensibility: some thoughts on the teaching of literacy', Occasional Paper No. 3, Reading and Language Information Centre, University of Reading. Reprinted in R. Beard (ed.) (1993) *Teaching Literacy: Balancing Perspectives*, Hodder and Stoughton, London

Hurry, J. (1995) 'What is so special about Reading Recovery?' *Curriculum Journal*, 7 (1), 93–108

Kennedy, M. M., Birman, B. F. and Demaline, R. E. (1986) *The Effectiveness of Chapter 1 Services*, Office of Educational Research and Improvement, US Department of Education, Washington, DC

McGaw, B., Long, M. G., Morgan, G. and Rosier, M. J. (1989) *Literacy and Numeracy in Australian Schools*, ACER Research Monograph No. 34, ACER, Hawthorn, Victoria

Piluski, J. J. (1994) 'Preventing reading failure: a review of five effective programmes', *Reading Teacher*, 48, 31–9

Riley, J. L. (1996) *The Teaching of Reading: The Development of Literacy in the Early Years of School*, Paul Chapman Publishing, London

Slavin, R. E., Madden, N. A., Dolan, N. J., Wasik, B. J., Ross, S. M., Smith, L. J. and Dianda, M.(1996) 'Success for all: a summary of research', *Journal of Education for Students Placed at Risk*, 1, 41–76

Wells, C. G. (1987) *The Meaning Makers: Children Learning Language and Using Language to Learn*, Hodder and Stoughton, London

**Acknowledgements**

A number of people have provided me with advice and encouragement during the writing of this book. I would like to acknowledge their contribution and in particular thank Ian Browne, Neal Marriott and Jeni Riley.

The author and publishers would also like to thank the MIT Press for permission to reproduce the figure on page viii. Every effort has been made to contact copyright holders, and we apologise if any have been overlooked.

# About writing 1

*When you have read this chapter you should:*

- understand some of the functions of writing

- understand the processes involved in writing

- appreciate the conditions which enable writers to write effectively

- be aware of a range of writing types.

To become an adept and confident writer involves learning how to write and learning about writing. Fluent writers are at ease with the writing system and know when and how to use writing in their lives. This chapter begins by examining the uses of writing. It then looks at how writing is produced and the stages a piece of writing passes through before it is completed. The later sections of the chapter describe the conditions which enable writers to write appropriately and show how knowledge about the processes of writing and the context in which each piece of writing is under-taken influence the form and presentation of text. This chapter introduces readers to the background knowledge within which the activity of teaching children how to write needs to be set.

## THE FUNCTIONS OF WRITING

When thinking about writing it is helpful to make a distinction between writing as an activity and writing as a set of symbols and conventions. Separating the activity from the system helps us to consider the following questions:

- What is writing for?
- How does writing work?

These are questions that anyone might ask about something that is unfamiliar to them, and they are likely to be asked in this order. If we do not see the use of an item we are unlikely to bother to learn how to use it.

## How writing works

Mastering the art of writing involves learning a great many things about the system and how to manipulate it. It entails learning to:

- use writing implements
- write legibly
- spell correctly
- use punctuation
- satisfy grammatical rules
- take account of an audience
- construct and organise texts
- select from a range of styles.

There is a great deal to know about writing in order to be able to make the system work, and adults are very conscious of how much young children need to learn about the conventions of writing. For that reason much of this book is concerned with explaining how to equip children with the skills and knowledge that will enable them to write. However, there is more to writing and becoming an effective writer than knowing how to operate the system. We need to know what the system is for.

## What writing can do

Writing has a number of uses and has an important functional role in our lives. The visible form of written language means that it provides ideas and thoughts with a degree of permanence and enables meaning to be conveyed to others or recorded without being constrained by distance or time. As a method of communication writing can be used to establish and maintain contact with others, transmit information, express thoughts, feelings and reactions, entertain and persuade. As a personal or private activity it can be a powerful tool for learning and remembering. It can be used to explore and refine ideas, organise thoughts and record information. In school writing often has another role. Children are asked to use writing to display what they know, and writing is usually the medium through which pupil learning is measured.

When children have been asked about why they are learning to write their replies frequently show that they have a very limited understanding of what writing is for. They know more about how adults use their writing to make judgements about them than they do about the other functions of writing. The reasons that children give for writing at school include: 'because the teacher tells us to' and 'so we don't get told off' (National Writing Project, 1990; Wray, 1994). They know more about the system of writing than they know about the activity, describing good writers as those who spell well

and present their work neatly. They rarely talk about writing in terms of its real-world uses.

Understanding what something can do and being convinced of its usefulness is the starting point for finding out how it works. Knowing how to make something work does not guarantee that it will be used unless it is regarded as personally useful. It is for this reason that this section about the functions of writing occurs at the beginning of this book. Lessons about the contribution that writing can make, immediately and in the long term, to the personal, social, emotional, cognitive and functional areas of everyone's life need to accompany the lessons children are given about the system. Since writing is a powerful tool for living and learning young learners need to be shown what writing can do as well as how to do it.

## THE PROCESS OF WRITING

The act of writing involves three important elements:

- composition
- transcription
- review.

All writing passes through these three stages at least once. Simple writing, such as a note to the milk deliverer, is given some thought (**composition**), is written (**transcription**) and is quickly read through to make sure that it conveys the writer's message clearly (**review**). More significant writing, such as a letter to a newspaper, may go through each stage several times. Each stage does not necessarily take place discretely. Writers continue to compose and engage in reviewing their writing as they transcribe as well as reviewing and editing their work after it seems complete. When we write, we:

> ... plan, gather materials, search our memories, imagine our audience, make decisions about form, tone or structure, seek for the right word or image, check back over what is written, ponder about outcomes, revise and correct. However, we are rarely, if ever, doing these things one at a time.

> (Protherough, 1983, p. 146)

As composition, transcription and review are the writing processes that all writers use, it is important that children are introduced to each of these aspects, taught the strategies needed to undertake each stage and given time to undertake each part of the process.

**composition**
the act of making decisions about content, style and organisation

**transcription**
the secretarial aspects of writing, including spelling, handwriting and punctuation, which are used to record what is composed

**review**
the act of reflecting on what has been written, often resulting in changes to aspects of composition and transcription

**audience**
the recipient of a piece of writing

**setting**
the context in which a narrative is located

**purpose**
the author's reason for undertaking a piece of writing

## Composition

Composing involves making decisions about the content of writing. There are two parts to this: first, generating ideas, and second, selecting what to include in order to meet the demands of a particular task most effectively. While at this stage the emphasis might be on thinking about content, intending authors may also be thinking about style and format. The nature of what they are writing, its purpose, its **audience** and the type of text that they are producing will shape the ideas that emerge. For example, if embarking on writing a fairy tale an author will not only be thinking about characters, events, **settings**, openings and endings but will also be thinking about these in relation to the typical characteristics of fairy tales, such as their location in an imaginary past time and the tradition that the small, vulnerable or young character usually triumphs. The age and experience of the audience will influence the choice of vocabulary and the number of complications that are included in the story. Ideas will be pursued or rejected according to their potential interest and their suitability for the **purpose**. This act of brainstorming is often recorded as notes or in a list. When all the writer's thoughts are exhausted the notes are reviewed, some ideas may be abandoned and different ones added. The writer then begins to organise the content so that it fits the conventions of the type of writing. It is only when these preliminary but vital activities have been completed that the writer can begin to write.

Children should not learn that once the topic for writing has been identified the next step is to immediately write down everything that they know or think in connected prose and then keep writing until they run out of ideas. This may lead to quantity but is unlikely to result in quality. Teachers need to help children understand that composition is not just about the physical act of putting pen or pencil to paper. It begins with understanding what is to be written, to whom and in what way. It then involves a period of thought and making a brief record of ideas. These ideas need to be considered, changed, added to, deleted and sequenced in order to produce a plan or a first attempt. Even at the transcription stage, when using a plan to produce a first draft, the writer still needs to think about what is being written and how, and is free to introduce changes as the writing emerges. Re-reading and discussing the first draft may lead to further thoughts about composition. Although composition is one of the processes involved in producing writing it can continue during the transcription and review stages.

## Transcription

This is the process of converting composition into marks on the page using recognisable spelling, readable handwriting, punctuation,

grammar and layout. It is dependent on composition since the way in which some aspects of transcription are used depends on the content, format and style of what is written. Transcribing is a time-consuming part of writing and can be difficult for young children, particularly if teachers give it more attention than it merits. Focusing too much on transcription deflects attention from composition. If children are to represent their ideas successfully in writing they need to be given support that eases this part of the process. Writers generally concentrate on transcription after writing a first draft and before a final copy is made.

## Review

Very little writing is perfect after a first draft because writing what we intend in the best possible way is difficult. Reviewing usually involves changing aspects of composition and transcription in order to improve what we have written. Introducing young children to this last part of the process of writing is often neglected, particularly in the early years. Teachers are often reluctant to ask young children to re-read and alter their writing. They may think that after children have put a great deal of effort into composing and transcribing some writing they deserve a well-earned rest. Children, like all writers, may readily agree with this view. However, if children have spent time and taken care with a piece of writing, there is all the more reason to review what they have produced. At this stage the writing should merit re-reading and afford the child the opportunity to enjoy and take pride in what they have written. If changes are needed to make the writing more interesting, clearer and more accessible to others it is worth making these, particularly as the hardest work, that involved in composing and transcribing, has already been done. Teachers who omit the review stage may themselves believe that writing is difficult, rather than demanding but satisfying, and may be teaching children to endure writing rather than enjoy it. They may also be demanding the impossible by asking for a best copy from the start. It has been suggested that they are issuing children with a 'Mastermind challenge' by implying 'try to be right first time: don't pass on any item; do as well as you can in the short time available; don't stop to correct your first attempt' (Martin *et al.*, 1989, p. 102). Not only is this unrealistic, it denies children the opportunity to write like real authors who are well aware of the usefulness of the review stage. When planning writing activities it is important to allow sufficient time for children to undertake the three stages of writing, and when responding to children's efforts to analyse how they have approached composition, transcription and review. This is in line with the Key Stage 1 National Curriculum Orders for English, which require pupils to

'have opportunities to plan and review their writing' and to 'assemble and develop their ideas' (DfE, 1995, p. 9).

**Activity**     Think about a piece of writing that you did recently. Identify the stages your writing went through from your first intention to write to the final draft. Can you match some of these processes to the ideas in the preceding section of this chapter? Does your own experience of the processes involved in writing have implications for the way you organise for writing in school?

## CONDITIONS FOR WRITING

### Purpose

Purpose describes the author's reason for undertaking a piece of writing. In the world outside school this will generally coincide with one of the many functions of writing, but in the classroom there may be a difference. This is because at school the teacher usually initiates writing activities and the children write because they have been asked to rather than because they have decided to write to fulfil a real and important purpose of their own.

In general, learners learn most effectively when they understand the reasons for developing the skill that they are learning and when they are aware of the uses of that skill. They benefit from understanding why they are doing something as well as knowing what they are doing. Whenever possible children need to engage in writing activities that have a genuine purpose that they recognise as relevant and that is made explicit to them. Adults need to involve children in writing activities which explore the different uses of writing and make sure that these make sense to young children.

### Audience

Since writing is, for the most part, a communicative activity it has both an author and an audience. Before beginning to write authors need to know not only why they are writing but also who will read their writing. We write for ourselves, family members, friends, acquaintances and people who are unknown to us. As experienced writers write they recognise the relationship that exists between the author and the audience. This may depend on the relative age and status of the writer and the recipient, but it may also depend on the nature of what is written. It is possible to write to a known audience informally when sending holiday postcards or formally when inviting them to important events such as weddings. The tenor of the

relationship between authors and audiences can be friendly, hostile, intimate, correct, cautious or polite. Knowing about the audience has a number of implications. It affects what is written, how it is presented, the time that is spent on it and even the choice of writing implement. When writing to an unknown audience or formally to a known audience writers may take a great deal of care to organise the content, present information clearly, ensure that the writing is legible and that words are used accurately and spelt correctly. Such writing might be drafted a number of times and shown to others to be checked before the author is satisfied. Children need to experience communicating with as wide a range of audiences as possible in order to learn how to write in different ways and to suit their writing to the situation and the reader if they are to use writing well in and out of school. With thoughtful planning teachers can offer children a range of audiences for their writing, as Table 1.1 indicates.

## Outcome

Outcome means what happens to writing when it is finished. It is linked to the purpose of the writing, why it was undertaken and whom it was intended for. Writing can be read by others, replied to, kept as something worth re-reading at a later date or used as a starting point for a talk or a discussion. A frequent outcome for writing is the waste paper basket. Once writing has served its purpose it is generally disposed of. Making this clear to children can help them to realise that writing does not always have to be undertaken with trepidation. The apparent permanence of writing can lead to anxieties that curtail risk-taking and experiment and lead to the 'getting it right first time' syndrome. Of course we would not want to throw away all the writing that children do. This could be very discouraging to them, and much of their writing will have been intended to have a permanent outcome on displays and in class books. However, once children begin to write at greater length and with greater ease it is worth discussing what is worth keeping and what can be discarded without devaluing what the writer has done. Outcome also influences decisions about drafting. Not every piece of writing is worthy of redrafting. Those which are intended to have a public or permanent outcome probably are but others may be left after the first draft and review stage.

| Self | Teacher | Peers | Other known audiences | Unknown audiences |
|------|---------|-------|-----------------------|-------------------|
| notes | maths story | first draft | class dictionary | letter seeking information |
| journals | drafts | books | letter to parents | competition entries |

**Table 1.1**
*Possible audience for writing at school*

Examine some recent examples of one child's writing. Can you identify the purpose, audience and outcome for each piece? How varied were these? Can you think of ways to widen the range of purposes, audiences and outcomes for this child?

## TYPES OF WRITING

In the past the primary school writing curriculum has been criticised for allocating too much time to personal writing while neglecting to teach children to use writing to convey information or to craft and develop their imaginative writing. The National Literacy Strategy *Framework for Teaching* (DfEE, 1998) expects schools to place a strong emphasis on non-fiction and literary writing and includes many experiences that are necessary for children to become familiar with these modes. Britton (1972) wrote of the expressive, transactional and poetic forms of writing, each with a different range of functions and styles. **Expressive writing** is often the first to develop as it closely resembles speech. **Transactional writing** is more impersonal and **poetic writing** more finely crafted than expressive writing, and so they tend to develop later and need to be taught and learned systematically.

### Expressive writing

Expressive writing is personal and can be used to record feelings and impressions or clarify ideas. It is typically found in anecdotes, notes and journal entries. The earliest writing that children produce is usually in the expressive mode. They often use writing to represent their experiences and, appreciating that writing, like speaking, is a way of communicating, are often eager to tell others what their writing says. Children may tell adults that their writing 'is about my dog'. Teachers of young children capitalise on these very personal communications by encouraging children to write about their favourite toys or TV programmes, to describe their holidays and to record their news, encouraging children to write sentences such as 'This is my dog' or 'I like playing with my dog'. This kind of writing exploits the relationship between speech and writing by showing that what is said can be written down, and draws attention to the communicative purpose of writing, both of which are helpful to children who are just beginning to find out what writing is for and how speech and ideas can be represented on paper.

However, expressive writing has limited application in the world outside school and its overuse in the classroom can lead to a

**expressive writing**
informal writing in the first person

**transactional writing**
writing used to convey or record facts

**poetic writing**
carefully crafted writing often intended to interest, stimulate or entertain others

restricted and tedious curriculum. While there are parallels between the uses of talking and writing we would rarely write something down when it could be told to someone who is in the same room. Writing is rarely used if speech can be used instead, largely because it demands more care and is more time consuming. Tann has suggested that 'what can be said in 1 minute . . . takes 6 minutes to write' (1991, p. 175). In school children are sometimes asked to write something that would normally be communicated orally. Writing down news that has already been shared with peers and the teacher is an example of this. This can confuse children about the distinct uses of writing and does not encourage them to see writing as a means of adding to their existing communicative abilities. Teachers may be familiar with reading a one-sentence summary of a piece of news that earlier had taken two or three minutes to say in a much more exciting or interesting way. When this happens we should recognise that children, rightly, cannot see the point of doing this, and by producing work that is cursory and often careless they are rejecting this writing task. They are asking why they are repeating something that can be and has already been communicated in another way. In school children need to explore authentic uses for writing, so the range of writing they are asked to undertake should be wide and mirror the way that writing is really used.

Rather than asking young children to write down experiences that have already been shared orally, teachers who work with young children in the nursery or reception class can continue to develop children's understanding of the expressive function of writing by examining all the uses of this mode. Personal journals, writing notes to friends and making predictions about investigations and experiments all involve using expressive writing for different purposes and audiences.

## Transactional writing

Non-fiction writing is impersonal and is used to convey information through reports, records and notices. A balanced writing programme includes opportunities for children to learn how to write factual texts. Early years teachers are expected to introduce children to recognising and writing non-fiction so that this type of writing can continue to be developed throughout the primary years. The most obvious form of information writing that very young children see and write are labels and signs, such as 'The Book Area' and 'Three children can play in the sand'. From this children should gradually be introduced to more complex, extended non-fiction writing including recipes, instructions and accounts (DfEE, 1998). Writing non-fiction usually takes place across the curriculum as a

part of learning about science, geography and history. It is rarely undertaken for its own sake. Its central function is to convey information clearly and accurately and it often includes lists, headings and diagrams. In order to write well in this way children need to be clear about the purpose and audience for the writing and the ways in which the form, style and language differ from expressive and literary texts.

## Poetic writing

The function of poetic or literary writing is to entertain through careful attention to vocabulary, style and structure, and examples include stories, poems, plays and songs. The starting point for developing poetic writing is storying. When we talk we often share experiences with others in story form: 'Last Tuesday, just as I was going out, the telephone rang and . . . ' is the beginning of a story even though it is an account of a real experience. Children are familiar with this way of using language from their own oral experiences. However, stories in books are not just anecdotes in story form or 'talk written down' (Stauffer, 1980). They are usually third-person, fictional **narratives** which have been composed and crafted with care in order to entertain others. Through frequent book-sharing sessions, stories become so familiar to children and teachers that it is easy to underestimate how difficult it can be to write them. Many people have analysed stories and identified the essential elements they contain (Applebee, 1978). A simple form of the many story grammars that have been described indicates what writers need to know in order to write stories well. They need to appreciate that stories have

**narrative**
a text which relates a series of events, often in chronological order

- an opening
- an ending
- plot
- structure
- characters
- setting
- a narrative voice.

Many stories written by children start in a rush with the writer as the central character, contain a list of 'and thens' and suddenly peter out. Or they contain a collection of unrelated items and events. This can happen because children have not thought their story through or made a plan before starting to write, or are not clear about story forms. They may not appreciate that one of the characteristics of writing is that it offers the writer the time and opportunity to reflect on what is to be communicated and how it will be transmitted, and they can take their time to think about the content and the

organisation of their writing. It is important to make this clear. Children can be helped to write good stories by examining texts by well-known children's authors to see how they have used the six elements of story grammar in their writing. By doing this and ensuring that children plan and draft their writing adults will place children in a better position to produce truly satisfying, high-quality stories that will merit a permanent place in the class reading area or school library.

### Openings and endings

All stories have a beginning and a resolution. The opening has to signal that what follows is a story rather than a report or a list. 'Once upon a time' or 'One day' are frequently used by young children to give this signal. However, openings are more complicated than this. They often establish the characters and the setting and may signal the type of story that is to follow. Examining how some familiar stories begin reveals that authors introduce the reader to their stories in many different ways. The following examples show writers using quite clear opening statements to identify characters, settings and times.

> Monday was a bad day in Mrs Lather's laundry.

(Ahlberg, 1981)

> It was Saturday, and Jo wanted to go out.

(Bradman, 1988)

Isolating endings can be equally revealing.

> After all – *what could be worse than an elephant?*

(Ahlberg, 1981)

> Jo and her mum laughed. 'You'll have to wait and see!'

(Bradman, 1988)

Very few stories end with 'it was all a dream' or 'and then I woke up', or even 'they all lived happily ever after'. The range of possibilities is much greater than this. Whilst the aim of an ending is to bring about a satisfactory resolution to a sequence of events it may also be surprising or humorous or leave the reader with something more to think about.

### Plot

Even very young children appreciate that things happen in stories. They learn this from all the experiences they have had when sharing books with others. Involving the class when sharing a known text is often a time when children are given demonstrations that stories contain events. Adults frequently pause as they read aloud and ask questions such as 'What's going to happen next . . . ?' and 'What will happen in the end . . . ?' Children show their understanding of plot when they tell stories as they look at wordless picture books and retell familiar stories using the pictures as a prompt.

What they find harder to demonstrate in their own writing is the connection between events. Applebee (1978) found that these connections need to be made through chaining (events related to each other) and centring (events related to the same character or issue). For example, in *Mrs Lather's Laundry* (Ahlberg, 1981) the events all follow on from Mrs Lather's bad day and describe the various solutions she tries in an effort to have good days. The events are related to the central character and to her problem. The following example shows a child struggling with the idea of chaining and centring.

> One day the little girl had a dog. It was black. She met her uncle. She liked her dog.

Here the events are not necessarily related to each other, and although they relate to the central character as there is no issue in the plot they appear discrete and do not make a satisfactory story.

### Structure
Besides thinking about the content of their stories authors also have to organise the events so that they lead logically to the resolution. Often this means ordering events chronologically over the course of a day, a week, a year. Children's use of a series of 'and thens' shows them experimenting with, but not usually in control of, this idea. After the opening the story moves on to the events. The first event might be quite simple then, because stories generally contain a problem which has to resolved; the events become more compli-cated and the final event resolves the problem. Each event follows on from the one before. For example, in *Mrs Lather's Laundry* the initiating event is Mrs Lather's refusal to wash laundry; the conse-quence is the increasingly bizarre things she does wash. This leads to the next problem, which is that now Mrs Lather does not want to wash anything and the final solution is to close the laundry and begin again next week.

### Characterisation
Characters are an integral part of stories. The number of books that include a character's name in the title and the way children ask

adults to tell them 'the one about Jack' or 'the one about Jo' testify to their importance. There are a number of ways in which writers can portray characters in stories. They may select from a character type such as a princess or a monster, or they can describe how characters look, their behaviour, their conversation or their thoughts. The way in which the events in a story proceed is often related to the kind of character at its centre, and decisions about characterisation should influence the choices that are made about events, consequences and endings. At the simplest level this may mean that giants and monsters frighten people and little children do kind deeds.

*Setting*

Very often the context for stories in books for young children is provided or supported by the illustrations. This could be why it is common to find the setting implied through the use of phrases such as 'going out' or 'coming round' rather than described in many stories written by children. Such phrases mean that the reader has to assume that the context is the character's home. All stories take place in a particular location and at a particular time, and this can be important for the story and to the reader. The setting provides the backdrop and gives readers clues about the type of story they are reading. The type of narrative, whether it is a traditional tale or a contemporary story, affects the setting. The choice of location – a palace, a forest, a living room or outer space – is likely to influence the behaviour of the character and the type of events that are included in the story. Learning about the importance of including details about place and time can widen children's appreciation of the differences between speech and writing. By thinking about what the audience needs to know and realising that the reader will not necessarily have the same knowledge as the writer, children may begin to see that written language has to be much more explicit than spoken language.

*Narrative voice*

The third-person 'he' or 'she' is a much more usual way of telling stories than 'I'. Even when 'I' is used the writer is generally reflecting on selected experiences rather than simply recounting them. Writers need to distance themselves from their writing. They need to become spectators rather than participants in the stories they write (Britton, 1972). Moving from the I of the expressive mode into the third-person narrative is something that children have to learn as they extend their story-writing skills. They can find this difficult to use and sustain. It is quite common to read young children's writing that begins with 'she' or 'he' and then lapses into 'I'.

Learning to write stories involves learning to become a narrator who can lead readers into experiences and worlds that are different from their immediate concerns. It necessitates learning about changing fact into fiction. It is much more complicated than is often thought, and children need to be helped to do this well. They need to be given information about how to write stories. They need many opportunities to explore and experiment with the different features of narrative writing separately and within complete stories. Effective story writing rarely develops naturally, but the craft of creating enjoyable narratives can be learned even by young children.

Rhymes, poems, songs and plays are other forms of poetic writing. Like narratives they have particular characteristics that children need to recognise before they can write them. As with stories, nursery rhymes, rhyming texts, poetry and plays need to be read, explored, discussed and modelled by the teacher before children begin to write them effectively for themselves.

## THE FORMS OF WRITING

Although there are three broad categories of writing there are a great many ways in which writing, drawn from each type, can be presented. In the first instance identifying why a piece of writing is being undertaken and what it is for can help the author to think about the way in which it might be presented. Table 1.2 gives an indication of how function affects format. It is based on the National Curriculum and the National Literacy Strategy *Framework for Teaching* requirements for writing at Key Stage 1.

Although the function of writing largely determines the form, it is the content, the relationship between the author and the recipient and the specific use of the writing which enable the writer to make an exact choice about format and language. For example, knowing that writing is being used to give information does not take account of the distinct linguistic demands of writing book reviews or writing a set of rules. Both of these are structured and use language differently. Nor does it identify the differences that arise when the same form is used for different reasons. For example, a book review can be written as a report or to persuade others to read the book. The structure and language of a book report is likely to be different from that used in a text written to encourage others to read the book.

### Genre
Writing can be organised and presented as lists, jottings, notes, labels, journal entries, letters, articles, descriptions, accounts, stories,

| Function | Form |
| --- | --- |
| organise ideas | plans, lists, diagrams |
| develop ideas | drafts, journals, predictions |
| explore ideas | notes |
| communicate personally | letters, postcards, messages |
| record experiences | diary entries |
| explore experiences | descriptions, personal accounts |
| remember | notes, lists, observations, records |
| present information | captions, labelled diagrams, signs, formal letters, book reviews, rules, keys, definitions, posters recipes, instructions, directions, comparisons, arguments, drafts, charts, maps, sequences |
| gather information | questionnaires, notes |
| advise | invitations, explanations, notices |
| persuade | advertisements, book reviews |
| enjoy language | rhymes, alliterative patterns, jokes |
| entertain | stories, poems, riddles, play scripts |

**Table 1.2**
*The relationship between the functions and forms of writing*

advertisements, notices and instructions. These can be written with different audiences in mind, be concerned with many topics and used in varied ways. The combination of the audience, outcome and purpose of the writing affects the way each piece of writing is presented. Genre theory has shown that the way that all language is organised is determined by the social context in which it is used as well as by the purpose of the communication.

The social context takes account of three factors:

- *field:* the content of the exchange
- *tenor:* the relationship between the author and the audience
- *mode:* the use of spoken or written language.

Awareness of these contextual factors enables writers to make decisions about the vocabulary they use and the organisation of the text. Genre theory has clarified the way in which the combination of function and social context results in a text that employs a particular sort of language and is structured in a particular way. The types of writing that result from the interplay between purpose and social context are known as **genres** and each distinct genre is governed by different conventions and has particular characteristics.

**genres**
types of writing with their own specific characteristics which are related to purpose

**register**
the vocabulary and grammar appropriate to a particular genre

## Register

**Register**, the choice of vocabulary and the type of grammatical constructions which contribute to the tone of writing, is related to function, content, audience and the relationship between the author and the recipient. A telephone message is usually recorded briefly in note form. Letters to friends or family members may be quite long, describe events and feelings in some detail, contain advice, comment and opinion and vary in tone from humorous to serious. There may be references to shared experience and interests and overall the letter may reflect the personality of the writer. Poems and rhymes may incorporate unusual or rhyming vocabulary, and words are usually used economically and have been selected with great care.

The analysis of generic structures and their language features is particularly relevant to non-fiction texts. It has raised awareness of what needs to be understood in order to write, discuss and read non-fiction, and by identifying the characteristics of different text types may make it easier for practitioners to identify what children need to learn and what needs to be taught. Table 1.3 shows how the specific function of non-fiction texts, which are often used in school, leads to writing that employs a particular genre or text type and uses a specific register.

Both the National Literacy Strategy *Framework for Teaching* (DfEE, 1998) and the English National Curriculum (DfE, 1995) identify non-fiction writing as an essential element of the Key Stage 1 curriculum and include a number of references to genre.

**Table 1.3**
*Purpose, genre and register in non-fiction writing*

| Purpose | Genre | Register |
|---|---|---|
| to retell events, to inform | recount | chronological order, past tense |
| to describe an object | report | classification, identification of attributes, present tense |
| to describe a process | explanation | temporal and causal connections, sequenced, present tense, passive voice, action verbs |
| to describe how to do something | procedural | may include diagrams, chronological, present tense |
| to present a point of view | persuasion | argument, reasons, present tense |
| to present evidence for and against | discussion | argument, evidence, conclusion, present tense |

**Activity**

Select an article from a magazine or a newspaper. Try to identify the purpose of this text and its genre. Examine the language used in the article to see whether there are patterns in the type of vocabulary it contains.

**Summary**

This chapter has introduced readers to some important research and ideas that have shaped the writing curriculum and the way it is organised in schools today. One of the most significant of these is that children need to recognise the use of writing to themselves and in the world outside the classroom if they are to learn to write easily and well. The processes of composition, transcription and review and the effect that knowledge about the purpose and audience has on what is produced have been described. The final part of the chapter outlined the contribution genre theory has made to our knowledge of writing and our understanding of how to write effectively.

In the next chapter these ideas are related to the documents that practitioners work with: the National Curriculum for English (DfE, 1995), the Desirable Outcomes for Children's Learning (SCAA, 1996) and the National Literacy Strategy *Framework for Teaching* (DfEE, 1998).

*The key points covered in this chapter were:*

- the functions of writing

- the writing processes of composition, transcription and review

- the conditions which enable writers to write effectively

- the range of writing genres commonly used by adults and children

- the characteristics of different types of writing

- what writing is for.

**Further reading**

Czerniewska, P. (1992) *Learning about Writing*, Blackwell, Oxford
 Drawing on the author's experiences as the director of the National Writing Project this book provides a comprehensive overview of the theory of writing as it relates to the classroom.

Graves, D. H. (1983) *Writing: Teachers and Children at Work*, Heinemann Educational Books, Portsmouth, New Hampshire
A classic text which describes the process of writing and the process approach to writing.

Martin, J. (1989) *Factual Writing: Exploring and Challenging Social Reality*, Oxford University Press, Oxford
This book provides a thorough analysis of factual writing and is one of the key texts about genre theory.

Wray, D. (1994) *Literacy and Awareness*, Hodder and Stoughton, London
A book which provides a great deal of useful background information about reading and writing.

# Writing in school 2

**Objectives**

*When you have read this chapter you should:*

● understand how and why the writing curriculum has evolved

● recognise the contribution of research and practitioner experience in its development

● understand how children develop as writers

● appreciate the present statutory requirements for writing

● understand the practices used in schools.

**Introduction**

In schools there are many different ways of teaching children about writing and how to write. Many schools mix established practices with newer ideas. In order to create a writing curriculum which is able to accommodate the individual needs of children and the statutory requirements it is necessary to understand present practice, evaluate it and substitute more effective practices when appropriate.

This chapter takes some of the ideas introduced in Chapter 1 and shows how they have influenced practice. It also describes how they have been incorporated into the Desirable Outcomes for Children's Learning (SCAA, 1996), the National Curriculum for English (DfE, 1995) and the National Literacy Strategy *Framework for Teaching* (DfEE, 1998).

## WRITING AT SCHOOL IN THE 1950s AND 1960s

Learning to write at primary school in the 1950s was characterised by copying from the board, tracing activities, weekly spelling tests, producing regular pieces of 'news' on demand, and occasional opportunities for writing stories and simple rhyming poems. Teaching focused on the product, and correct spelling and neat handwriting were valued. Transcription rather than content was emphasised This was a formal, often dreary and repetitive curriculum where little attempt was made to link writing that was practised in school with the writing demands of everyday life. Learning to write was considered to be difficult by pupils and teachers and there was little expectation that writing could be enjoyed. Many children were expected to fail and many did.

The next decade saw the emergence of the creative writing movement (Clegg, 1964). Here the emphasis was on children producing personal responses to direct stimuli such as music or unusual artefacts. Children were encouraged to express their ideas, feelings and imagination in their writing. Individuality, spontaneity and creativity and the use of vivid and unusual vocabulary were prized. In the main, composition was valued more than transcription. During this period many teachers felt uncertain about their role in the writing development of their pupils. Although they recognised that becoming a writer includes having control of the system, learning techniques, being able to spell, punctuate and write clearly, they worried that their intervention might interfere with creative potential.

## PURPOSE AND AUDIENCE

During the 1970s the limitations which resulted from placing too much emphasis on creative writing were generally acknowledged, and the need for a broader approach to writing was recognised. Britton's (1972) work on the functions of language and audience led to an important shift in the way that writing at school was viewed. He proposed that writing could be categorised into three modes, expressive, transactional and poetic. Expressive writing is personal. It verbalises the inner consciousness of the writer, is relatively unstructured, and is the language that is typically used in diaries or letters to friends. Transactional writing employs the language of 'getting things done'. It is used to give instructions, persuade, advise, record, report and inform. The poetic mode is valued for its artistic merit, including the form, style and choice of vocabulary. Britton also showed the importance of remembering that writing is produced in order to communicate with a range of audiences. His research in schools (Britton *et al.*, 1975) revealed that the audience for most of the writing undertaken by children was the teacher, who often responded by assessing transcription and identifying errors rather than replying to what had been communicated. Britton's work on writing functions and audiences broadened the curriculum in school and continues to be important and influential.

## THE PROCESS APPROACH

The work of Graves (1983) and others throughout the 1980s added to practitioners' understanding of the strategies writers use by examining the processes involved in writing. Before beginning to transcribe, writers compose their writing by thinking about the content of what they are about to write and how they will present their writing. Important pieces of writing are drafted and revised in order to realise the writer's intentions. After a first draft is made this is read through and if necessary altered. Reflection, planning, composition, transcription, revision and editing are important processes in writing. Graves's work showed that in order to learn to write well children need to learn about the processes that are available to them and need to be given time to move through each stage if they are to produce a complete and satisfying piece of writing. Within this movement, establishing purposes and audiences for writing continued to be important and transcription skills were seen as having a supporting rather than a dominant place in the writing curriculum. As children do not automatically learn about writing through their own efforts, the teacher's role was to pass on knowledge about the craft of writing and provide guidance that was closely related to children's needs.

## DEVELOPMENTAL WRITING

The **process approach** to teaching writing coincided with research that revealed that even very young children know a great deal about writing and that they can and do produce unaided writing that demonstrates their understanding of the system (Clay, 1975; Ferreiro and Teberosky, 1983). Similar studies of children's early mark-making and writing have added to our appreciation of how young children make determined and intelligent attempts to explore the writing system and become writers (Kress, 1997). They have revealed how children's early experiments with writing are an important first step in the development of literacy. Research that has looked at the changes in children's writing over time has shown how independent practice and exposure to writing enables children to refine their experiments and produce writing that gradually approximates to conventional models. When teachers recognised that the ability to write develops when children are encouraged to write independently many of them rethought their approach to writing. They could see that it was not necessary to train children in transcription and limit their early writing to copying under adult writing. Instead they created a climate in which children were encouraged to write alone and where adults provided support and guidance rather than instruction. Teaching children to write through working with them on their independently produced writing to extend their existing knowledge and abilities is known as a **developmental approach** to writing (Temple *et al.*, 1993).

**process approach**
a way of organising the teaching of writing so that children are introduced to and use all the stages involved in producing a piece of written text

**developmental approach**
teaching children to write by first analysing what they can do alone and then working with them on their independently produced writing

Children learn through their experiences and observations. From the earliest stages all children gain some experience of writing through seeing adults around them produce and use writing and noticing examples of writing in their environment. They often begin to experiment with producing marks that are intended to represent writing. They try out the patterns of writing initially because it seems to be a satisfying activity (Dyson, 1983) and then later they begin to attribute meaning to their marks. These early child-initiated experiments with writing are now recognised as being the earliest stages of learning to write. As children produce more writing and take more notice of print their own writing shows an increasing resemblance to that produced by mature writers. Their early attempts at writing reveal how they learn to manipulate the principles of the writing system which are fundamental to becoming a writer (Clay, 1975).

Children's earliest writing often contains shapes that are repeated. These may look like letters but can also take the form of joined-up scribble. At this stage children are imitating the behaviour of writers they have observed and trying to reproduce the written symbols they have seen them produce. Often the child asks the reader to tell them what the writing says. They do not yet know that the meaning is fixed by the writer but think that it is ascribed to the text by the reader. When this early writing takes the form of repeated shapes children have realised that writing uses particular shapes and involves particular movements (see Figure 2.1). They may not yet know exactly what these are but they do know that in writing some shapes occur repeatedly. The way that writing depends on the use of repeated shapes is known as the **recurring principle** of writing (Clay, 1975).

**recurring principle**
understanding that writing contains repeated shapes

To use writing it is necessary to appreciate that writing is a symbol system. It uses a set of symbols to represent something other than itself. Writing stands for the author's meaning and written symbols convey a recoverable message. Clay (1975) called this understanding the **sign concept**. When children realise that the writer's own meaning is represented by the symbols that are produced they have reached another significant learning point in their development as writers. At this stage children begin to express their own thoughts and experiences in written form. The message may still be unreadable to others but the child will be able to ascribe a meaning to the symbols and say what the marks mean (see Figure 2.2).

**sign concept**
understanding that writing is a symbol system which can be used to represent meaning

Young children are keen to show their spontaneous, independent writing to others and to join in with others as they see them write. As a result they receive feedback from adults and are invited to look

**Figure 2.1**

Daniel is playing with me and kissing and cuddling me.

**Figure 2.2**

closely at models of mature writing. This helps them to refine what they know about writing. As a result of their observations of writing and feedback from others children begin to notice the specific features of writing. They start to separate writing symbols from other written marks such as drawing and numbers. Their writing often contains some of the letters that are found in their names, probably because these are the symbols that are most familiar to them (see Figure 2.3). They may be able to identify and name some of the letters they include in their writing, particularly the ones which are taken from their names. Fluent writers know that they can combine a limited set of symbols in different ways to produce all the words and sentences they want to write. They understand the **generative principle** of writing (Clay, 1975). Making use of the letters they do know in order to write demonstrates children's increasing awareness that the set of symbols for writing are limited, regular and can be combined in different ways to produce words.

**generative principle**
understanding that writing contains different combinations of a limited number of symbols

Another principle of the writing system, which children have to learn about, is its flexibility and the limitations to this. English is flexible in that it contains 26 letters which can be represented in different ways. For example, *a* may be written as *A* and may vary in size and decorative features. However, although each of the 26 letters can be written in different ways, not all characters that include curved and straight lines are acceptable as English language symbols. Although *b*, *d*, *p* and *q*, which employ the same shapes but are orientated differently, are all acceptable as letters, *a* does not become a letter shape if it is turned around. The gradual elimination of numbers and non-letter shapes from writing indicates children's growing knowledge about the writing system, what is permitted and what is not acceptable.

Over time the writing that children produce shows a growing awareness of directionality and page-arrangement principles. It is often arranged horizontally and vertically on the page rather than being placed randomly on the paper, and indicates that children are becoming more aware of the conventions of writing.

Studies of young children's writing have helped teachers to understand that as children learn to write and learn about writing their writing passes through a number of stages, and each of these stages represents an important achievement in learning to write. They have also shown that composition or the intention to convey meaning develops in advance of transcription. With increased practice and guidance, and in response to exposure to models of writing and discussions about writing with mature writers, children are able to produce pieces of writing which they are able to read back. They

**Figure 2.3**

learn to arrange their writing conventionally and use the sounds of the language to write words. Although it is impossible to state exactly when children achieve each aspect of writing described in the developmental sequence, most children are able to produce recognisable writing with confidence sometime between the ages of four and six.

This knowledge has influenced what and how teachers teach children about writing. As a result of the work of Clay (1975), Ferreiro and Teberosky (1983), Goodman (1990) and others the early writing curriculum now includes many opportunities for young children to experiment with and see demonstrations of writing. Practitioners place less emphasis on children producing correct writing through copying or using word books. Instead, in their individual responses to what children write, teachers discuss both the content and the transcription of writing. They help children to progress towards the next stage and towards conventional writing by providing them with correct models, and they offer reasons and explanations about writing that match the child's present level of understanding.

**Activity**   Collect some pieces of writing that children have produced independently. If possible try to gather these from nursery, reception, Year 1 and Year 2 children. See if you can match some of the features in the children's writing with the developmental characteristics described in this section. Can you recognise an increasing ability to manipulate the writing system?

## THE NATIONAL WRITING PROJECT

The findings of the National Writing Project (1985–8) confirmed that writing is learned developmentally, promoted the process approach to writing and reiterated the importance of providing children with as wide a range of purposes and audiences as possible. The project, which depended on research and experiments undertaken by teachers in their own classes, had a major impact on how writing is taught in schools. It also influenced the first and subsequent editions of the National Curriculum programmes of study for English. The most recent version of the National Curriculum (DfE, 1995) urges teachers to acknowledge and build on children's 'early experiments and independent attempts at communicating in writing', provide a range of audiences and purposes for writing and distinguish between composition and presentation.

## GENRE THEORY

Recently, research into writing has been examining the relevance of genre theory for literacy development in school (Littlefair, 1992; Martin and Rothery, 1986). Genre is a word that is used to describe types of text. There are literary genres and non-fiction genres. However, the significance of this work is not that it allows the word genre to be substituted for type or form. Genre analysis is important because it has drawn attention to the social factors which affect the way in which texts are constructed and has identified the characteristics of different texts in detail. Martin (1989) has suggested that by becoming more aware of the forms, functions and variations of language, teachers will be in a better position to teach children how to write for a variety of purposes in a range of situations.

Although a number of literary genres have been identified, such as fairy stories, poetry, plays and contemporary fiction, many writers believe that genre theory has a particular relevance to non-fiction writing (Wray and Lewis, 1995; Wing Jan, 1991). It is probably true that in the past, and particularly in the early years, transactional writing has been less well taught than expressive or poetic writing. As both the National Literacy Strategy *Framework for Teaching* (DfEE, 1998) and the English National Curriculum (DfE, 1995) identify non-fiction writing as an essential element of the Key Stage 1 curriculum the application of genre theory may help to develop practice in this area.

**Activities**

1 Collect some examples of a range of different types of writing that children have undertaken. Can you match the writing with a genre? Which genres are represented most often and which are sparsely represented? Has this any implications for the writing curriculum?
2 Examine the writing you collected again. What is it about each piece of writing that enabled you to make a judgement about its genre? Could the children have used more genre-specific features to improve their writing and fulfil the purpose of the task?

## THE NATIONAL CURRICULUM

The most significant influence on the writing curriculum in England and Wales since 1989 has been the statutory and official guidance that has been provided for schools. This has led to a great deal of consensus about the content of the writing curriculum. Drawing on much of the research and good practice that have emerged during the past twenty years, the Desirable Outcomes for Children's Learning (SCAA, 1996), the National Curriculum (DfE, 1995) and the National Literacy Strategy *Framework for Teaching* (DfEE, 1998), which are all linked, describe what constitutes an appropriate writing curriculum for young children at the end of the twentieth century.

At Key Stage 1 the programme of study for writing is divided into three sections, Range, Key Skills and Standard English and Language Study. Range concentrates on the composition and content of writing and draws on much of the research undertaken in the past three decades. There are references to introducing children to the purposes of writing, to allowing children to write independently as with a developmental approach, to varieties of writing types, to audiences and to learning about text structure. The section on Key Skills, which in the main refers to transcription, opens with the words, 'Pupils should be taught to write with confidence'. This is a reminder that although punctuation, spelling and handwriting are important they need to be taught sympathetically and without undue or inappropriate emphasis. The section on Key Skills reiterates the importance of knowing the purposes of writing and urges teachers to show children the similarities between writing and speaking. Both are acts of communication which are directed to an audience and anticipate a response. This section highlights the need to give children time to work on their writing and to learn how to plan and review as well as to write. The final section of the programme of study, Standard English and Language Study, describes how what children already know about oral language can be applied to writing if they are given appropriate guidance, and indicates how teachers should extend children's existing knowledge about language by developing their ability to organise texts and explore and experiment with an increasing variety of vocabulary.

Readers will be able to see the influence of Britton, Graves, Ferreiro and Teberosky, genre theorists and the National Writing Project on the emphases expressed in the programmes of study. This is also true of the Desirable Outcomes for Children's Learning (SCAA, 1996) and the National Literacy Strategy *Framework for Teaching* (DfEE, 1998), both of which have evolved from the National Curriculum Orders.

## THE DESIRABLE OUTCOMES FOR CHILDREN'S LEARNING

The Desirable Outcomes were written after the programmes of study and identify what children need to understand and be able to do in order to successfully embark on the National Curriculum. As with the programmes of study, understanding that writing is a meaningful, communicative activity and appreciating the purposes of writing are stressed. Transcription is emphasised only in relation to children's names, which are probably the most significant words for them and ones that they will want to learn to spell and write accurately.

The Qualifications and Curriculum Authority is undertaking a review of the desirable learning outcomes and intends to publish revised guidelines on the education of children aged between three and five in September 1999. These are intended to ensure continuity between nursery, reception and Key Stage 1 and will have links with the National Curriculum and the National Literacy Strategy. The proposals and consultation document (QCA, 1999) suggest that there will be many similarities between the outcomes for language and literacy expressed in the existing documentation (SCAA, 1996; DfEE, 1998) and the proposed early learning goals.

## THE NATIONAL LITERACY STRATEGY FRAMEWORK FOR TEACHING

In the summer of 1998 the National Literacy Strategy *Framework for Teaching* was published by the Department for Education and Employment. It resulted from the findings of the Literacy Task Force and the work of the National Literacy Project where the techniques it recommends had been trialled.

The Framework expands upon the Desirable Outcomes for Children's Learning and the National Curriculum for English by translating both documents into a set of detailed objectives covering what children are required to learn from Reception to Year 6. As described above, the National Curriculum programme of study for writing contains three sections, Range, Key Skills and Standard English and Language Study. The Framework sets out the range of writing pupils are expected to undertake. Each term they should write stories, poems and information. For example, in Year 1, Term 1, children are expected to write personal experiences, stories, rhymes, captions, lists, instructions and labels. The Key Skills and Standard English and Language Study sections of the National Curriculum are covered by sections on word-level work, sentence-level work and text-level work, which are concerned with spelling, punctuation, handwriting, vocabulary, text structure, text types, review, organisation, and writing with an understanding of purpose and audience. As in the National Curriculum, composition and transcription are separated. Composition is described in the section on text-level work and transcription in those on word- and sentence-level work.

The difference between the National Curriculum and the Framework, apart from the detail about what children are expected to learn, is the advice it contains about how children should be taught. It describes how the teaching of writing should be linked with the teaching of reading and how both aspects of literacy teaching should be covered in an uninterrupted hour of teaching. During the hour the teacher should work for part of the time with the whole class and with groups of children Both whole-class and group teaching should include a balance of reading and writing.

**Activity**     Select one of the termly plans in the *Framework for Teaching*. Read this through and then try to relate the objectives for writing to the English National Curriculum programme of study or the Desirable Outcomes for Children's Learning. Can you see how all these documents are connected?

## THE PICTURE IN SCHOOL TODAY

Despite the agreement about what has to be learned about writing, as outlined in Chapter 1 and in official documents, the way it is taught is far from uniform. Readers of this book are likely to encounter a variety of practices in school. In some settings children might be observed working on a piece of writing over a number of days as they plan, draft and revise a story for publication or write a letter for an outside audience. Children may be making independent attempts at spelling and freely using the many resources for writing available in the classroom. As each stage of the writing is completed the teacher might be discussing content and, when appropriate, transcription with the author.

Other teachers instruct children in writing through activities such as copying and tracing over adult writing, copying from the board, copying and tracing handwriting patterns and using individual word books in which the teacher writes correct spellings for children to copy. In some classrooms little attention is paid to the purpose, audience and outcome for writing, and discussions about content, structure and style are rare. Writing is generally expected to be finished in one session and is rarely redrafted unless it is to be displayed, when it might be copied out once it has been corrected by the teacher. Readers might want to think about the strengths and limitations of the different approaches to developing writing that are presently used in school and how far they contribute to the requirements of the writing curriculum.

1 Think back to your own experiences of writing at school. How do the ideas in this chapter match the teaching you received? If there is a close match how helpful were these ideas about writing? If they are unfamiliar do you think your own writing would have benefited from some of the research findings and practical advice that are now available?

2 How many of the ideas introduced in this chapter have you seen in practice in school? How are they interpreted and presented to children? Are some practices more helpful than others? Which ones and why?

## COMBINING RESEARCH AND PRACTICE

Learning to write is a developmental process. Children learn about writing and learn to write as they learn more about the world they live in and as they explore different ways of communicating and representing meaning. Once they have begun to experiment with writing they need support and encouragement to continue and refine their abilities. This needs to be provided within a curriculum that takes account of the appropriate conditions for writing.

All writing takes place in a context. It is undertaken for a reason, for an audience and with regard to conventions. It is composed, transcribed and reviewed. Decisions are made about content, structure, style, vocabulary, spelling, punctuation and handwriting. The lists below summarise this and are a reminder of the number of factors that need attention when writing and the complexity of the activity. Keeping this in mind should help when planning a varied and interesting writing curriculum which covers all the elements of writing as described in the National Curriculum for English and identifying what young children need to learn.

Children need to know about:

- the *purpose* for a piece of writing
- the *audience* for their writing
- the *outcome* of their writing.

They need to learn how to:

| Compose | Transcribe | Review |
|---|---|---|
| content | spelling | clarity |
| form | punctuation | appropriateness |
| structure | handwriting | |
| style | grammar | |

They are more likely to produce effective writing when they have:

- an understanding of the functions of writing
- a reason for writing
- an audience to write for
- opportunities to explore style
- access to different forms of writing
- opportunities to evaluate what they have written
- chances to change their first attempts
- discussions with others about how to improve their writing
- time to spend on writing.

The conditions and curriculum that support young writers can be provided when adults themselves understand what writing is for, identify the processes involved in writing, and are aware of the vast range of writing that is used in daily life.

## Summary

At the end of the twentieth century teachers have a detailed plan to help them to teach writing effectively. The National Literacy Strategy *Framework for Teaching* (DfEE, 1998) and the National Curriculum for English (DfE, 1995) have resulted from more than fifty years of experience and research into literacy and language. This chapter has shown how some of the key discoveries about writing and learning to write have been incorporated into these two documents and into the writing curriculum at school.

*The key points covered in this chapter were:*

- **an account of how and why the writing curriculum has evolved**

- **the contribution that research and practitioner experience have made to the development of the curriculum**

- **the way children develop as writers**

- **the present statutory requirements for writing**

- **some of the writing practices currently used in schools.**

## Further reading

Temple, C., Nathan, R., Burris, N. and Temple, F. (1993) *The Beginnings of Writing* (3rd edition), Allyn and Bacon, London
A classic text about the developmental approach to writing.

Wing Jan, Lesley (1991) *Write Ways: Modelling Writing Forms*, Oxford University Press, Australia
This book illustrates how genre theory can be applied in the classroom and contains many helpful examples and illustrations.

# Organising writing 3

*When you have read this chapter you should:*

- understand classroom procedures for developing writing
- appreciate the teacher's role in teaching children to write
- be able to support children as they learn to write.

In order to teach writing well teachers need to know about writing and about teaching. Both what and how are important. The way that teaching is organised and the experiences that are offered in the classroom can either support or hinder children's learning. This chapter outlines organisational strategies that can be employed when practitioners are considering how to implement a broad, balanced and purposeful writing curriculum in the early years.

## TEACHING AND LEARNING PROCEDURES

Children need to learn about writing as well as learning how to write. If they are encouraged to engage in each stage of the writing process they are being given the chance to understand how to write. They may also learn that writing is important and worthwhile. The process approach (Graves, 1983) involves children in composing, transcribing and reviewing and enables teachers to provide real teaching about writing through conferencing. Drafting, shared writing, **scribing** and publishing all help children to learn about the process of writing, behave like writers and gain satisfaction from writing. As you read the descriptions of the procedures described in this chapter you will recognise that they have implications for the management of resources, time, children and the curriculum. Writing will be one of the many activities that teachers offer children each day, and like any classroom activity it depends on effective classroom management skills for successful outcomes.

**scribing**
the process whereby a more experienced writer transcribes the composition dictated by a less competent writer

Many of the teaching procedures described in this chapter can be used with all early years children, from the nursery to Year 2. However, some of the practices are more suited to the developmental needs of children who have accumulated more experience as writers. Within the descriptions of each strategy there are some suggestions about the age of the children for whom the practice is most appropriate and how it can be adapted to cater for older or younger children. The procedures described are arranged chronologically, beginning with independent writing and ending with guided writing. The earlier activities are most suitable for nursery age children while teachers working with Key Stage 1 children can use any or all of the procedures.

## Independent writing

Teachers should expect all children, regardless of their age or experience, to write independently. Children should always write without copying or waiting for the teacher to help them with spellings. Working in this way has a number of advantages; it:

- acknowledges the knowledge and ability that children already have about writing
- is in harmony with good early years practice since it offers opportunities for learning through active exploration
- provides the teacher with useful information about what the child can do and understands
- enables the teacher to identify each child's needs and to address these individually
- develops children's belief and confidence in their own abilities
- places the emphasis on the content and composition of writing rather than transcription
- fulfils the National Curriculum requirement, 'Pupils should be taught to write independently'
- gives the teacher time to teach rather than spending her time giving children correct spellings.

### *Organisation*

The children need to know that they should write without seeking assistance. The ethos of the classroom needs to foster independence and risk-taking so that the children feel confident about writing alone. Initially children should be encouraged to write without worrying about spelling and handwriting, but they should be encouraged to think about the content of their writing and how to convey this. The classroom needs to contain resources which help children write independently, and the children need to be aware of strategies such as writing the first letter of a word then leaving a gap if they cannot spell a word. They can be given support in conferences before, during and after writing. After the writing has been produced the teacher gives the children feedback on the content of what they have written and help with the transcriptional elements in order to help them to revise and extend their understanding of writing. The teacher does not correct every error that the child makes when writing; instead she teaches through providing correct models for the child to see and working positively and sensitively with the child on one or two mistakes or difficulties.

## Shared writing

Shared writing involves a group of children composing a text collaboratively, with the teacher acting as the scribe for the group. It is a way for teachers to 'help pupils to compose at greater length by writing for them, demonstrating the ways that ideas may be recorded in print' (DfE, 1995, p. 9). When children are familiar with the format they may take over some of the scribing, but initially it is more helpful if an adult does this. This is an excellent way of teaching children about writing in the nursery and reception classes, as the skills and practices that are explained and demonstrated during shared writing sessions provide a model for children to draw on when they write.

Shared writing encourages children to reflect on all aspects of the writing process. The children see and participate in all the stages of writing, including composing, planning, drafting, editing, evaluating and redrafting, and from this model they can learn valuable lessons about how they might work on writing they undertake alone. As the teacher writes she may draw the children's attention to spelling patterns, punctuation, word boundaries, layout of text, and the patterns and conventions associated with different genres of written language. Seeing how writing is transcribed helps children to learn about and incorporate the conventions of writing into their own writing.

Writing in this way enables children to work collaboratively and to draw on and value each other's strengths and ideas. As the transcriptional aspects of writing are taken over by the teacher, the children can focus on the composition and as a result can participate in producing longer, more complex texts than they could if they were writing alone. Less confident or less able writers benefit a great deal from shared writing since they can see that writing does not have to be perfect at the first attempt and that writing is as much about composition as about transcription.

### Organisation

Shared writing sessions are generally best organised by having the children sitting as a group on the carpet and the teacher writing on large sheets of paper on a flip chart or an easel. It can be undertaken with the whole class for writing that is of interest to all the children, such as a letter to be sent home or the final results of an experiment. With a new class it is best to begin with a simple, short piece of writing. Alternatively it can be used with a group of children who share a specific learning need, such as the need to learn about story structure, drafting, or to spell frequently used words correctly. Rules about how to make a contribution may need to be established so that children listen and develop each other's ideas. Shared writing is particularly suited to the class teaching requirements of the literacy hour since it teaches children about writing and reading, and if it is used to produce a large class book this can be used later for shared reading.

The activity usually begins with the teacher and children discussing the topic for the writing. If shared writing is new to the class it may be best to use it to retell a familiar story, write a letter, produce an account of a visit, make a sign to go with a display or compose a poem, as these have a clear structure that can be followed by the children. It is important to be clear about the aims and purposes of the writing and make them explicit to the class, as these affect the style and content and guide the children's contributions. After the initial discussion the teacher takes the children through all the processes of writing as she scribes for them. The first stage is to brainstorm ideas to be included in the writing. As the children contribute their ideas the teacher records these as a list or diagram. After collecting the ideas on content the group consider which ideas should come at the beginning, middle and end of the writing. The teacher then numbers the ideas in the order that they will occur in the text to form a plan. Working from the plan, the children and the teacher begin to compose the writing. The initial ideas are reworked, words are changed and sentences are composed as the group focus on the writing. At the end of this stage the first draft of the writing, probably containing false starts and crossing out, is complete. The first draft is read through and may be revised or edited before the final draft is produced by the teacher or the children.

A piece of shared writing may take a number of sessions to complete. This is a useful example of the permanence of text and illustrates how writing things down helps people to remember ideas and organise their thinking. It also signals that writing that is worth doing need not be completed in one session. Writing often benefits from taking place over a longer period than one session since the writer has had time to consider what they have written and to think of new or better ideas. Reading and reviewing what they have written at the beginning of each session usually leads to further revisions and helps children to see the benefits of re-reading a piece of writing.

The completed writing may be copied out by the children. With a long piece individual children may copy out one section of the text to form the writing for one page of a class book. They can then illustrate their page. Alternatively the teacher may write the final draft in a large class-made book, and the children's role is to provide the illustrations. This can be used for shared reading. Sometimes the teacher may stop scribing before the final draft of the writing and the children can use the plan and the draft to compose their own individual ending to the story, poem, letter or account. Whatever the final outcome of shared writing sessions it is important that the teacher has thought beforehand about how the activity will end.

## Scribing

More experienced writers, such as older children, parents, carers or other adult volunteers, can be invited into the classroom to write with and for the children. They can transcribe for individuals or small groups. As with shared writing, because the adult is transcribing, the children are free to concentrate on the composition of text. As they write, adults can discuss the choice of words, spelling, the use of punctuation and layout with the children. They can also act as prompts if the composition dries up, and encourage the children to get ideas by reading and reflecting on what they have written so far. The scribes may do all the writing involved in planning and writing first drafts. They can write by hand or on the computer. They may tape-record a child's story and then work with the child as she writes her story using the tape recording as a first draft. Experienced writers, writing alongside children, can encourage children to compose at greater length than they could manage alone and enable children to see how writing should be tackled. Often children gain enormous satisfaction from seeing their words in print, and through scribing can be motivated into wanting to write alone (Smith, 1994).

### Organisation

Before volunteers or teaching assistants start to work with the children it is essential that they know exactly what is required of them. The teacher may need to explain the purpose of the strategy and explain the way that she would like them to work with the children. It can be helpful to provide guidelines on suitable prompts.

## The process approach

It was the work of Graves (1983) that first drew attention to the importance of organising the writing curriculum and classroom routines to allow children to experience all the processes of writing. This has had a significant influence on the way that the teaching of writing is now thought about in schools. In the account that follows each stage is explained in detail so that readers can think about ways of incorporating this approach into their classroom routines.

### *Getting ready to write*

The teacher may have suggested a subject or type of writing that she wishes the children to tackle or individual children may have identified a topic of their own. Whatever the starting point, at this stage, children are engaged in preparing to write and getting ideas about what they might include in their writing. They can do this through class and group discussions, or brainstorming with their response partner.

### *Planning*

Selecting from the ideas generated in the previous stage, the child makes a plan for the writing. This might take the form of a drawing, a list or a spider diagram.

### *First draft*

Using the plan the child writes a piece of continuous text without worrying too much about spelling, handwriting and punctuation.

### *Revising*

The child proofreads what they have written in order to see whether the content, organisation or style can be improved. While checking the writing the child might be asking:

- Does the writing make sense?
- Has anything been missed out?
- Could anything else be included?
- Does it sound right?

The teacher and the response partner can also contribute at this stage. Revisions to the text such as deleting, reordering, inserting and elaborating are undertaken. If necessary a second draft can then be written; if not the child passes on to the next stage. Revision is not concerned with cosmetic alterations to the text such as correcting spelling. This is left until the next stage.

### *Editing*

This is when corrections to spelling, handwriting and punctuation are made, using classroom resources and help from the teacher.

## Preparation for publication

At this stage thought is given to the final layout of the text and the best way of presenting what the child has written. This will vary according to the purpose and audience for the writing but may include breaks in the text, the use of illustrations and regard to the writing implement to be used.

## Publication

The child writes the final version of the text. It incorporates all the changes that have been made and is presented in a way that invites and enables others to read it. Before the text is used in the way intended the writer may 'publish' or read it aloud during a whole-class conference or plenary at the end of a session.

Readers will be able to make connections between the process approach and the three elements of writing, composition, transcription and review, described in Chapter 1. Not all pieces of writing need to go through all of these stages. Depending on the purpose and the audience some writing, such as a journal entry or a reminder listing the equipment needed to make a model, may be considered finished after the planning or the first-draft stage. However, if all the stages are followed it will take several days to move through them, and the teacher needs to plan the week's work to allow for this.

## Organisation

When this way of working is adopted children need access to resources and they need to be capable of working independently. Initially they should be encouraged to write without asking for spellings or checking words with the teacher, and so need to be able to draw on self-help strategies. The teacher's planning needs to allow for children to work on one piece of writing over a number of days. It is it is unlikely that all the children in the class will be writing at the same time, and writing will probably be one of a number of different curriculum activities taking place in the classroom at any one time. This enables the teacher to work with the children on their precise learning needs, individually or as a group, as they are writing. Amongst those who are writing some may be planning, others editing and some publishing. The writing that children are asked to produce needs to be selected carefully so that children can see the purpose of what they are doing and are motivated to work on their writing for a number of sessions, sustained by the knowledge that the final outcome will be used or read by others.

## Writing conferences

These are an important part of the process approach. They are discussions about writing and occur as children are developing their writing. Conferences provide the teacher with opportunities to assist children with content, organisation and use of conventions and give children opportunities to ask questions and get feedback about writing. Different types of conferences can be held depending on pupil need. These are roving conferences, individual conferences, group conferences, peer conferences and whole-class conferences. The programme of study for English acknowledges the value of conferencing: 'To encourage confidence and independence, pupils should be given opportunities to collaborate, to read their work aloud and to discuss the quality of what is written' (DfE, 1995, p. 9).

### Roving conferences

These are usually held at the beginning of a writing session while children are settling down to write and organising their thoughts. The teacher might quickly ask selected children simple questions about the writing they are about to start, look at what children have done so far, note the stage they are at and what they have to do next and keep track of children having problems. One question similar to the ones in the following list may be all that is needed:

- What are you working on?
- What is the story about so far?
- Do you need any help?
- Did you make the changes we discussed yesterday?
- How are you getting on with your writing?

The purpose of the roving conference is to motivate and to check progress. It can help teachers identify children who would benefit from a more sustained conference or a common need that can be addressed in a group conference.

### Individual conferences

Normally these occur while children are writing and are used to discuss work in progress. They often occur at the end of a writing stage, for example after the plan has been drawn up or after a first draft has been written. During this time the child reads what they have written to the teacher, and the child and the teacher discuss any possible improvements. Individual conferences with young children can be used for providing correct versions of writing and comparing these to what children have written. One teaching point may be considered, and after a short discussion the child goes away to make the changes and work on the next stage. During individual conferences teachers need to be positive and comment on what children have achieved as well as how the writing can be improved. The number of suggested improvements should be limited. One or two teaching points are sufficient for young children. Children can also be reminded to consult other sources of help in the classroom, including books, dictionaries, word lists and other children.

### Group conferences

These are held during a writing session. They can address a specific need that has arisen simultaneously for a number of children, for example how to use question marks, the use of interesting beginnings for stories or the use of headings in information texts. They can be times to teach or check that children understand the look copy cover write check strategy. They may also be a time when children discuss their writing with their peers. In the group each child reads their writing and the other children offer suggestions to improve the writing, such as adding detail or making the meaning clearer. When group conferences are held to discuss and improve writing the teacher participates and facilitates the children's contributions. She may take the lead by asking children questions such as:

- Have you finished the piece of writing?
- Is there anything you want to add?
- Which part do you think is best?
- Is there anything you want to change?
- Is there anything that you would like help with?

During these sessions children are learning the skills that they need during peer conferences and the sorts of questions that eventually they will be able to ask themselves as they review their writing. So the questions the teacher asks provide a model that children can follow.

### Peer conferences

These involve two children working together to improve each other's writing. During the course of the National Writing Project (1989) some teachers were particularly impressed with the way that children, as young as five, were able to help their peers and work successfully in this way. Working in pairs, children listen to or read their partner's writing and comment on how the writing might be improved or extended. They can comment on clarity of meaning and order as well as helping with spelling and punctuation. After sharing their work the children then continue to work on their writing using the comments of their response partner to help them. Peer conferences should take place before individual conferences, as the children may be in a position to make some changes before discussing their writing with the teacher. This develops children's independence and ability to be self-critical as well as saving the teacher time.

### Whole-class conferences

These are usually most productive if they take place at the start or end of a writing session, and may fit into the whole-class period or plenary session during the literacy hour. They can be used to:

- discuss ideas before getting started on a piece of writing
- share successful writing
- teach editing skills
- discuss and teach spelling
- discuss the structure of different sorts of texts and look at published examples in books
- teach any aspect of writing that will be of use to the class.

During whole-class conferences it is important not to include too many teaching points or cover too much ground. Only teach what the children are ready for and select points that are relevant to the majority of the children, as the teaching required by small numbers of children can take place in group conferences.

### Organisation

It is unrealistic to plan for an individual conference for each child every day. The intention should be to see each child individually once a week. Children will still be receiving teaching through roving, group, whole-class and peer conferences. Keep a record of children who have had conferences to help you to plan.

The teacher of younger children may need to allocate more time to roving conferences to help children focus their thoughts and decide on the next step. With older children, who are familiar with the routines of evaluating the writing of others, the teacher can include more peer conferences in her planning.

The purpose and structure of peer conferences needs to be explained to children. Initially they will need to be instructed about how they can best help to improve the work of others, and they will probably benefit from their own experiences of working in similar ways during individual, group and class conferences and shared writing sessions with the teacher. They can be given simple instructions about how to act as a supportive partner, such as:

- Say two good things about the writing.
- Ask questions if anything is not clear.
- Suggest two ways of making the writing better.

The pairings can be arranged by the teacher, or children can consult any child who is free to help. As children become more practised at helping each other the benefits of this strategy increase.

Make sure children understand what you expect them to have done before they ask for an individual conference, and be consistent about these rules. For instance, you may want children to re-read their own writing or to have shared it in a peer conference or to have consulted resources for spelling before they are ready for a conference with the teacher.

## Writing workshop

This employs practices similar to those described in the section earlier in this chapter outlining the process approach. The difference is that a workshop is a specially timetabled writing session when all the class write at the same time. The session begins with a whole-class planning time, when the children discuss with a partner what they are going to write. This is followed by an uninterrupted and quiet period of writing when the children write independently. The teacher is also expected to write during this time. Alternatively she may spend her time working with a group of children who need extra help or who are revising their first drafts. After the children have finished their writing they can share it with the rest of the class. The class comment on each other's writing, making suggestions and commenting on the content of what each has written. The children can then revise their own writing and the teacher can work with a group or individuals to provide focused teaching, or she can work with the whole class on one aspect of writing that has general application to the children's needs.

### Organisation

Writing workshops are a regular feature of the weekly timetable. The children need to follow routines, know their partner, understand the need for quiet concentration and be clear about how to give feedback. The way that the teacher participates alongside the children provides a model for them to imitate. The length of the session will vary according to the age of the children but sufficient time needs to be allowed for the discussions at the start and end of the session. Some teachers have found that the structure of the writing workshop beginning with a whole-class session followed by individual or group writing where the teacher can work intensively with one or two groups and individuals and ending with a whole-class period fits well into the format of the literacy hour. Although Calkins (1986) recommends that a writing workshop should take place every day, some schools prefer to schedule it once a week.

This gives the class a regular opportunity to work on some writing of their own choice if they wish. During the remainder of the week children engage with writing that arises from other work in the class.

### Drafting

Very few writers have the skill of producing perfectly crafted writing at the first attempt. Most writers, whatever their age or experience, need to draft important pieces of writing before producing a final copy. The programme of study for writing tells us that children at Key Stage 1 need to be introduced to drafting when it states: 'Pupils should have opportunities to plan and review their writing' (DfE, 1995, p. 9).

Drafting gives children the opportunity to shape and reshape their ideas on paper, on the computer or on tape before producing their final version. It encourages children to reflect on their writing and to evaluate and self-correct as they read through what they have written. Not every piece of writing needs redrafting – this depends on its purpose and its audience – but all writing can benefit from applying some aspects of the drafting process.

Before writing a first draft writers need to focus on what they are about to write. They may spend time recollecting and remembering information, incidents or feelings. This is a very important part of the composing process. They then need to make a note of the ideas that they have thought of, maybe in the form of a picture, a spider diagram or a list. Key words and expressions as well as ideas can be noted. Less experienced writers can recollect and plan by drawing either one picture or a sequence of pictures that help them to organise their thoughts and consider what they are going to write. Next the ideas need to be organised into a coherent plan, maybe by making a list or numbering the ideas in sequence.

After the planning stage the writer is ready to write. A first draft is for getting one's ideas down quickly without worrying too much about spelling, punctuation or handwriting. As long as the child can read what they have written there is no need to interrupt the creative flow of the writing to make corrections. At this stage the child may make false starts and rethink as they write, and this may result in what looks like a messy piece of work containing misspellings and crossing out. This does not represent careless or poor work; many adult writers' first drafts look like this. A first draft represents the writer's struggle with the process of translating thoughts and ideas into the written form. There is no need for the child to use an eraser to conceal mistakes at this stage; crossing out is far quicker and interrupts one's thoughts less. It is also unnecessary for the child to check spellings by asking the teacher or consulting a dictionary. As long as the words can be read back they can be checked after the first draft has been completed. The mistakes made at this stage can give teachers useful insights about the aspects of writing that children are finding difficult and how these are tackled. They may provide the teacher with starting points for a writing conference.

When the first draft is complete it is time to read the writing through. Children can look for clarity of meaning and change words, phrases and sentences to make a more satisfactory piece of writing. They can also proofread for spelling and punctuation errors. It is at this stage that children might use a dictionary to check or find spellings. They can use a highlighter pen to indicate problems that they cannot resolve independently, such as altering parts of the writing that do not make sense or correcting difficult spellings. Then, if the children have response partners, their partner may read what they have written and offer suggestions. At this stage individual children will be ready for a writing conference with the teacher. During this the child and the teacher can discuss the work so far to see if further revision or more ideas are necessary. It is also at this stage that the teacher will respond to the child's own queries and work on transcription.

The writing may go through another draft to incorporate the ideas and changes which have been discussed. Alternatively after the first draft the child may move straight to the final draft. At this stage the child should be clear about how the work is going to be presented. Is it going to be in the form of a book, a letter, or for display? This will affect layout and the choice of writing materials. The focus at this stage is on presentation. If the work is to be read by others the child will need to write carefully, attending to spelling and using clear handwriting. The teacher should expect the final version to reflect the help that has been given. If appropriate, it is at this stage that the child will incorporate illustrations into the writing. At the end of the final draft the child should have a piece of writing that is personally satisfying and interesting for others to read.

The time spent on drafting will vary depending on the child's age and experience as a writer, as will the exact drafting procedures that are used. Very young children may plan by thinking before they write. They can consider what they are going to write as they draw a single picture or a sequence of illustrations, talk to the teacher or to other children about what they want to write, or dictate into a tape recorder before beginning to write on their own. After this the teacher will discuss with the child what they have written. She can then either write the correct version under the child's writing or correct one or two errors and ask the child to rewrite the sentences incorporating the changes that have been discussed. This is the final draft. Older, more experienced writers who can write at greater length can be expected to go through all the stages of planning, editing and producing a final draft. They may be helped in this by using a double-page spread of an exercise book for planning and making first drafts. The left-hand page can be used for plans and notes and the right-hand page for writing in complete prose. If the writing is to be published the draft on the right-hand page can be corrected before the final copy is made on a separate piece of paper. If the first draft is also the final version it can be responded to and corrected in the usual way.

Drafting takes children through all the stages that real writing passes through. In particular it encourages children to think before they write. Children are free to take risks when they write first drafts since mistakes can be rectified later. Drafting helps children to separate content and transcription and concentrate on these at different times, and can result in a very satisfying piece of writing.

### Organisation

Shared writing sessions when the teacher models the way in which writers plan, draft and redraft their writing provide children with an introduction to drafting. However, children need further explanations about why it is helpful to work in this way and examples of how to draft and redraft before they are confident with the procedure. This can be done by introducing each stage of the drafting process separately and demonstrating each stage to the children. For example, the teacher might begin by telling the class that their writing today is going to consist of collecting ideas and making plans. This can be modelled and the children asked to undertake a similar activity. The teacher should give feedback to individuals and to the whole class on the results. Some of the children's plans can be used to demonstrate the next stage, translating a plan into a first draft. Some first drafts can be shared and discussed during a whole-class conference at the end of the writing session. At the beginning of the next writing session a few of the children's first drafts can be used to illustrate revision and editing and the children given the opportunity to practise this. Finally the children can write their best copies. Examples of the children's plans, drafts and final versions can be displayed to show children how writing can be developed and improved.

In order for drafting to work, the class has to be organised so that a piece of writing can be worked on over a number of days. One day's writing may cover only the planning and first draft stage. Children need to be able to store their first drafts in their own writing folder or in their first draft book. They can then return to these during their next writing session.

When children spend time drafting and redrafting their writing it is essential that the outcome for the writing is important enough to demand this degree of attention. It is also important that before the children write they know the purpose and the audience for the writing, as this will affect the content, style and organisation of the writing. For example, a letter to a friend reads very differently, is set out in a different way and includes different sorts of information than a letter written to an unknown audience.

## Publishing

Publishing means making writing public, often in books made by the children or the teacher but also in other forms such as posters, notices or letters. Not every piece of writing done by a child needs to be published. Personal writing, diaries, notes, diagrams or plans may never have been intended for an audience beyond the writer or the teacher. Some writing may become public through being used as a prompt when speaking to other children or telling a story. The child and the teacher should discuss whether a piece of writing should be published. The original purpose of the writing as well as the quality of the finished product will influence the decision. Publication in written form should be viewed as the end of a long process where the teacher has worked through the drafts with the child and both have agreed that the writing is good enough to be published. Quality must take account of each child's experience and the degree of effort that they have invested in the writing. This will differ from child to child even in the same class or age group.

The subject matter and purpose may determine what form publication takes. Accounts of learning or the description of a process may become part of a display. Captions, labels and explanations may be placed next to models or drawings. Stories or information may be published in books that are placed in the class library to be read by the writer and other children in the class.

### *Organisation*

Resources for publication need to be available and the children need to know how to use them. Blank books can be prepared in advance for stories, but showing children how to make their own books gives them greater control over the length of their writing. If children know how to use the paper trimmer and have access to glue they can mount their writing for display. All the resources that are needed for publishing can be kept in the writing area of the classroom.

## Guided writing

With guided writing the teacher works with a group of children on a piece of writing which offers an appropriate level of challenge to the group. It enables teachers to develop and refine children's abilities beyond their independent capabilities, and to plan work that exactly meets the needs of a small group of children. It can be a time when writing in progress is returned to and improved and extended. Guided writing sessions can focus on:

- planning
- supporting work in progress
- evaluating and improving writing.

### *Organisation*

An adult works with a group of about six children on a specific and preplanned aspect of their writing. All the children in the class should receive a guided writing session once a week. Group guided writing offers the opportunity to use some of the techniques mentioned earlier in this chapter, such as response partners and group conferencing. It should enable children to make changes in their writing or learn and use a new writing strategy that will help them to write more easily or more appropriately. It may also be used to introduce transcription techniques such as look copy cover write check, or reinforce handwriting or punctuation skills.

**Activity** Select one of the suggestions for organising writing. Think about how you could use this strategy with the children you work with. After considering the way in which you might make use of it introduce it to the class. If it is an unfamiliar way of working be prepared to give it a trial period of a couple of weeks or longer in order to give the children sufficient time to become familiar with the routines. During this time evaluate the way in which the procedure is supporting the children's learning and your teaching. At the end of the trial period compare it with earlier methods of organising for writing. Has it contributed to the children's learning? Is it worth permanently incorporating this way of working into the curriculum?

## THE TEACHER'S ROLE

In order to teach well the teacher needs to be aware of her many roles in the classroom. This applies as much to writing as to any other area of the curriculum. Not every situation requires the use of the complete repertoire of teaching strategies, but all will have a place at some time over a period of learning. A number of reports and documents (HMI, 1996; DfEE, 1998) have identified the following aspects of teacher behaviour as likely to result in effective teaching and learning:

- knowledge about literacy
- high expectations
- the effective use of time
- a clear focus on what needs to be learned
- careful classroom management
- systematic and challenging teaching
- a mixture of whole-class, group and individual teaching
- a mixture of direction, demonstration, explanation, questioning, guidance, discussion
- providing opportunities for investigation and exploration
- careful monitoring of what can pupils do
- making connections between writing and reading.

All of these play a part in the daily teaching programme, and need to inform the way the teacher manages the literacy curriculum and thinks about the most appropriate way of extending children's learning. In particular the teacher draws upon all the following aspects of her role as an educator.

### Expert

None of us ever feels that we know everything that there is to know about individual curriculum areas, how children learn and the best ways to teach in every situation. For this reason teachers frequently participate in courses in order to extend their knowledge and skills. However, whatever their background and experience, teachers are the expert writers in the classroom. They know how to write and they use writing in their daily lives. They can call upon their own experiences of writing and maybe those of learning to write to support young children who are taking their early steps along the same route. A good teacher uses her own experiences not as a standard but to benefit others. Teachers who understand the processes of writing and how children learn to become writers will share their expertise with children in ways that make sense to them and encourage their development. They will do this when they offer support and advice about writing during conferences and when they teach specific aspects of writing that are creating difficulties for children.

### Facilitator

As a facilitator the teacher sets up an effective learning environment which contains the resources that children need when they write. She makes sure that there are sufficient resources to support the children as they write independently. Such resources include alphabet friezes, collections of words, dictionaries and models of writing. She arranges the classroom to accommodate a writing area, literate play areas and a well-resourced book area. She sees all the children in the class as a resource for their own and other children's learning. She knows the value of children working together to foster their independence. As a facilitator the teacher plans writing activities that are necessary, purposeful, varied and relevant, that, wherever possible, allow children to work through each stage of the writing process and result in a visible, valued outcome. If available, she makes the best use of additional adult help and word-processing facilities.

### Model

Through her own attitude to writing and her own use of writing and resources in the classroom the teacher demonstrates how writers behave. The importance of demonstrating the composing, transcribing and reviewing processes and providing examples of the sort of writing she is expecting the children to try cannot be over-emphasised. Shared reading and shared writing sessions should be regarded as important teaching opportunities although these should not be used mechanically nor take precedence over enjoying literacy experiences. Writing demonstrations are also given when adults scribe and engage in written dialogues with children. These visual models of the kinds of writing and writing behaviours that children need to develop provide children with props for their independent work.

### Teacher

Direct instruction or telling do not necessarily result in learning; however, there may be times when the teacher needs to call upon her management, questioning, advising, explaining and directing skills as she focuses on what children need to know. These professional attributes are grouped together in this section under the heading of 'Teacher'. Teaching skills are just as important and should be used alongside the other roles of expert, facilitator and model. Some teachers consider that teaching conflicts with, for example, their role as a facilitator. This need not be the case. Developing learning draws on a repertoire of professional skills which can be used to suit the purpose of the activity and the learner's needs. Within the positive ethos she establishes in the classroom, the teacher has the authority to constructively criticise the work that children do. Children expect teachers to be able to give them the guidance that they need, and respect them for this. Interpreted in this way teaching incorporates guidance and intervention. It should be varied and include whole-class demonstrations, class discussions about writing and participation in focused group and individual conferences. All teaching will have learning aims based on the teacher's knowledge of the children's abilities and interests, and it will be informed by her observations of the children as they write. At all times the teacher will be positive about children's achievements whilst looking for appropriate ways to extend their abilities. Individual teaching may be given through writing correctly transcribed models beneath children's writing and an accompanying discussion. It may take the form of encouraging children to think about the letters contained in words or teaching children to use the look copy cover write check strategy. It will almost certainly include making suggestions about the content, organisation and language of their writing. Future teaching will be carefully planned and will be based on the children's successes and their needs.

Table 3.1 suggests some guidelines which may be useful when considering how to organise and teach writing successfully.

| |
|---|
| • Develop your own knowledge about writing. |
| • Recognise and exploit children's existing abilities. |
| • Encourage children's belief in their ability to write. |
| • Involve children in their own writing development. |
| • Encourage risk-taking. |
| • Allow children to make decisions about what, how and when to write. |
| • Develop self-reliance and independent use of writing resources. |
| • Foster positive attitudes to writing. |
| • Explain to children that writing is primarily about communication of content. |
| • Give children reasons for writing and audiences for their writing that are relevant to them. |
| • Provide opportunities for children to discuss their own and other children's writing. |
| • Analyse the precise demands of each writing activity and organise teaching to support this. |

**Table 3.1**
*Guidelines for developing writing effectively*

**Activity**   If possible observe another skilled adult as he works with children on writing. Try to identify the range of pedagogical skills he uses. Could you incorporate any of these into your own teaching?

## MAXIMISING OPPORTUNITIES FOR WRITING

Early years settings need to be amply resourced with varied, good-quality literacy resources, for reading and for writing, if children are to benefit from a wide variety of experiences that will support their development as writers. In order to foster independence and exploration of writing the resources need to be accessible to the children. They need to be well maintained and replenished regularly so that they are always available when needed. They can be stored in the writing and reading areas in the classroom and incorporated into other activities according to the teacher's intentions for the children's learning.

Daily or sessional routines need to maximise the time available for learning. Even arrival at school can be productive if coat hooks are labelled with children's names and they are expected to read them in order to hang up their personal possessions. Similarly entry into class is a literacy opportunity if children are expected to sign in or self-register in other ways. Whole-class sessions can be used to introduce new activities, teach through demonstration or share children's written work. Story time can be used to reflect on an author's style or message.

The teacher needs to plan for the most effective use of time for all the adults who are available. If teaching assistants or volunteers are not supervising activities at the start of sessions they might be able to assist children who are changing reading books or they can help individuals to sign in on the flip chart. During class time all the adults should be allocated to working with activities, groups of children or individuals, and they should know who or what they are working with as well as the purpose of the activity. The teacher may be observing, working with individuals, groups or the whole class; the specific role she takes should be planned ahead. The composition of groups and the focus of the teaching they will receive will also have been decided in advance. The introduction of the literacy hour has indicated how much of each day or session should be spent on reading and writing and how important it is to use this time to maximum effect.

When children are clear about the teacher's expectations and her routines they are more likely to settle quickly and contribute to the

calm, purposeful atmosphere of the classroom. If the classroom ethos encourages independence and collaboration the children are likely to initiate their own learning through writing in the writing area or in the imaginative play area. If all the opportunities for literacy development are to be used by the children, it is vital that the children are confident and feel happy to have a go at writing and reading without waiting for the teacher to instigate this, provide spellings or give her permission for them to begin or continue some writing.

## Summary

It is now clear that teachers who understand how to teach writing and combine appropriate procedures with a curriculum composed of meaningful and important writing activities are in the best position to help children to develop as enthusiastic and capable writers. This chapter has described a number of classroom procedures for developing writing with early years children from the nursery to Year 2. All of these strategies are compatible with the organisation expected in the literacy hour. They can also be used in classes that adopt other arrangements for the teaching and learning of literacy and language. The procedures can be used with individual children, groups and whole classes. The chapter ended with a section which described the many aspects of the teacher's role as she extends children's writing abilities.

*The key points covered in this chapter were:*

- **the variety of classroom procedures for developing writing**

- **ways of supporting children as they learn to write**

- **the teacher's role in teaching children to write**

- **ways of maximising opportunities for writing in early years settings.**

## Further reading

Campbell, R. (1996) *Literacy in Nursery Education*, Trentham Books, Stoke-on-Trent
This short book focuses exclusively on teaching reading and writing before Key Stage 1. It includes examples of some of the organisational strategies described in this chapter.

CLPE (1990) *Shared Reading Shared Writing*, Centre for Language in Primary Education, London
This practical and easily accessible book includes a number of accounts of shared writing sessions with children.

Dawes, L. (1995) *Writing: The Drafting Process*, National Association for the Teaching of English, Sheffield
This booklet contains a number of practical ideas for drafting fiction and non-fiction writing.

Graves, D. H. (1983) *Writing: Teachers and Children at Work*, Heinemann Educational Books, Portsmouth, New Hampshire
A key text which describes the process of writing and the process approach to writing.

Wyse, D. (1998) *Primary Writing*, Open University Press, Buckingham
This is an up-to-date account of the process approach to writing. It includes a number of case studies and examples.

# Developing writing in the nursery and reception class

**4**

**Objectives**

*When you have read this chapter, you should:*

- recognise the importance of developing positive attitudes towards writing

- appreciate some imaginative and developmentally appropriate ways of teaching writing

- be aware of ways of organising children, teaching episodes and resources

- understand the requirements for writing development in nursery and reception classes.

**Introduction**

This and the next chapter draw on the information contained in earlier chapters. Using the information about writing, classroom organisation and teaching strategies this chapter illustrates how activities that support children's learning and meet the statutory requirements for writing development can be incorporated into an early years curriculum. The Desirable Outcomes for Children's Learning (SCAA, 1996) and the National Literacy Strategy *Framework for Teaching* (DfEE, 1998) provide the core elements of a writing curriculum for nursery and reception classes. The aims they outline need to be addressed through a variety of imaginative and stimulating activities that are in keeping with what is known about children as learners and as developing writers, and are embedded within a curriculum and a classroom ethos that fosters positive attitudes to writing and develops children's confidence in their own ability to write.

The experiences and activities that are suggested in this chapter are intended to fulfil the statutory requirements for writing in nursery and reception classes and adhere to the principles of established good practice in the early years. They are suited to early years classes which are organised into workshop areas, which have

well-resourced curriculum areas and where children are used to accessing activities and equipment independently and responsibly.

## DEVELOPING POSITIVE ATTITUDES TOWARDS WRITING

Learning means becoming more knowledgeable through adding to one's understanding and skills, and it occurs in response to experience and teaching. However, increases in knowledge or ability are not the only consequences of learning. Learners also develop attitudes towards what they learn and construct a picture of themselves as successful or unsuccessful learners. Attitudes, perceptions of the subject's relevance and self-concept can affect how much learning takes place and how easily it is acquired. The curriculum that is offered to children, the way it matches and builds on their existing abilities and understanding and the way adults respond to what children do can have an important and lasting impact on their attitude towards writing and their interest in learning to write.

We now know that children commonly engage in independent writing without relying on a teacher to show them how to do it. Young children have already learned a great deal about writing before they are four, and are aware of print, are experimenting with it for themselves and are able to talk about writing (Bissex, 1980; Clay, 1975; Ferreiro and Teberosky, 1983; Hall, 1987; Kress, 1997). At this age they are also very optimistic about their ability to learn. Because they are developing and acquiring skills rapidly and have been successful at this, most children feel confident that they will continue to learn with comparative ease (Hills, 1986). The curiosity young children have about the world around them and their eagerness to explore new ideas leads them to embark on learning eagerly and with confidence when they first enter educational settings.

At one time children were prepared for writing through pre-writing activities such as tracing and copying handwriting patterns, letters and words using chunky crayons, chalks and large pencils. These activities were intended to introduce children to the writing system and to develop the motor skills needed to control writing implements. Pre-writing exercises were followed by set writing tasks. These often began with the child being asked to draw a picture and explain the content to the teacher, who then wrote down what the child said in an abbreviated form. Finally the child was expected to trace over or copy the adult's writing (Beard, 1984). Practices such as these emphasised correct letter formation and spelling. They reflected the belief that children have to be taught and then practise transcription skills before they can begin to write independently.

In order to write the child was expected to follow the teacher's instructions but was not necessarily expected to understand the purpose of the writing. These sorts of practices did little to widen children's understanding of the uses of writing and awareness of its relevance to them as young communicators. It is easy to see how this approach to teaching writing could lead to children thinking that writing is about getting the words right rather than being an act of communication, since this type of activity involves:

- learning by rote
- developing skills in isolation
- direction by the teacher
- getting it right
- the possibility of failure.

When writing means getting the words right, being told exactly how to do it and having to practise, it suggests to children that they are engaging in a difficult activity where failure is possible. Although children sometimes express satisfaction with prescribed and decon-textualised tasks, the satisfaction gained from succeeding at imposed activities that have little relevance to the learner is generally short term and derives from pleasing others rather than from intrinsic enjoyment or interest. Children who encounter practices that make writing difficult and do not make its use and relevance clear can become uninterested in it. They are unlikely to develop enthusiasm for this area of the curriculum or enjoy and explore the possibilities of writing. When their work is constantly corrected they may also lose confidence in their ability to learn.

Children in nursery and reception classes do not have to wrestle passively with tasks that stress transcription above composition or that introduce them to failure when they are learning to write. There is no official requirement to work in this way. One of the most recent documents from SCAA (1997c) suggests that effective practice should incorporate a wide range of activities, and HMI (1993) have criticised the formal curriculum that is offered to children in some reception classes. SCAA's recommendations and HMI's criticisms are supported by more recent research which suggests that a formal curriculum in the early years can in the long term 'lead to poorer performance, disincentives to learn and low self-esteem' (Sylva, 1997, p. 20).

Young children learn best when they actively engage with ideas and materials and when they are given reasons for learning that are relevant and make sense to them. They will learn a great deal about writing through observing others who write, examining print in books and exploring and experimenting with the tools, the system and the uses of writing. Taking risks, making mistakes, constructing and testing hypotheses are a valuable part of the process of rehearsing, revisiting, evaluating and extending what is known. Operating in this way in a well-prepared environment with the support of knowledgeable adults enables children to acquire the foundations of writing that will serve them well for the future.

By the time most children attend the nursery or reception class, writing development has already begun. The writing curriculum they are presented with should build on what they can already do and take account of the way they learn. It should include opportunities for children to:

- freely engage in mark-making and writing activities
- engage in purposeful and relevant activities
- spend time gaining real understanding of new concepts
- discover through active exploration
- learn through experimentation
- develop motivation and interest in what is learned
- become confident learners
- acquire positive dispositions towards writing.

**Activities**

1  Think about a successful learning experience that you have had. Try to identify the conditions that helped you to learn easily. Can you make some connections between the conditions which you have found helpful and the learning environment we can provide for children?

2  Think about something you find difficult, such as parking a car in a busy road. Do you feel confident about your ability to do this? Is it a pleasurable experience? Why are difficult activities often unpleasant? What would help to make them less intimidating? What can be done to give children confidence in their abilities as writers and make writing a pleasurable and rewarding experience for them?

## WRITING DEVELOPMENT BEFORE KEY STAGE 1

During their time in nursery and reception classes teachers have a number of goals for writing development. Amongst many other things, they want children to learn:

- that writing is a purposeful, communicative activity
- that what is said can be written down

- that there are many different types of writing
- how to use a variety of writing implements and other resources
- to write their own names
- to read or tell others what they have written
- to understand that speech sounds can be represented by letters
- to develop the skills needed to form letter shapes.

During these early years children's writing will take many forms and will not immediately resemble mature writing. Instead it might appear as:

- drawings
- random scribble
- scribble in lines
- letter-like shapes mixed with real letters and numbers
- groups of letters
- letters standing for words with recognisable connections
- words that are complete although not necessarily spelt correctly.

All of these features are typically found in nursery and reception children's writing, and the teacher's role is to help children move through this developmental sequence. Children who are learning that writing conveys meaning and who are able to make their meaning more accessible to others over time are making progress in writing.

Collect samples of one child's writing spanning a month or longer. Examine these and consider what the child knows about writing and what skills the child has as a writer. Look back at the section on developmental writing in Chapter 2 for more possibilities. Identify differences in the pieces of writing and consider whether these demonstrate progress, and if so in which aspects.

**Activity**

## WRITING EXPERIENCES AND ACTIVITIES

Most nursery and reception classes contain many opportunities for writing development within their normal, daily routines. In these settings teachers also teach children directly about writing during discrete writing sessions, as well as planning opportunities for children to independently practise their developing skills in varied ways. The opportunities to learn about writing that are offered enable children to learn through:

- observation
- exploration

- direct instruction
- practice.

This means that children are able to learn in different contexts and return to their learning many times over in order to consolidate and extend what they know.

These different types of provision for fostering writing development – routine activities, direct teaching and opportunities for practice– are used as headings for the activities which are described in this section. However, the distinction between them is not always clear cut. Routines are often implemented because of their intended learning outcomes and so are the result of planning, and independent activities may also be occasions when direct teaching is given. Readers will know that children's learning depends on careful thought about every aspect of the curriculum and the resources that are offered, and that opportunities for teaching occur at many points during the day.

## Routine activities

Many seemingly commonplace practices and resources in early years classrooms enable children to appreciate and explore literacy and experiment with writing. When children incorporate writing into their play and write freely in the writing area they are discovering that they can manipulate literacy for their own immediate purposes and their confidence as literacy users grows. Through their active involvement with reading and writing they are discovering that learning to be literate can be a pleasurable and satisfying experience. Provision of this kind also gives children time and space to explore writing at their own pace and at a level that is appropriate to their existing abilities.

### Literacy models

Demonstration is a very powerful form of teaching since it enables learners to see and remember how something is done. This helps the inexperienced to attempt similar activities for themselves. Adults and older children at home provide children with models of writers and writing which are very beneficial in children's early writing development. Adults in school can demonstrate and talk about other ways and other purposes for writing to children as they make records and notes during the day.

### The reading area

Reading areas filled with carefully chosen books including a selection of enlarged texts, non-fiction and books made by the teacher and the children provide examples of writing for many purposes, and their use helps children become familiar with how texts are constructed. Tapes and story props give children additional opportunities for becoming familiar with stories and texts.

### Displays of print

Classrooms contain a considerable amount of writing. Cupboards, equipment and specific areas of the classroom are labelled. Lists, charts and alphabets abound. Displays of art and design work are accompanied by explanations and titles. All these examples of print provide children with models for their own writing. Children can also write captions and other contributions for displays. Displays can be resourced with paper and pens so that children can add their own thoughts, reply to questions or comment on the work that has been included. When children are involved in producing the environmental print in the classroom they become more aware of the writing that is displayed and are more likely to refer to it when they are writing alone.

Displays that are related to letters and sounds, such as a 'letter of the week' table, can support writing as well as reading, particularly if they are designed to be interactive. Besides featuring objects that relate to the letter they can include chalks and a chalking board, rice or sand in a tray, plastic letters and other resources that encourage children to explore and make letter shapes This helps to reinforce the link between letter sounds and shapes. Letter displays can also contain words that relate to the objects and the collection of items, and the words can be used by the children for sorting and matching. Questions and answers related to displays can be written in speech bubbles and help children to recognise the connection between speech and writing.

### Art work

Through painting and drawing young children can explore how drawn and written forms stand in place of actual objects and experiences. They are discovering that symbols can be used to represent something other than themselves. This understanding is important for writing, which employs a set of symbols to represent actual and imagined events.

Art activities also give children practice at manipulating mark-making implements with increasing control. Sometimes children include letters and numbers in their painting, and adults can suggest that they paint patterns which use the strokes that are used to form letters. They can also encourage children to write their own names on their paintings. These activities help children with transcription.

**onset**
the opening unit of a syllable or word, e.g. <u>b</u>oy, <u>sw</u>ing

**rime**
the end unit of a word, e.g. bo<u>y</u>, sw<u>ing</u>

### Whole-class sessions

Saying and learning nursery rhymes, singing songs and encouraging children to join in the repeated refrains of stories is an excellent way for children to develop phonemic awareness (Goswami and Bryant, 1990). Children who can hear patterns in language and **onsets** and **rimes** in words are taking their first steps in developing phonic knowledge and spelling abilities.

## Planned opportunities for independent practice

Before and after children receive direct instruction in writing they need opportunities to explore the uses and the system of writing. Once they have been shown a model of writing and maybe had the opportunity to practise with guidance from an adult they are in a position to experiment further. Providing resources and reminding children that these are available encourages them to explore, gain practice and extend their skills in their own ways and at their own pace. Activities which permit children to do this should be freely and frequently available. They provide children with experiences that will enable them to 'use writing in a variety of ways' 'for a range of audiences', 'experiment with writing' and engage in 'independent writing' (DfEE, 1998, p. 19).

### Writing across the curriculum

In order that children see writing as a normal part of all their activities, and to give them opportunities to experiment with their developing skills, all activities can be resourced with writing materials. Teachers may select particular activities and learning areas to resource with literacy materials at different times. Paper and coloured pencils can be placed in the construction area so that children can record their plans for the models they intend to build. Pieces of card and felt tip pens can be used to label models with the maker's name, make notices asking others not to touch, and write identification labels. Large pieces of paper on an easel or smaller pieces on a clip board can be used to record children's findings as they experiment with sand and water. The results of matching, sorting and classifying activities can also be recorded. Sequences of notes and instruments can be written down so that the children's tunes can be played to the class during circle time. Pictures cut out of catalogues can be stuck into a blank book by the children, and later they can add their own explanatory text when they are working in the writing area. Plastic, wooden and foam letters can be used for sorting and matching activities so that children become familiar with the shapes of upper- and lower-case letters as well as learning their names and sounds. During outdoor play children can be given buckets of water and large paintbrushes to write on the playground and the outside walls of the school. When exploring touch and texture, Plasticene, clay and individual trays containing small amounts of sand or damp cornflour can be used to practise making letter shapes and patterns.

### The writing area

This is an important part of the provision for exploring writing in early years classrooms. It needs to be well equipped with as wide a range of paper, card and writing implements as possible. Other resources such as blank books, folders, a stapler, hole punch, glue, Sellotape, paper clips and scissors will give children additional ideas for their writing. Reference materials such as displays of letters, writing styles and scripts in many languages, alphabet books, simple dictionaries, word lists and a notice board are also useful. These need to be kept in an orderly and inviting state to encourage participation.

This should be an area that children can use independently and purposefully. They will be helped to do this if they are shown how to use the resources and are involved in organising the area. Working with the teacher they can compose notices and labels for the equipment. These could be written in a shared writing session by the teacher or by the children. Some of the writing that is produced in the writing area can be shared with the class, responded to or displayed.

Writing areas give children the chance to experiment with writing regularly and when they choose. They can write for their own purposes, at their own pace and without needing adult support. They can also explore the different uses and formats for writing as they use envelopes or blank books, as they write lists and letters and as they make cards. The writing area can provide opportunities for children to practise activities that have been introduced by the teacher. For example, if the children have been introduced to letter writing during shared writing or have been making greetings cards they may spontaneously practise these different forms of writing in the writing area. Lally (1991) described a teacher working with nursery children to make a sign for the nursery gate. Over the next few days the children, imitating the teacher, wrote a great many signs themselves.

### Imaginative play areas

These are an important resource for all of sorts of learning in the early years classroom, and need to be organised as carefully as any other planned learning activity. Adding literacy materials which encourage children to read and write provides opportunities for them to explore print in many forms. Books, magazines, brochures, telephone directories, calendars, diaries, maps, notices, forms, notepads, paper, envelopes and a range of pencils and felt tip pens all have a place in the home, cafe, shop, garage, or office. The children's use of the resources benefits from adults who spend time modelling literate behaviour in the play area. They quickly imitate adult writing and reading behaviours and incorporate these into their play. To remain effective and stimulating the focus and the resources in role-play areas need to be changed regularly. Involving the children in making the changes draws their attention to what they can use and how.

### Dramatic play

A few well-chosen props can be used by children to re-enact familiar stories and explore characterisation and the sequence of events in books. For example, a box and a collection of toys might be sufficient for children to re-enact *Bet You Can't!* (Dale, 1987).

### Signing in

Instead of taking a register the teacher can set up a large signing-in sheet on a small easel. As the children come into class each day they can write their names on the sheet. If necessary parents can help with this in the early stages, but it is important for children to try to write for themselves. This activity illustrates how writing is used to keep records and information. It can also be used by the teacher to note the children's developing writing skills.

### Puppets and story props

Sets of props or puppets that can be used to retell a known story can be used to give children valuable practice at rehearsing plots and sequences of events, and investing characters with personality traits, all of which add substance to the content of children's written stories. Their use should be modelled by the teacher as he shares a story with the children. Story props made by the teacher or by the children, and mounted onto a small magnet for use on a magnet board, can be kept in the listening area with the accompanying book and tape for the children to use independently when they read the book again.

### Making letter shapes

Children can experiment with making letter shapes using a variety of materials such as Plasticene, play dough, clay and pipe cleaners. They can create letter stamps out of string to print with or trace letters in rice and other tactile material. They can paint letter shapes or chalk them on the playground or outside walls. All these activities will help them to become familiar with letter shapes and letter formation. Children who need additional practice with letter shapes can sort plastic or wooden letters before they attempt to make letters for themselves.

**Activity**

Examine the way you plan for writing opportunities across the curriculum and in play. Could your provision be extended in any way? It might be helpful to look at the section on role play in Chapter 9 when you address this question. If appropriate try linking writing to other non-literacy activities.

## Direct teaching

A great deal of direct teaching in the early years takes place through demonstration, which allows children to observe how writing is done and why. Demonstrations present children with models that they can then use in their own early investigations of print and independent experiments. Direct teaching also occurs when teachers plan supervised writing activities which are supported by adults. As the children write or experiment with letters and words the adult's role is to guide them and extend what they know. This can be done by reminding children to think about their writing before they write or by helping them to visualise letters and words as they write.

### Writing books at home

Before children start in the nursery or reception class parents are often invited to make a book with their child at home. This is then brought to school. Such books usually include photographs of the child at different ages, their siblings, other family members and pets. The child and the adult compose the sentences that are written in the book, and these relate some of the child's interests, achievements, likes and dislikes. Making a personal book that will be read many times by others and by the author provides children with many lessons about writing. They learn about authorship, audience, the functions of writing, composition and transcription as well as 'to think about and discuss what they intend to write, ahead of writing it' (DfEE, 1998, p. 19). At a later stage children can use their personal books for reference if they want to spell their names, those of other family members or words of personal significance.

### Making alphabets

Alphabet friezes and books that are made by the children are a valuable resource for writing as well as providing opportunities for learning during the time that they are being made. By drawing the pictures to illustrate an alphabet frieze or dictionary the children learn a great deal about letters and words. Using topics such as food, flowers, countries or their own names and those of their friends can make the alphabet, letters and sounds relevant and interesting to children.

### Shared reading

Sharing a large book with the class or a group of children provides another demonstration of the uses of writing, the enjoyment it can bring and the way it is constructed and arranged. During shared reading sessions teachers can read and re-read stories, poems, rhymes, songs and non-fiction texts to and with children. During story times children can be some distance away from the books that are being read, and it can be difficult for them to see the details of normal-sized books. Commercial or class-made enlarged texts enable all the children to see the print as the teacher reads it.

Before beginning the reading the teacher might talk to the children about the cover, the title, the illustrations. As he reads he may point to the words. After the reading he may talk to the children about the contents and draw attention to the structure of the story, the way it begins and ends, the sequence of events and the characters in the book. Children can also be introduced to other forms of writing when texts other than stories are shared. This helps children to learn about books, different types of writing, text structure and the vocabulary of writing, and provides children with models for their own writing.

Once the children are familiar with the text and are ready to focus a little more on the writing the teacher can introduce enjoyable follow-up activities that introduce children to letters, sounds and letter patterns, all of which help with spelling. The group can be asked to look out for a particular letter as the teacher reads. They may be looking for the first letter of someone's name or a letter that frequently appears in the text. They can be asked to look for lower- or upper-case versions. Enlarged texts can also be used to demonstrate punctuation. Because shared reading teaches children so much about reading and writing it can be tempting to overuse the teaching opportunities it presents. Teachers need to be careful not to do this and to always remember that the main reason for sharing books is to enjoy a good read and that teaching should take second place to this.

### Visits

Taking groups of children on visits provides them with other models of literacy. Outings to local shops or a walk in the local environment will reveal writing in use and demonstrate many of the functions and purposes of writing. Street signs, advertisements, shop names, newspapers and magazines in the paper shop, menus, order pads and bills in the take-away are just some of the types of writing they may see. An outing can be prepared for by making a list of things to take and of people who will be going. A shopping trip may require a written shopping list. After a visit children can try to incorporate the environmental print they have seen into their modelling, construction play and imaginative play in the classroom. If appropriate the teacher and children can write a letter together in a shared writing session to thank the shopkeepers they visited. Alternatively the children can write their own thank you notes. Visits and follow-up activities stimulate discussion about language, its functions and its appearance and can raise children's awareness of writing.

## Shared writing

In shared writing sessions children observe how words are written down, the structures of words, letters and sounds. Teachers can use shared writing sessions to write stories based on known texts, to demonstrate story structure, plot and sequence, and to introduce children to aspects of the composing process.

## Modelling on known texts

This involves using a familiar text as a framework for writing which can be transcribed by the teacher or the children. A story, which may be made into a class or individual books, is created by following the structure and sequence of a published book. The characters or the objects in the story may be changed, but the language and the structures of the original text remain the same. For example, the teacher might use the model provided in *Where's Spot?* (Hill, 1980) to write a book entitled 'Where's Jacquie?' ... Is she in her office? ... Is she in the hall? ... This helps children to become familiar with writing stories and with the composing process. It also provides children with a clear structure for their own independent writing. Rhymes, poems and songs can be used in a similar way.

## Sequencing

Sequencing activities help children to become familiar with story structure and narrative language. Pictures and words taken from a book, or photographs and sentences recounting an activity the children have undertaken, are given to pairs of children. The activities might include an experiment, a school event, an outing, or a cooking activity. Working together the children arrange the pictures in order. After the children have sequenced the cards they can use them as the framework for narrating a story or event to other children or to an adult. The children can also make their own cards for this activity based on their own favourite books or class events.

### Sound and letter patterns

After rhyming texts such as *It's the Bear* (Alborough, 1994) have been shared with the class a number of times the teacher can take the opportunity of specifically discussing some of the rhymes in the text. Some of the words can be written on a flip chart, and the sounds and the letter strings that make up the rhyming parts can be discussed and compared. This helps to draw children's attention to the phonic and visual aspects of words and helps them to become aware of how words are spelt. Once children have begun to think about letter sounds, displays of items and words that begin with individual letters associated with the sound can be set up to support further exploration of letters, their sounds and their shapes.

### Teaching through response

Much of the direct teaching in the early years will take place when adults respond to and discuss children's early writing. This may have been produced spontaneously or during one of the planned opportunities for writing. All the writing that children produce needs to be treated seriously. It merits comment that focuses on the content and the author's intention. Responses such as 'lovely writing' are of little value as they do not do justice to the effort that the child has expended and do not give feedback that is helpful for the future. Responses drawn from the list that follows, and based on the teacher's knowledge of the child's previous experience and understanding, will help to extend what children know and can do.

- Respond with respect to what children have done.
- Ask the child to read back or tell you what they have written.
- Be positive about what the child has written.
- Talk about the content.
- Then comment on any significant aspects of the transcription.
- Respond in writing with a comment, a question and a correct version.
- Write a reply if a child has written to you.
- Display the writing on the writing noticeboard.
- Use the writing if it has been produced for a play area or a display.

Once children begin to experiment with making marks and print the teacher can plan for experiences that will stimulate further writing. Teachers can offer support and devise activities that are informed by observation, knowledge about writing and the child, and are appropriate to children's development.

*Writing for a range of audiences and purposes*

With inexperienced writers it can be difficult to devise activities which are purposeful and have an audience other than the teacher. The writing area, where children can write notes to peers and family members or greetings cards for others, encourages children to write in different ways for an audience of their choice. A post box which is regularly emptied can stimulate children to write messages to their friends in the class. Writing for displays will also be read by others. In addition teachers can set writing activities that grow out of themes or familiar rhymes and books. The children might make a get well card for Humpty Dumpty, or a shopping list for Mrs Grindling in *The Lighthouse Keeper's Lunch* (Armitage, 1977), or record the recipe for the Queen of Hearts' jam tarts after making them.

**Activities**

1 Consider the modelling techniques you use to foster children's writing development. Do these help children to become aware of the many uses of writing as well as demonstrating skills and techniques?
2 Observe two children who engage in literate activities during the course of a day. How might you support their learning through your response to their writing and the provision of future activities?

## TEACHING TRANSCRIPTION

The National Literacy Strategy *Framework for Teaching* (DfEE, 1998) identifies the following as areas for attention before children are five:

*Grammar and punctuation*

- Know that writing is ordered from left to right.

*Spelling*

- Recognise letters of the alphabet.
- Write initial letters of words.
- Distinguish between letter sounds and names.
- Be aware of alphabetical order.

*Handwriting*

- Form lower-case letters correctly.
- Form upper-case letters correctly.

As these concerns are returned to in Years 1 and 2 it is not expected that children's command of all of them will be complete by the end of the reception year. Some of the activities described in this chapter address these aspects of writing directly, develop children's presentation skills or provide practice. In addition adults will, when appropriate, provide individual and group teaching of some of the elements of transcription through direct teaching.

All aspects of children's writing will be helped when early years teachers provide children with opportunities to:

- see that their writing abilities are valued
- browse, share and read books
- see displays and models of writing
- use a variety of resources for writing
- talk about and investigate writing and language with others
- write in many different situations.

In a positive environment where children are undertaking valid and purposeful activities they will be learning to become writers rather than merely learning the skills of writing.

**Activity** Consider the range of writing opportunities, planned and unplanned, that children have access to during each day. When, what and how do they learn about spelling, punctuation and handwriting in these situations? What additional support is needed from adults if children are to achieve the outcomes listed in the Desirable Outcomes for Children's Learning?

**Summary** This chapter has suggested that confidence and positive attitudes towards writing are fundamental if children are to learn to write easily and recognise the significance of writing to their own lives. Taking this as the starting point the chapter then introduced readers to some ways of teaching and organising for the development of writing in the very early years of schooling.

*The key points covered in this chapter were:*

- **the need for young children to develop positive attitudes towards writing**

- **the need for young children to feel confident about their writing abilities**

- some developmentally appropriate ways of teaching writing

- ways of organising children, teaching episodes and resources

- coverage of composition and transcription in nursery and reception classes

- the requirements for writing development before Key Stage 1.

Campbell, R. (1996) *Literacy in Nursery Education*, Trentham Books, Stoke-on-Trent
This short book focuses exclusively on teaching reading and writing before Key Stage 1.

Hall, N. and Robinson, A. (1995) *Exploring Writing and Play in the Early Years*, David Fulton Publishers, London
A book which amply illustrates the possibilities for writing during play.

SCAA (1997) *Looking at Children's Learning*, SCAA Publications, Middlesex
This book contains a number of examples of teaching and activities for nursery and reception classes.

Whitehead, M. (1996) *The Development of Language and Literacy*, Hodder and Stoughton, London
This is an account of how young children learn language and of developmentally appropriate practice in the early years.

# 5 Developing Writing at Key Stage 1

## Objectives

*When you have read this chapter you should:*

- be familiar with the content of the writing curriculum at Key Stage 1
- be able to develop children's abilities to compose text
- be aware of some strategies that can be employed when introducing children to the expressive, transactional and poetic uses of writing.

## Introduction

The National Literacy Strategy *Framework for Teaching* (DfEE, 1998) has been designed to cover the requirements of the National Curriculum for English (DfE, 1995) and to take account of the Desirable Outcomes for Children's Learning (SCAA, 1996). It has been organised to ensure progression and coverage of a range of writing styles and formats. In the sections on writing the emphasis is on children learning about how to convey content and meaning, organise writing, use features of language and recognise the differences between spoken and written language. Like the programmes of study it stresses the importance of teaching children to compose. The skills of transcription, handwriting, spelling and punctuation are treated separately. This chapter is concerned with how to develop composition in the early years. Although some elements of transcription need to be taught alongside composition, as in the *Framework for Teaching*, teaching children about transcription is considered separately and is covered in later chapters.

### THE STATUTORY REQUIREMENTS

The main elements of writing in the *Framework for Teaching* are summarised in Table 5.1. This should help readers to appreciate the progression in writing ability that is expected. The table indicates which aspects of composition are to be developed in Years 1 and 2. It also shows the range of writing which children should undertake.

**Table 5.1**
*National Literacy Strategy Framework for Teaching: curriculum content for writing*

## Year 1

**Term 1**
- Write stories based on personal experiences
- Write rhymes and stories based on familiar texts
- Write captions
- Write lists
- Write instructions

**Term 2**
- Adapt and play with patterns of language in books
- Represent plots using diagrams
- Represent story plots in a variety of ways
- Write character profiles in a number of ways
- Use story elements to structure writing
- Write labels
- Write extended captions
- Organise information into non-chronological reports

**Term 3**
- Write about significant incidents from known stories
- Include settings in simple stories
- Use poems as models for writing
- Compose poetic sentences
- Write simple recounts
- Use the language and features of information books
- Make information books

## Year 2

**Term 1**
- Use story structure to write stories based on personal experiences
- Structure a sequence of events using the language of time
- Write poems based on published poems
- Write simple directions and instructions for others
- Organise instructions sequentially
- Use diagrams
- Use appropriate register in writing instructions

**Term 2**
- Use story settings from known books in own stories
- Write character profiles of characters in known books
- Write poems based on the structure of known poems
- Make class collections of poems
- Make class dictionaries and glossaries
- Produce flow charts and diagrams to explain a process

**Term 3**
- Write sustained stories using narrative, settings, characterisation, dialogue and story language
- Write humorous verse, riddles, jokes and language puzzles based on published examples
- Write a simple evaluation of a book
- Make simple notes from an information text to use in own writing
- Write non-fiction texts
- Write non-chronological reports

In order for children to learn about all the aspects and types of writing in Table 5.1 teachers will need to widen children's knowledge about:

- the functions of writing
- types of writing
- the distinguishing features of different types of writing.

**Activity**  Read the National Literacy Framework requirements for writing and identify how the content of children's writing is expected to become more sophisticated over the six terms they spend in Years 1 and 2. This should help you to see how composition in writing progresses.

## WRITING AT KEY STAGE 1

During their time in nursery and reception classes children will have become increasingly familiar with writing and the writing system. They will have been exploring what writing is for and what they can do with it. As they embark on the programme of work for Key Stage 1 some children may be quite experienced at writing brief stories, captions and notes, and may have been introduced to simple drafting techniques such as planning through drawing, composing in their heads, and editing writing on the word processor. They may be able to form many letters clearly, spell simple words correctly or recognisably and know that there are resources that they can consult to help them with their writing. Other children will still need to acquire more experience before they demonstrate this level of competence. All children in Year 1 and Year 2 classes will continue to benefit from activities such as those described in Chapter 4, and these should continue to be offered to them. For some children the degree of challenge may have to be increased and for others the aim will be to continue to build confidence and competence. The activities described in this chapter are suitable for children who are at ease with the writing system and ready for Key Stage 1.

Young writers have to learn how to manipulate a communication system that is both demanding and time consuming; being able to control both composition and transcription simultaneously is not easy. As Newman (1984) suggests, writers have to:

- have something to say
- know how to say it
- know how to organise it
- employ the necessary secretarial skills.

Initially children's ability to write is supported by their recognition of the similarities between written and spoken language. However, as children become more competent at writing and move from expressive writing to using the more formal modes of transactional and literary writing the differences between print and speech become more apparent. This is because with writing there is:

- no immediate response from the audience
- no shared context
- no help from intonation and stress.

This means that there is:

- a greater need to use formal language
- a need to express meaning explicitly and clearly
- a need to use correct forms of language.

Just as the writing activities that children are expected to undertake become more demanding, the support from their experience as oral language users lessens.

Adults as well as children can be inhibited by all the demands writing places on them, but in the classroom it is the teacher's responsibility to prevent these challenges from deterring children from writing. If they do occur children may write very little or rarely finish a piece of writing, and will not get the practice that is required to become a competent writer. The role of the teacher in Key Stage 1 is to retain children's motivation to write and to help them come to grips with the demands and the complexity of writing. The teacher can do this in four ways, by:

- teaching children about the different parts of the writing process
- limiting the number of writing activities children undertake and selecting these with care
- ensuring that all writing is purposeful and has an audience and a motivating outcome
- not expecting children to have complete control of transcription when they are composing.

## DEVELOPING CHILDREN'S AWARENESS OF THE USES OF WRITING

Teachers develop children's knowledge of the functions and forms of writing as they use the teaching procedures described in Chapter 3, since these are intended to make writing in school a meaningful activity with purposeful outcomes. Additionally, if the type of writing and the purpose and audience for each piece of writing that children undertake is selected with the intention of widening their awareness of the requirements and characteristics of different sorts of texts, children's understanding of the possibilities of writing will be increased.

As children see and read text that is used for different purposes, and as they begin to use writing in different contexts and for different reasons, they will begin to recognise an increasing range of uses for writing. Increasingly children will be using writing to accompany their work across the whole curriculum, which will include writing to plan, predict, explain and record. They will be continuing to write in the expressive mode in journals and in contributions to class accounts of shared events, and they will be extending their literary writing abilities by writing more extended stories and more sophisticated poems.

The environments in Year 1 and Year 2 classes should contain displays of writing that reflect its different uses. Lists, charts, instructions and rules show how writing can be used to remember special days, special people or how to do something. Similar messages are given by literacy resources, such as telephone directories and recipe books in the play areas and dictionaries and reference texts in the writing area. Letters, notes and greetings cards indicate the communicative function of writing. Brainstorms, plans and drafts show how writing can be used to organise and develop ideas. The books in the reading area and all the stories, poems, rhymes and songs that are read by and shared with the class demonstrate that writing is a source of pleasure.

*The Jolly Postman* (Ahlberg and Ahlberg, 1986) and its sequel *The Jolly Christmas Postman* (Ahlberg and Ahlberg, 1991) contain examples of writing used to fulfil many different functions, including maintaining relationships, giving information and persuading. Discussions about the different types of communications that are included in these two books could introduce children to the notion of register and how it changes to accommodate the audience and the message. Books such as *Dear Daddy* (Dupiasquier, 1986), *The True Story of the Three Little Pigs* (Sciesza, 1989), *The Magic Fountain* (McGough, 1996), *The Baby's Catalogue* (Ahlberg and Ahlberg, 1985), *Messages* (Thompson, 1993) and *The Truth about Cats* (Snow, 1996) demonstrate how writing fulfils a number of purposes. *The Shopping Basket* (Burningham, 1980) and *Don't Forget the Bacon!* (Hutchins, 1976) demonstrate, by omission, the value of writing as a means of remembering. Sharing books with children such as those mentioned in this paragraph, and discussing the characters' motives for writing and the types of writing the books contain, will add to children's awareness of the many uses of print.

*I Like Books* (Browne, 1991) catalogues a number of different types of books written in different styles. Imitating the narrator in *I Like Books* the children could classify some of the books in their own classroom. They could list their findings using some of the headings suggested in *I Like Books*. As the entries on the charts accumulate the children could be asked to justify their decisions. This might be a productive introduction to analysing types of writing.

## LOCATING WRITING IN A CONTEXT

Texts are produced with an awareness of purpose, audience, outcome, form and register. These conditions determine the sort of writing that should be produced, and when they are known make it easier to write well. In order to learn how to compose effectively children need to be aware of the uses of writing, be clear that what is being written and to whom affects how it is presented, and be starting to recognise that particular grammatical constructions and vocabulary items are used in different types of writing. When planning to teach children about how to compose different types of writing teachers will need to make the following factors clear to children before they begin to write:

- the function of the writing
- the audience
- the content
- the register
- the format
- the outcome for the writing.

For example, if the children were asked to write to their parents to invite them to an open day at the school they would have to consider all the following information before beginning to plan and compose their individual letters:

| | |
|---|---|
| function | give information |
| audience | parents, carers |
| content | what, why, when |
| register | formal vocabulary, clearly organised |
| format | invitation, reply slip |
| outcome | sent to, read by and responded to by the recipients. |

Teachers will also want to give children the time to plan, draft, discuss and revise their work. Each of these stages provide valuable learning opportunities. Class and group brainstorming sessions generate ideas that children may use when they are planning their own writing and prevent them from feeling they have nothing to say. Drafting followed by conferencing provides vital, purposeful teaching and learning opportunities. Children's writing will not develop merely through writing every day. Learners need to be given explicit feedback and be provided with strategies for improvement through individual and group teaching and teacher demonstrations.

**Activity** Plan a writing activity for a group of children. Identify the function of the writing, the audience, the content, the register, the format and the outcome. How might you explain these features to children to help them complete the task well?

## DEVELOPING EXPRESSIVE WRITING

Writing 'news' is one of the most familiar formats for expressive writing undertaken in school. However, this is a limited activity. It rarely serves any purpose beyond giving children opportunities to practise and the teacher the chance to assess writing. The sole audience is often the teacher and its overuse can lead to stale offerings and uninterested writers.

A more productive way of allowing children to write about their personal experiences is to provide them with writing journals. Children should be able to use these when they choose rather than at set times. Used in this way they are rather like diaries. To demonstrate what can be written in them the teacher might read some extracts from diaries to the children showing how thoughts ('I hope that . . . ', 'I really enjoyed . . . '), events ('At school we are having a book fair . . . ', 'Tomorrow is a special day . . . ') and experiences ('Yesterday my nan came . . . ', 'Last night I had a horrid dream . . . ') can be recorded. Sometimes journals contain notes for oneself, reminders, things to find out or questions to ask. Journals can also be used to communicate with the teacher. If they are used in this way the teacher needs to write back to the child and respond to what they have said. Keeping journals presents children with many opportunities to use expressive writing authentically.

Introspective and autobiographical writing that is often linked to a theme or derived from work across the curriculum is another type of expressive writing. Likes, dislikes, ambitions, past experiences, favourite toys and friends are examples of writing being used to express something about the writer. Art, history, geography and religious education often give rise to writing in this way. In science and design and technology children are sometimes required to speculate and clarify their developing ideas; this also allows children to record their personal thoughts in writing.

## DEVELOPING TRANSACTIONAL WRITING

The ability to produce clear factual texts such as lists, reports and records is needed in order to meet the writing demands of schools and society. The emphasis on 'range' in the National Curriculum Order for English (DfE, 1995) is intended to ensure that non-fiction writing is given an important place in the literacy curriculum. Developing children's abilities to read and write factually is an important element in the *Framework for Teaching* (DfEE, 1998). This document refers to captions, lists, factual statements, recounts, directions, instructions, explanations, evaluations and reports as the forms of writing that should be familiar to children by the end of Year 2. Non-fiction writing is organised, explicit, impersonal, and often incorporates specialist terminology and formal sentence structures. It is very different from the expressive mode. In order to write factually children need to learn about and understand the distinctive features of the genre.

Learning about non-fiction is likely to begin with reading and discussing information books. Initially children can discuss the differences between fiction and non-fiction texts. They might talk about their different functions, the way they are organised and the linguistic and pictorial devices they employ. Children may also have had some experience of non-narrative writing through producing labels, captions and notices for the classroom. These too can be compared with the other sorts of writing they have produced.

### Explanation

One of the simplest types of information writing is that of chronological non-fiction writing, such as a description of the life cycle of a plant or an animal. This is logical writing that has order and a clearly identifiable starting point. Children's early attempts to describe a life cycle often take the form of a diary: 'Today I planted a seed . . . today my seed has grown two leaves . . . '. An explanation is somewhat different from this. It should explain the processes that are involved in natural and social phenomena. It opens with a general statement identifying what is to be explained, and continues with a series of sentences arranged logically and chronologically which explain how or why something occurs. In style it is impersonal and often employs the third person. Children need to be shown how to shape their diary writing into an explanation. The teacher can demonstrate this through modelling in shared writing. The opening statement might be the title for the writing, 'The Life Cycle of Plants'. The sentences which follow might include: 'First seeds have to be planted . . . After two or three days they develop roots . . . '. Comparing the child's example with the teacher's model illustrates what children will need to learn. After seeing the teacher write in this way and after discussing the characteristics of an explanation children will need to practise transforming their own accounts into an explanation. They might do this by rehearsing their explanation orally with a partner or an adult before beginning to write.

### Report

Reports are descriptions of objects. Children are often asked to describe objects such as the classroom, their bedroom or the park. They can be helped to produce a successful piece of report writing if they are shown how this type of writing is structured. They need to know where the description should begin and what information should be included. They need to be aware that descriptions are written in the present tense and include some of the following features:

- the name of the object
- its appearance
- its qualities
- its parts and their function
- what it is made of
- how it is made
- what it is for.

If children are given the headings appropriate to the object they are describing they should be able to organise their writing clearly and succinctly.

### Recount

Children are often required to use non-fiction writing to retell events such as a class outing to a place of interest. Using the elements of genre theory, the textual requirements can be identified as shown in Table 5.2.

Following the three stages in the structure section will again support children as they remember and organise the event in writing.

### Procedural

Writing recipes, instructions and rules involves using the procedural genre. The characteristics of tasks such as these can be analysed as shown in Table 5.3.

Children are often asked to write explanations, reports, recounts and procedural texts in school. Without guidance their writing tends to combine expressive and information styles and the result is writing that is not clear and that does not suit the purpose. When

| Purpose | to retell events, inform others |
|---|---|
| Tenor (relationship with audience) | a known familiar and receptive audience such as the teacher, peers, family |
| Field (subject matter) | autobiographical, personal experience |
| Language | personal pronouns *I*, *we*, words that show the passage of time: *first*, *then* past tense, action verbs: *went*, *saw*, *found* |
| Structure | introductory scene-setting statement chronological ordering of events closing statement |
| Other examples | giving an account of a child's day in a Victorian school |

**Table 5.2**
*An account of a class trip using the recount genre*

| Purpose | to direct the behaviour of others |
|---|---|
| Tenor | unspecified, general audience, formal |
| Mode | written, diagrammatic |
| Field | how to do something |
| Language | addresses the reader as *you* or does not include pronouns words for chronological order: first, next, second present tense, imperatives: get, find, do, mix, pour explicit, clear |
| Structure | traditional format, title, ingredients, method |

**Table 5.3**
*Characteristics of the procedural genre*

introducing an activity that involves non-fiction writing teachers have to be clear about requirements of the sort of text that is being composed. Using genre theory helps with this. For example, it would show that the differences between describing a life cycle and describing an object arise because one is likely to be an explanation and the other a report. When the characteristics of the text are identified teachers are able to give children precise guidance about what is required and provide them with a framework for their writing.

Factual writing is a skill that needs to be learned. It makes many demands on young writers and we cannot assume that because we show them examples of recipes, brochures or invitations they will know how to write in that genre. They need to be made aware of the formal characteristics of such texts through analysing them with the teacher's guidance, practising the features orally and experimenting with them in purposeful writing activities drawn from all areas of the curriculum.

In order to write non-fiction well children need to:

- understand the difference between factual and narrative writing
- understand the function of different forms of factual texts
- be aware of the characteristic features of factual texts
- plan for factual writing
- use diagrams, tables and other graphic forms.

**Activity**  Design a prompt sheet with brief headings that can be completed with words or pictures that children can refer to and use to write a recipe using the procedural genre.

## DEVELOPING POETIC WRITING

Poetic writing is writing that can be appreciated for its own sake. At its best, the content, the structure and the style all contribute to the reader's enjoyment. It can be found in stories, poems, songs, rhymes, jokes and plays. The starting point for literary writing is literary reading. Children who enjoy listening to and reading books and who enjoy a substantial diet of stories and poems by a variety of authors will already have an appreciation of the power of language to entertain. They may also have an implicit understanding of how texts work (Meek, 1988). Although it is easy to enjoy well-written literary forms it is far more difficult to write them. Children do not find the composition of literary texts easy (Bereiter and Scardamalia, 1985). They find it difficult to plan the structure of a composition before writing it. So just as with other types of writing, children need to be taught about the characteristics of poetic writing and engage in activities which enable them to appreciate that stories and poems are carefully organised and have their own particular structure.

### Story

In conjunction with discussions about familiar books children can begin to explore story forms by drawing on their own experiences. These might include oral anecdotes or descriptions of events that have been recorded in journals. An account of a special occurrence can be related as a sequence of events with a beginning and an end. As children become used to writing in this way and become more aware of story structure teachers can help them to extend their ability to use events in their own lives as the basis of a story by asking them to think of a title before they begin to write. Titles such as 'Adventure in the Supermarket', 'The Day My Sister Got Lost' or 'The Birthday Outing' encourage children to think about the difference between an account and literary writing. Giving writing a title and an audience raises its status and may encourage children to structure their work more carefully and experiment with style by including humour, surprise or dialogue. It is this crafting of personal experience into story form that is recommended in the National Literacy Strategy *Framework for Teaching*.

The next stage is to examine and then write more sophisticated stories. All stories include a number of elements. These are:

- openings and endings
- plot
- structure
- characterisation
- setting
- a narrative voice.

Children can be helped to write more effectively if they engage in activities which help them to examine the conventions of literary writing. The first step is to reflect on the elements of familiar texts. Big books, that are read and re-read with the class, provide an excellent starting point for discussing how stories are written.

### *Openings and endings*
Working with some of the books available in class the children could start to compile charts of beginnings and endings. This can help them to see that stories often begin with a clear statement and an introduction to the central character. They do not just begin with the first event. For example:

> Titch was little.
>
> (Hutchins, 1974)

> This is a story about a young man called Patrick, who set out one day to buy a violin.
>
> (Blake, 1968)

Endings often contain a final event which ensures that order is re-established and the characters are happy.

> And Titch's seed grew and grew and grew.
>
> (Hutchins, 1974)

And they all got back to the town before dark.

(Blake, 1968)

This activity and the discussions that accompany it would add to children's understanding of how stories are constructed and help them to avoid starting their writing with an instant entry or ending with an abrupt conclusion. Later the charts listing openings and endings, compiled by the class, could be used as a resource for their own writing.

### Plot and structure

All writers benefit from help with organising their ideas. Careful plotting is one of the most crucial aspects of effective writing. Young children can be helped to appreciate story structure by examining stories that are familiar to them. As they re-read familiar stories with the teacher they can listen for and identify the events. These can be recalled and listed by the teacher and used to support an oral retelling.

Once children have rehearsed plots orally during story and individual reading sessions, they can be asked to rewrite a familiar story. They can be invited to select four events from a story and draw or write these in sequence. For example:

Mrs Lather washed laundry.
Mrs Lather washed babies.
Mrs Lather washed an elephant.
Mrs Lather closed the laundry.

(modelled on Ahlberg, 1981)

### Adapting known texts

At times, either working with the teacher or writing alone, children can base their own stories on known texts. For example, *Where's Spot?* (Hill, 1980) could lead to a class version which substitutes the teacher or a child for Spot as in the example of 'Where's Jacquie?' that follows.

| opening | Where's Jacquie? |
| events/development | Is she in the cupboard? |
| | Is she in the office? |
| ending/resolution | She's in the playground. |

To write a different version while using the structure of the published story the children will have used a number of conventions – an opening, a set of events and an ending – although they may not have been consciously aware that they were doing this.

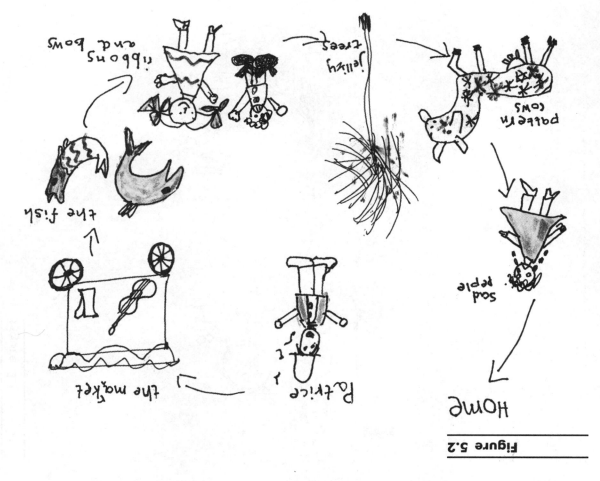

**Figure 5.2**

they are writing. The activities that are selected need to introduce children to thinking about the appearance, personality and behaviour of people in stories.

Painting and drawing familiar characters taken from favourite books is one way of considering appearance and, as dress often reflects behaviour and personality, beginning to think about personal qual-ities. The children's pictures can be made into posters and displayed. Discussions about the posters will encourage the children to use words that can be incorporated into their writing.

A later activity might be to ask the class to think of words that describe a known character. The words could be recorded on a flip chart. If working with *Princess Smartypants* (Cole, 1986), words like *pretty, rich, pet lover, untidy, adventurous* and *naughty* might emerge. The children could then explore characters in other familiar books in a similar way. At a later stage the children could be asked to group the words describing personality and appearance separately.

**Figure 5.1**

and provide further practice in learning how to compose stories. A single picture drawn by a child can be extended into a story by drawing what happened before and what happened after the orig- inal picture. Using the three pictures children can narrate their story orally or in writing (see Figure 5.1).

Using a sequence of pictures is another way of helping children to plan their stories. A piece of A4 paper can be folded into four sections and children asked to represent four events in each of the sections. When these are discussed with the teacher a possible sequence can be explored, the pictures can be numbered and the story told and then written.

Individually or collaboratively children can draw a set of pictures that answer the Who? Where? What's the problem? What happens next? and What happens at the end? questions. The pictures can be arranged in sequence and captions or key words can be added to the pictures before the story is written in full.

Making maps can be a helpful way of thinking about stories that tell of a journey. For example, the plot of *Patrick* (Blake, 1968) or the Jolly Postman's delivery round (Ahlberg and Ahlberg, 1986) could be represented as shown in Figure 5.2.

Using timelines to examine and then support writing can be another useful way of introducing children to ways of structuring stories. Many books that have been written for young children follow the sequence of the days of the week, for example *The Very Hungry Caterpillar* (Carle, 1969), *Mrs Lather's Laundry* (Ahlberg, 1981) and *Jasper's Beanstalk* (Butterworth and Inkpen, 1992). Later the vocab- ulary that signals the development of a narrative over time, words such as *once, then, after, afterwards, next, finally, at last,* can be intro- duced. Bradman's *Through My Window* (1986) and *Wait and See* (1988) could be used to introduce the use of this type of vocabulary.

All these techniques intended to explore, recreate and plan new stories can be used on the left-hand page of a writing book. The facing page can then be used to write the first draft of the story (see Figure 5.3).

### Characterisation

Exploring character begins when children talk about the heroes and heroines in the stories they hear and read. However, children need more help than this in order to include characterisation in their own writing. It is probably best to begin by examining characters in known stories before moving on to inventing characters. Working in this way gives children examples that they can draw upon when

The next stage is to make this method of organising stories explicit so that children can consciously incorporate similar frameworks into their own writing. The following example, using *Princess Smartypants* (Cole, 1986), illustrates a framework that the teacher can use with the class:

*Opening*
Who? Princess Smartypants
Where? Castle
What's the problem? She does not want to get married.

*Development*
What happens? Lots of princes ask her to marry them.

*Ending*
What happens at the end? She changes one of the princes into a frog and lives happily ever after.

This could be written up by the teacher, who might want to emphasis the sequence of:

- Who?
- Where?
- What's the problem?
- What happens next?
- What happens at the end?

Using this simple set of questions the teacher and the children could rewrite *Princess Smartypants* together in a shared writing session. Next the children could write their own version of the published story using the questions as a framework and drawing on some of the ideas generated while discussing what to include in the class version. The next stage would be to write a different story using the framework. Again this should be modelled by the teacher before the children use the questions to construct their own stories. This sequence of teaching episodes introduces children to the concept of story structure, introduces the appropriate vocabulary to discuss stories, provides them with a simple framework for their own writing, presents them with a demonstration of how to use the framework and gives them an opportunity to experiment with story structure in their own writing. As with all work with young learners the teacher will need to revisit story structure and repeat the teaching steps before children are confident with the process.

*Composing with pictures and diagrams*
As well as providing headings and questions teachers can demonstrate structure and sequence through the use of pictures. This method can be used by the children to plan and draft their writing

**Figure 5.3**

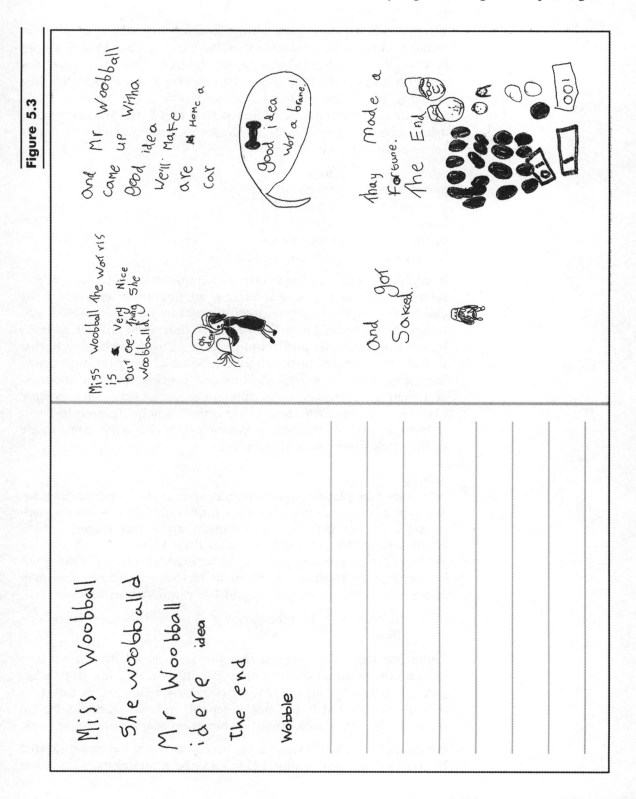

When creating a new character the simplest first step is to give him or her a name. Asking children to name the characters in their stories is a simple but effective activity for children. This often gives the reader a number of clues about character type and personality. Just thinking about the names Mary, Robert and Ms Jones is likely to create different images in the reader's mind. The next stage is to ask children to assign some attributes to their character. A simple series of prompts can help:

| | |
|---|---|
| name | Tom |
| appearance | small, brown hair |
| personality | lonely, kind |
| likes | animals |
| dislikes | noisy people |
| behaviour | asks for a puppy. |

It might be useful for the children to think about describing themselves in this way before depicting an imaginary character. The children's simple character descriptions can be incorporated into passports or personal files. They can also draft their characters' traits by drawing portraits and framing their pictures with objects that would be significant to the character. Some of the paintings, drawings, diagrammatic representations and profiles could be collected and included in class books of different character types such as *Brave Characters* or *Kind Characters*. These activities help children to begin to think about how they can make their own characters come to life in the stories they write themselves.

### Setting

All stories take place in a particular location and at a particular time. The type of narrative, whether it is a traditional folk tale or a contemporary story, affects the setting. Children can be encouraged to think about settings by considering stories they know. A book such as *Wait and See* (Bradman, 1988) could be mapped out on a flip chart by the teacher to draw attention to location and time. The map could record the shops that Jo and her mum visit as follows:

> the baker's → the greengrocer's → the fish shop → the post office

These familiar sights suggest that the story is set in a street in a contemporary urban environment. We are told that the story takes place on Saturday but the teacher could ask what else in the story tells us this. Jo is at home, not at school, and, for readers who are familiar with other books about Jo, her mum is at home, not at work.

Similar activities that examine familiar stories will demonstrate that the type of narrative, traditional folk tale or contemporary story, has an effect on the setting. When we share books with children we may think that these are obvious, but discussions about what can be taken for granted can give children information that will be useful when they write.

*Narrative style*

Stories incorporate a number of linguistic devices which set them apart from everyday anecdote. They are usually related in the third person using the past tense, they include particular phrases and combinations of words, and the language that writers select adds interest and detail to the content.

Using and maintaining the third person in a narrative text is something many children can find difficult. To begin to use *she* and *he* rather than *I* involves being aware of the distinction between expressive and literary forms. Besides making this distinction teachers should avoid asking children to write stories when they mean an account of a personal experience or a journal entry. This confuses children about the characteristics of different texts. Retelling and rewriting published texts helps children to develop a sense of distance. It would be difficult to substitute *I* for Mrs Lather, for example. Rehearsing ideas and making first drafts of stories should also be of assistance and provide an opportunity for changing *I* to *she* or *he* if children have included them in their writing.

From the earliest stages of sharing books with children we draw attention to the special kind of language that is often found in stories. We talk about phrases such as *Once upon a time* and *Long ago*. When children are reading we may discuss the way words are ordered in written language and comment on arrangements such as *said the old man* or *Crash! Went the glass* which would be unusual in spoken language. The child who wrote the sentences shown in Figure 5.4 to describe his dog shows an ear for the grammatical structures of written language.

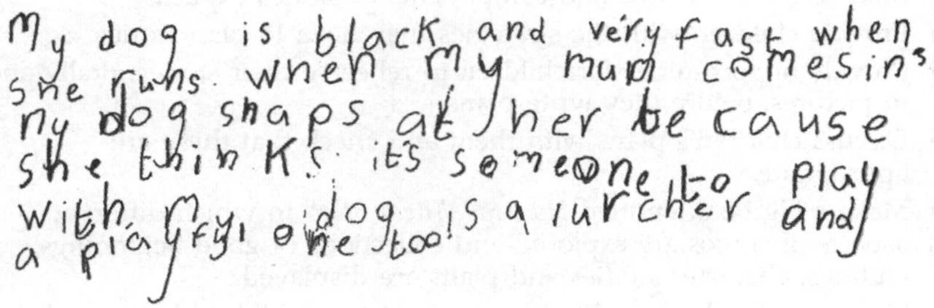

**Figure 5.4**

My dog is black and very fast when she runs. When my mum comes in, my dog snaps at her because she thinks it's someone to play with. My dog is a lurcher and a playful one too.

Had he written a more conventional set of statements, such as:

My dog is a lurcher. My dog is black. My dog is playful

the effect of his description would have been diminished and the impact of the ending lost.

Brainstorming interesting words to use when writing stories, compiling lists of words that have similar meanings and encouraging children to delight in language heightens their awareness of words, increases their written vocabulary and prompts them to make more adventurous choices in their writing. Young children who are confident enough to take risks when they write and who know that readers enjoy vivid language can with a little encouragement begin to explore style and their own narrative voice.

## Composing effective stories

Although the various elements of stories have been considered separately it is important that the routines described above do not prevent children from writing complete stories. Each activity needs to be integrated into writing experiences that result in significant outcomes. When the stories that result from these activities are illustrated and then published as wall stories, in large teacher-written books, in class anthologies, as individual small books and on tape, they can be added to the resources available in the reading and listening areas. The children will then see that their writing has an audience, a purpose and an important outcome.

Teachers can help children to become effective writers of narrative by incorporating some of the strategies listed in Table 5.4 into their regular literacy programme.

**Table 5.4**

*Strategies to help children become effective story writers*

- Tell stories to children using written prompts that they can see.
- Make the conventions and components of stories explicit.
- Provide children with the strategies they need to plan stories.
- Provide opportunities for children to rehearse their stories, orally and in pictures, before they write plans.
- Discuss children's plans with them and check that these are appropriate.
- Make a big book entitled *How to Write a Story* in which different aspects of stories are explored and collections of good beginnings, endings, character studies and plans are displayed.
- Give clear feedback and guidance about how children have used the elements of stories in their writing.

**Activity**

Select a book written for young children. Identify the different story elements it contains. How might you use the book as a starting point for developing children's writing?

## Poetry

Writing poetry gives children the opportunity to enjoy and play with language. Through the careful selection of words poetry can entertain, amuse or evoke feelings. All these aspects are present in the National Literacy Strategy *Framework for Teaching* (DfEE, 1998), which requires that children gain experience of playing with patterns of language, write rhymes and poems based on familiar models, experiment with structure, and write their own poems, riddles and jokes.

Saying and hearing nursery rhymes, songs, playground rhymes and stories with repeated refrains are among children's earliest experiences of poetry. They reveal how words and the rhythms of language can be manipulated into memorable and enjoyable forms. Re-forming nursery rhymes orally and in writing is a simple way of introducing children to experiments with language. Adding new verses to familiar songs such as *If You're Happy and You Know It* provides further opportunities to think about rhythm and rhyme.

Young children can compose alliterative alphabets, such as:

> Asvi Always Asks for Apples,
> Bobby Bakes Brown Bread ...

Simple poetic forms can be explored through shared writing based on lists and formulas, such as:

> One wiggly worm
> Two tired turtles
> Three thirsty thrushes

> Yellow is the colour of the sun in the summer.
> Yellow is the colour of a buttercup.
> Yellow is the colour of the butter on my toast.

These frameworks help children to structure their early experiments, but more importantly they require writers to maintain rhythms and patterns as they write so that they get a feel for language. As children become more familiar with poetry through poems that the teacher reads to them, their own browsing and reading, displays of poetry books and posters and reciting poems, they can be encouraged to become more original in their own writing. They might experiment with poems in their writing journals, identify favourite published poems and copy these out for a class anthology, try to imitate the style of a favourite poem, and make collections of jokes and riddles. Giving children paper of different shapes, colours and textures can be an added stimulus for their experiments. All of these activities help children to move towards an appreciation of poetry as 'the best words in the best order, language used with the greatest possible inclusiveness and power' (DES, 1975, p. 135).

## INTEGRATING LEARNING ABOUT WRITING

The different types and conventions of writing can be used and taught separately but sometimes they can be combined in one extended project. If the teacher selects a rich starting point for writing, children can work through a number of writing forms and explore a number of writing functions before producing a finished product. For example, producing a collection of stories that are published in a large book and that will be read by and with the class can involve the children in composing, transcribing and reviewing stories. This necessitates thinking about plot, character, setting and structure. Producing a list of contents, the text for the back cover and brief author biographies introduces children to some of the forms that factual writing can take. All the writing that is undertaken during a book-making project can have a purpose and an audience that are understood and relevant to children. The success of such a project depends on thinking carefully about component parts of the activity and the organisation of time. The teacher needs to know about the children's existing writing skills and knowledge about writing so that she can plan her teaching sessions and teacher–child conferences and allocate time for children to plan, draft and revise their writing. Careful planning of exciting and relevant writing activities should ensure that the outcome is worth all the effort that will be expended.

**Summary**

This chapter has developed some of the points introduced earlier in the book and related them to the provision for writing that should be made in Key Stage 1 classes. In Chapters 1 and 2 it was suggested that writing well and appropriately depends on having knowledge about how to fashion writing in a way that suits the particular situation. Although adults may be able to do this without identifying all the influences they are taking account of, children have not yet reached this stage of language awareness. They need to be shown that the purpose of the communication, the content and the writer's relationship with the audience affect the choices that are made about vocabulary, structure and style. Children need to be taught about the different functions and characteristics of expressive, transactional and poetic writing and the many different forms of writing within each of these categories. This chapter has suggested ways of helping children in Key Stage 1 to learn about writing conventions and composition.

*The key points covered in this chapter were:*

- **the content of the writing curriculum at Key Stage 1**
- **ways of teaching children about writing**
- **ways of showing children how to organise their writing**
- **strategies that can be employed when introducing children to the expressive, transactional and poetic uses of writing**
- **strategies to develop children's awareness of the match between written language, purpose and audience.**

---

Temple, C., Nathan, R., Burris, N. and Temple, F. (1993) *The Beginnings of Writing* (3rd edition), Allyn and Bacon, London
A classic text about the developmental approach to writing. It contains many ideas about activities and suggestions about how to support children's development.

Wing Jan, Lesley, (1991) *Write Ways: Modelling Writing Forms*, Oxford University Press, Australia
This book illustrates how genre theory can be applied in the classroom and contains many helpful examples of structures that children can use when writing fiction and non-fiction texts.

**Further reading**

# 6 Spelling

## Objectives

*When you have read this chapter you should:*

- have an understanding of the English spelling system
- appreciate how accuracy in spelling develops
- have appropriate expectations of young children's spelling
- be able to promote independent and accurate spelling.

## Introduction

Spelling is one the conventions of writing and is referred to as a presentation, surface, secretarial, mechanical, technical or transcription skill. Developing children's spelling abilities is one of the teacher's functions as he helps children to extend their writing abilities. Being able to use increasing numbers of correctly spelled words enables writers to communicate more clearly with others and to concentrate on the meaning of what they are writing. Learning to spell well is a skill that develops over a number of years. In order to begin to extend their spelling abilities young children need to be given opportunities to see and use written language and to be taught strategies that help them remember and make confident attempts at writing unfamiliar words.

### KEEPING SPELLING IN PROPORTION

It is easy for adults to become unrealistically preoccupied with children's spelling. When reading writing produced by children they often identify misspellings before considering the content, purpose or style of the writing. Everyone can feel confident when identifying the spelling errors that young children make. Harold Rosen once said 'Any idiot can tell a genius he has made a spelling mistake' (Graves, 1983, p. 188). Spelling, unlike style for example, is tangible; consequently it is easy to demonstrate the right version. Discussions about genre, organisation or characterisation are more demanding than explanations about transcription. It is important for teachers to remember that although correct spelling is important it is only one aspect of learning to write. This is recognised in the programme of study for English (DfE, 1995), the Desirable Outcomes for Children's Learning (SCAA, 1996) and the National Literacy Strategy *Framework for Teaching* (DfEE, 1998). The discussion paper which was used as a basis for the National Curriculum for English suggested that even by the end of compulsory schooling pupils cannot be expected to spell perfectly. At the age of 16

> pupils should be able to spell confidently most of the words they are likely to need to use frequently in their writing; to recognise those aspects of English spelling that are systematic; to make a sensible attempt to spell words that they have not seen before; to check their work for misspellings and to use a dictionary appropriately. The aim cannot be the correct unaided spelling of any English word – there are too many words in English that can catch out even the best speller.
>
> (Cox, 1991, p. 148)

By absorbing their teachers' values and listening to what they say about writing young children can learn that spelling is writing. When asked about the characteristics of good writing they frequently reply 'correct spellings' (Wray, 1994). When asked about the difficult aspects of writing they also respond with 'spelling' (National Writing Project, 1990). Research has not identified that children consider that organising content or telling a witty and exciting story are important or difficult, yet these are hard and are what separate successful from poor writers in the world outside school. *Mr Gumpy's Outing* (Burningham, 1970) is a good read, not because each word is correctly spelt but because the author uses language and story structure imaginatively and effectively. Spelling is for writing rather than being writing. If too great an emphasis is placed on spelling we run the risk of limiting children's experiments and learning about writing and damaging their enjoyment of writing.

## THE COMPLEXITY OF SPELLING

English spelling is in part an alphabetic system. It has also been influenced by other language conventions. These are the meaning and derivation of words and the rules of grammar. Understanding something of these helps adults to appreciate the spelling system and make it intelligible to children.

### Alphabetic conventions

English **orthography** has its origins in a largely alphabetic system in which each symbol represents a sound or a unit of sound. However, after a long evolution, during which words and methods

**orthography**
the writing system

of representing them have been taken from other non-alphabetic systems, English is now far from being strictly alphabetic. There is no simple one-to-one correspondence between sound and symbol; instead, 26 symbols or letters are used to represent approximately 44 sounds or **phonemes**. The sound that each of the 26 letters assumes is affected by its position in a word and the letters that surround it. For example, the letter *a* sounds quite differently in each of the following words:

*cat, make, day, ball, was, what, road.*

## Lexical connections

Sometimes the spelling system shows connections between words with related meanings. Although these can conflict with alphabetic correspondences their own consistency helps us to understand English orthography and provides clues about how to spell words correctly. A **root** is a word in its simplest form. Words that are derived from the root reflect its meaning and its spelling. For example, *plus* is a root which means more, and words derived from it include *surplus* and *plural*. The silent *g* in *sign* represents its lexical connection with *signal*. **Prefixes** and **suffixes** can be added to words to change their meaning. The prefix *dis-*, meaning 'not', is added to many words, including *agree* and *appear*, to give them contrary meanings. The suffix *-er*, meaning 'one who', produces *painter*, *speaker* and *reader* when added to the end of a word. Words that have distinct meanings but that sound alike are often spelt differently to indicate the lack of a relationship. Examples of these are *hair* and *hare* and *where* and *wear*.

## Grammatical markers

Words may also contain grammatical markers which affect the way they are spelt. The addition of the **morpheme** *-s* to a word is frequently used to represent the plural form, as with *cats*. Sometimes this distorts the sound of the word in its single form, as with *houses*. The morphemes *-ing* and *-ed* are often added to verbs to indicate different tenses, as with *jumping* and *jumped*. Distinct spellings of words that sound alike often signal that they are different parts of speech, for example *to* (preposition), *too* (adverb) and *two* (noun).

Although it can be complicated, English writing contains many clues which help us to think about how to spell. These are:

- alphabetic conventions
- lexical connections
- grammatical markers.

Acknowledging that English spelling draws on a number of language conventions and is not straightforward means that

**phoneme**
the smallest unit of sound in a word

**lexical**
pertaining to words

**root**
the simplest form of a word

**prefix**
an addition at the beginning of a word

**suffix**
an addition at the end of a word

**morpheme**
the smallest unit of meaning

expectations about children's developing abilities can be kept in proportion and teachers can offer children a range of strategies which will help them to learn to spell accurately.

Adults frequently call upon a variety of strategies to help themselves with their spelling. They may pronounce each syllable of the word in an exaggerated fashion as with *Wed-nes-day*, or write down several versions of a word comparing them to see which one looks right. Sometimes they use a known spelling to provide clues about the spelling of a more difficult word, for example using *finite* to spell *definite* or *lie* to spell *believe*. They may draw on their understanding of language features such as roots, prefixes and suffixes and common letter sequences. At times they consult dictionaries or use spell checks. When spelling difficult or unfamiliar words adults often use a combination of these strategies. The most reliable of these is visualisation, and activities which develop this strategy should be emphasised in a spelling programme.

## THE DEVELOPMENT OF SPELLING

Accuracy in spelling develops as children explore the writing system and as they become more familiar with written language (Read, 1986; Temple *et al.*, 1993). As children progress through the five spelling stages that are explained on the following pages their spelling becomes increasingly accurate and conventional. Each stage shows children developing new insights as they attempt to under-stand and use the English spelling system.

### The pre-phonemic stage
During this stage children imitate the writing that they see in the world around them. The writing that is produced may take the form of scribbles or pretend writing. It may incorporate numerals, random letters or letters found in the child's name. The child may be able to explain the meaning of the writing but the text is generally unreadable. At this stage the child has not yet begun to think about spelling (Figure 6.1).

### The early or semi-phonemic stage
When they reach this stage children show a developing awareness of the alphabetic and phonic principles of the language and they use their understanding of this complex relationship to write words. Letter names are used to represent words, for example *R* for *are*, and *T* for *tea*. Letter names may also stand for groups of letters, for example the *T* in *NIT* for *night*. Consonants are used more frequently than vowels. At this stage the children's writing and the message

**Figure 6.1**

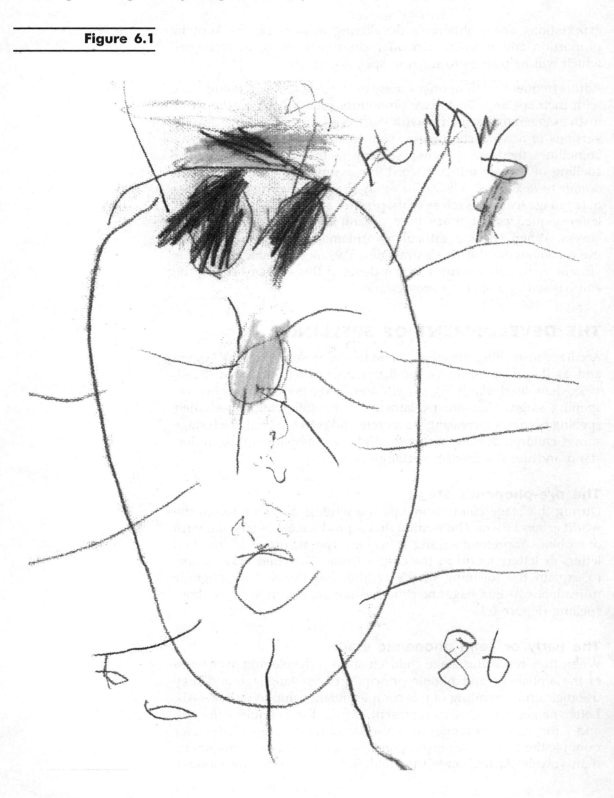

they wish to convey begins to be more easily understood by the reader (Figure 6.2).

**The phonetic stage**

At this stage children recognise that all the sounds in words can be represented by letters. More letters are included in words and the words become more complete (Figure 6.3). Spellings at this stage might include *baf* for *bath*, *wons* for *once* and *didemt* for *didn't*.

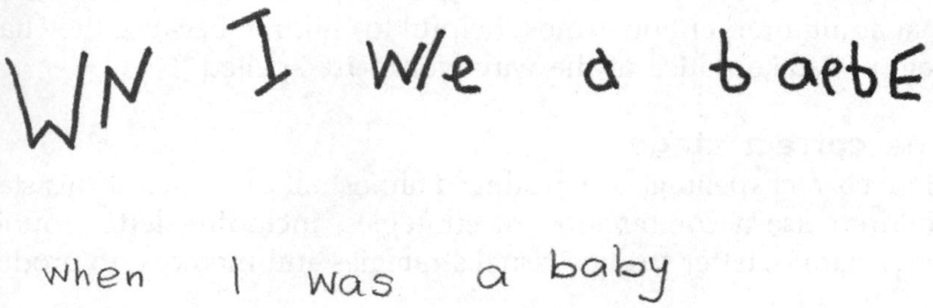

WN I W/e a boebE

when I was a baby

**Figure 6.2**

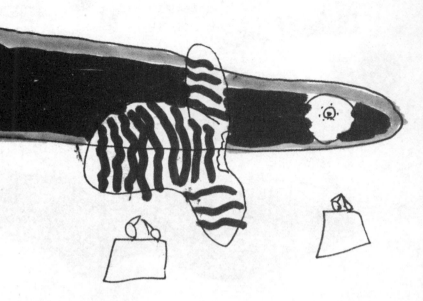

it cam5 from a Fatt-Roy.'

**Figure 6.3**

## The transitional stage

When children reach this stage they begin to move away from their dependence on phonic strategies and incorporate spellings that reflect their visual memory of words. They begin to combine phonic and visual knowledge. By this stage children will have become more familiar with written language through seeing adult models and through their own reading. This will have helped them to develop a greater awareness of common combinations of letters and letter patterns and enables them to write words that look right, such as *moterway*, or, in the example in Figure 6.4, *bnanan*. It is at this stage that adult intervention is most helpful to children because they have begun to take notice of the way words are spelled.

## The correct stage

Here correct spellings are produced almost all the time. At this stage children use a combination of strategies, including letter sounds, letter names, letter strings, visual strategies and memory, to produce

**Figure 6.4**

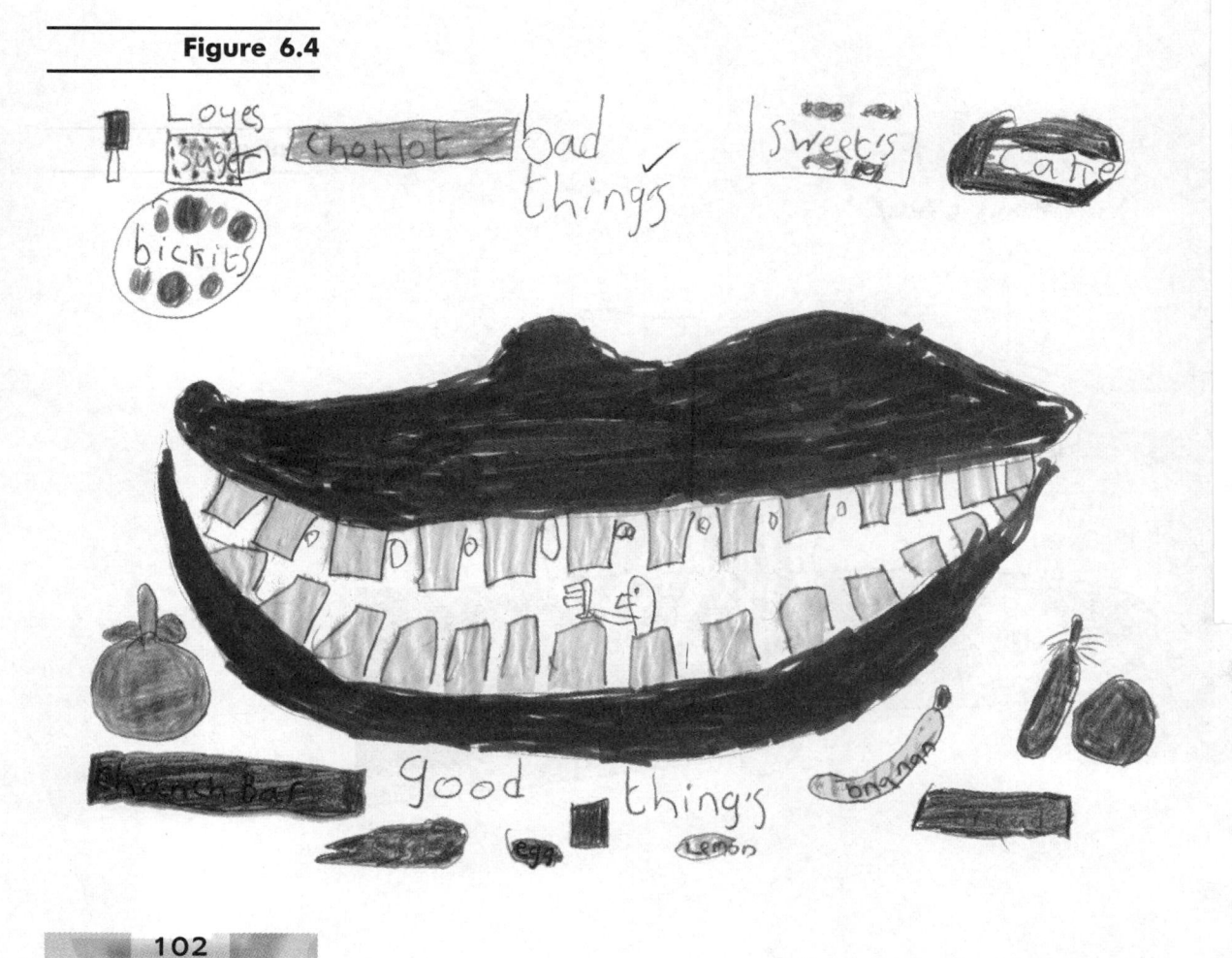

close approximations or correct spellings of short and multi-syllabic words. They have a good knowledge of word structure and a large body of known spellings, and their knowledge of the English spelling system is well established. The writing reproduced in Figure 6.5 is an example of this stage.

In their early attempts at spelling children seem to break down spoken words into individual speech sounds and match each speech sound with a letter. As they gain more experience of seeing written language they begin to realise that spelling involves making more complicated choices. They begin to move away from a phonic approach and experiment with alternative ways of representing words. Children from the nursery through to Year 2 will demonstrate some of the characteristics identified in the five stages. Many nursery- and reception-age children will be spelling using pre-phonemic and semi-phonemic strategies. Most children will only begin to reach the correct stage during Year 2 and beyond.

The developmental model of spelling, described above, shows that the spelling mistakes children make, as they experiment with writing, are usually systematic and often transitory. Independent experiments with words are a necessary part of children's learning about spelling, as they provide them with opportunities to make intelligent and informed attempts. The developmental model also reveals that inexperienced spellers almost always draw upon phonic strategies without being formally taught to do this. Adults who limit their teaching to pointing out auditory or phonic strategies may be teaching children what they already know and not helping them

**Figure 6.5**

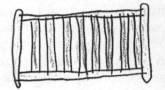

baby's need cots to sleep in. You can cradle them to sleep and sing them a song. They have gates on each side so they don't fall out. They are made of wood.

to progress. Appreciating how children's spelling develops helps teachers to respond positively to what children can do, appreciate progress, identify known strategies and establish a framework for teaching spelling.

## TEACHING SPELLING

Devising a programme for spelling begins with assessing what children can already do. It has been suggested that until children have reached the transitional stage of spelling they are unlikely to benefit from direct teaching (Palmer, 1991; Redfern, 1993). Children need to have some understanding of the principles of English orthography and to have had the opportunity to produce their own attempts at spelling before they can understand and absorb instruction about correct spelling. Overemphasising correctness too soon can make children anxious about writing and inhibit their experiments with language, which provide them with valuable insights into the principles of spelling. Learners need to feel positive about their ability and their achievements if they are to take the risks that new learning necessitates. If children receive praise for their spellings and their progress they will see themselves as able spellers in the making and feel sufficiently confident to use unfamiliar words in their writing.

Because spelling in English is complicated, most writers do not simply 'catch' spelling accuracy; they need to be taught carefully, systematically and sensitively (Peters, 1985). Good teaching does not merely consist of correcting children's mistakes but helps children to avoid repeating those mistakes. This involves giving children strategies for producing conventional representations of words and remembering the spellings of frequently used words. Learners are best able to make use of teaching when they appreciate its relevance to their own needs, so children are likely to learn most productively if they are taught to spell the words that they use in their own writing. Teachers need to respond positively to the ideas that are expressed and the spellings that have been attempted before discussing how spelling could be improved. When giving help it is important that teachers limit the number of errors they correct and consider when and which words to teach to individuals, groups and classes.

For many years teachers have recognised that children queuing as they wait for spellings to be written in word books wastes valuable teaching and learning time. While standing in line for words the train of ideas is interrupted, children forget what they intended to write, lose the opportunity to attempt to work out the spelling for themselves and learn to become dependent on adults. Copying the adult's version from a word book gives rise to the myth that every word needs to be spelled correctly in every piece of writing, and there is no evidence to suggest that copying words fosters good spelling or helps children to develop strategies for spelling well (Mudd, 1994; Redfern, 1993). Peters (1985) compares children's use of word books to the way in which telephone directories are used, describing how once the number is dialled it is forgotten so effectively that we probably need to look it up again if we dial incorrectly. This may explain why many children who use the word-book system ask teachers for the same words day after day.

Many of the teaching strategies that follow develop children's knowledge about spelling and their memory for words as well as promoting positive attitudes to spelling and a continuing interest in words and language. From these, readers should be able to select the activities which should be used regularly as part of a systematic approach to developing spelling in the early years.

## DEVELOPING AWARENESS OF SOUND–SYMBOL RELATIONSHIPS

### Segmenting words into phonemes

Learning the sounds and names of the letters of the alphabet helps children who are at the pre-phonemic and semi-phonemic stages of spelling development to move on to the phonetic stage. It gives them one strategy for making reasonable attempts at writing words. Many children are introduced to sound–symbol relationships through short phonic sessions which usually begin with initial letter sounds, move on to initial **blends** such as *bl*, *cl* and *fl*, then long vowel phonemes such as *ee* and *ai*, two-letter vowel and consonant combinations such as *er*, and finally three-letter combinations such as *air*.

However, using sound–symbol correspondences is only efficient where each single letter in a word corresponds with a simple phoneme, as in *hat* or *man*. Moseley (1990) has suggested that only one-third of the words used by young children contain a one-to-one correspondence between letter and sound. This means that relying on sounding out words is misleading when trying to spell grapho-phonemically (i.e. using sound–symbol correspondences)

**blend**
the sound produced when two or more phonemes are combined. In a blend each phoneme can still be heard, as in *cl* or *ng*. This contrasts with a digraph, where the combination of phonemes produces a new sound such as *ch*.

irregular words and words that are regular but that can be spelt in a number of reasonable ways. Adults who sound out words slowly by enunciating each letter sound and ask children to listen and to write down the sounds they hear are demanding a great deal from children, as translating auditory information into visual symbols is a complex act. So, although it is important that children know letter–sound correspondences, they need to be taught other ways of attempting to spell words.

## Using books to teach sound–symbol relationships

It is easy to match the choice of book to be read at story time to a letter to be learned by the class. Attention can be drawn to the letter when the title is read, and during the discussion that follows the reading the teacher can return to the letter he wishes to concentrate on and write it and some of the words from the story that begin with the chosen letter on a flip chart. Poems, rhymes and songs that emphasise particular letters can also be used. This activity draws children's attention to sounds in words and to how words look, and may help them to remember words that they will write.

Books and rhymes can also be found to support letter blends and other letter strings, for example *Amazing Grace* (Hoffman, 1991) for *gr*, and *The Three Billy Goats Gruff* for *gr* and *tr*. The value of embedding phonic work in stories is that children see how the sounds are written. It is this that supports spelling development most effectively.

## Splitting words into units

### *Onset and rime*

These terms were coined by Goswami and Bryant (1990). Onset is the opening unit of a syllable or word and rime the end unit of a syllable or word. For example, in the word *boy*, *b* is the onset and *oy* the rime, and in *swing* the onset is *sw* and the rime *ing*. It has been suggested that children's sensitivity to onset and rime can help their reading and spelling development as it is the precursor to phonemic development. Children can recognise the existence of onset and rime through saying nursery rhymes and using books which draw on rhyme and alliteration. Nursery rhymes are a particularly rich resource for developing **phonological awareness**, for example recognising the match between *Jill* and *hill* and *down* and *crown*. Books such as *Green Eggs and Ham* (Seuss, 1960) emphasise sound patterns in a similar way. While their research was originally intended to help with the teaching of reading, Goswami and Bryant found that children use their knowledge of onset and rime to help them with their spellings before they apply them to reading. Adams

**phonological awareness**
awareness of the sound system of the language and of sounds within words

(1990) added that children can be helped to learn regular spelling patterns through the methodical use of onset and rime, particularly when they see the letters that represent the sounds they are saying. She also suggested that when sound–symbol instruction occurs during an examination of meaningful connected text children achieve more highly. Sharing big books which contain nursery rhymes or rhyming texts, or making large, nursery rhyme and rhyming books with children provides teachers with opportunities to foster children's appreciation of onset and rime, make connections between sounds and symbols and develop their spelling abilities. Since the onsets that are easiest to identify are often single-consonant phonemes there is some overlap between phonic awareness and onset awareness.

Classroom games such as *I Spy* are based on onsets. They usually use simple single-letter onsets such as *b* for *books*. Extending them can encourage children to think about longer onsets such as *ch* (chair) or *str* (string). *I Spy* may also be adapted to use rimes instead of onsets. Playing other word games such as *Odd One Out* can also develop phonological awareness.

### Syllables
Separating a multi-syllabic word into syllables and saying it aloud can sometimes help with spelling. This is most helpful when the word contains phonically regular letter strings or chunks. Examples of such words include *re-mem-ber* or *jump-ing*. The danger of overusing this technique is that at each part of the word the child is presented with a new set of spelling possibilities. For example, *sta-ble* can easily and reasonably become *stay-bull*. Whilst sounding out words as they are spelt, for example *Wed-nes-day* and *rasp-berry*, can help to reduce some spelling uncertainties children have to know which words can be split in this way and have a good idea of how they are spelt in order to use this practice for themselves.

## Incidental oral activities
Reciting and singing rhymes and sharing poems and jokes provides a rich opportunity to interest children in language. Even young children understand the humour of 'Knock, Knock' jokes, which depend on the ambiguous sounds of words for their effect. Listening to and playing with words develops phonological awareness in an enjoyable way.

## DEVELOPING VISUAL AWARENESS

As the developmental model of spelling indicates, children need to be moved on from relying on phonic strategies to developing their visual awareness. Looking at words is important but it has to be 'looking in a specially intent way' (Peters, 1985, p. 37) so that children become accustomed to the probability of letter sequences in words and develop a memory for words. The following techniques are useful for drawing children's attention to words and their structure.

## Fostering awareness of words

When teachers draw children's attention to classroom displays, labels and notices they are providing opportunities for visualising and remembering words. Marking children's cloakroom pegs and drawers with names rather than pictures encourages children to look at and remember words. Children also benefit from activities which involve making letter strings in a variety of media. These can be used to make frames and borders for pieces of art, writing or displays in order to give them a purpose that children can appreciate.

Watching adults write, either as scribes or during shared writing sessions, provides children with visual models of words and letter patterns. As teachers conduct these sessions they can draw attention to aspects of words in order to develop children's awareness of spelling.

Shared reading and story sessions can provide opportunities to develop children's spelling knowledge. For example, after reading the big book *Birthdays* (Cowley, 1988) with the class, the teacher could ask the children to think of words that contain the letters *ay*. These could be recorded on a flip chart and the letters and letter strings emphasised by the teacher. After gathering a number of words the teacher could ask the children to read individual words. The sharing of *Birthdays* could also lead to a discussion about other compound words such as *firework* or *playtime* and these could be written down. These activities involve the careful visual examination of words, heighten sensitivity to acceptable sequences of letters, and encourage children to remember spellings.

Challenging children to find individual words, words within words, letter strings and compound words contained in print and books in the classroom are incidental activities that can be used productively in spare moments. This activity can begin with the children's own names, for example finding *it* in *Anita*, *trick* in *Patrick*, *lip* in *Philip* and *in* in *Esin*. Following on from this children can be helped to find similar letter strings in other words in order to help them build up a knowledge of generally occurring sequences. Philip's words could include *slip, clip* and *lipstick*.

## Letter strings

Teachers can talk about letter strings in words with children in order to draw attention to spelling patterns. For example, beginning with the word *heart* they could extract *hear* and *ear*. The next stage is to compile a list of words that contain the letter string *ear*. The list could include

*tear, hearing, bear, dear, fear, heard, near, pear, nearly, wear, year*

In each of these words the letter string could be highlighted or underlined. Although the spelling pattern is the same in each of these words it is sounded differently. It is helpful to explore this with children so that they become aware of the interesting inconsistencies of the English language.

## Language games

The games of word snap and lotto using the names of children in the class and later using common words that are familiar to and used by the children are enjoyable ways of encouraging children to examine words closely. To make this even more relevant and useful the children can be asked to make the game. Writing the words carefully on the cards will help to develop the children's memory for conventional spellings and provide them with a real reason for spelling carefully and correctly. Many commercial word games also help to foster careful visual examination of words.

## Analogy

Making associations between known words and unknown or troublesome words can help children to solve some of their spelling problems. To make an analogy, letters from a known word are used to spell an unknown word. For example, *what* and *when* are frequently misspelled by young children. Identifying and remembering that *what* contains *hat*, and *when* contains *hen*, can help. Another way to use analogy is to make lists of words that contain a common letter string. Start the list with a known word and highlight the pattern. Using the word *night* in this way will help with the spelling of a number of words that contain *ght* if this is pointed out to children.

## Look copy cover write check

One of the most helpful strategies for learning frequently needed words that are proving difficult to remember is the look copy cover write check routine originally devised by Peters and Cripps (1980). Selecting a misspelt word that has occurred in the child's writing that needs to be spelt correctly, because it is frequently used or important, the teacher writes the word and asks the child to look closely at it before copying it. The correct versions are then covered or removed and the child is asked to write the word from memory. The child's spelling is then checked against the correct version. If the spelling is correct it can be incorporated into the writing. If the word is incorrectly spelt the teacher and the child compare the two words, identify where the problem lies and repeat the whole procedure concentrating particularly on the parts that are proving difficult.

Children can be introduced to the look copy cover write check technique in whole-class or large group sessions using a flip chart in the following way:

- Select a word that many children are finding difficult.
- Write the word clearly on the chart.
- Say the word and ask the children to repeat it.
- Encourage the children to look at the word thoroughly.
- Point out the initial letter, final letter and letter strings.
- Ask the children to write the word in the air.
- Cover the word and ask selected children to try to reproduce it on the chart.
- Compare their versions with the original.
- If the children have spelt the word incorrectly underline the hard part and repeat the procedure.

Once children are familiar with the stages of this routine they can work on corrected spellings in a personal spelling book in the same way. It can be time-consuming to establish the look copy cover write check procedure and children are likely to need a great deal of practice with it. But since it uses the eye, ear, hand and brain to remember words it is effective and worth the effort.

### Personal spelling notebooks

These can be used to practise words that require the look copy cover write check technique. The notebook is an ordinary exercise book. Each double-page spread is a learning page and each set of double pages may have a letter of the alphabet at the top. The word to be learned is written at the left-hand edge of the left-hand page. After looking carefully at this word the child folds the edge of the page over and writes the spelling to the right of the fold on the same line as the original. This is compared with the correct version. If the child has not spelt the word correctly further practice is gained by trying again further along the line (Figure 6.6). The back pages of the notebook can be used for children to try out their spellings before deciding on a version that looks right. Both sections of the notebooks provide the teacher with a valuable record of children's

**Figure 6.6**

| better | Bater | Beter | better |
| because | Becos | Becase | because |

spelling development and can help him to identify words that could be used for a group or class look copy cover write check session. From time to time children can work in pairs to test each other on a few words selected from the front part of the notebook.

> **Activity**
>
> In school, use the look copy cover write check routine with individuals or groups of children. After a few days see how well the children you have worked with have remembered a spelling you worked on with them in this way.

## DEVELOPING AWARENESS OF LANGUAGE

Extending children's interest in and knowledge about words can support spelling development. Reflecting on word meanings, origins and simple grammatical markers can be encouraged when teachers discuss children's writing or talk about words and letters with groups and classes. Discussing how word endings such as *-ed* and *-ing* relate to verb tenses is an obvious example. Many teachers talk about and show children how to spell these morphemic units and letter strings when supporting spelling. Examining words, finding out why they are spelt in the way they are and how they resemble and differ from other words helps children to identify patterns and conventions. This can then provide clues for predicting the spellings of unfamiliar words as well as giving children opportunities to remember the spellings of words that are discussed.

Teachers can also foster awareness of language through discussions of proverbs, similes, abbreviations, words from other languages, palindromes, puns, figures of speech and jingles. In *Mr Gumpy's Outing* (Burningham, 1970) the play on words in Mr Gumpy's replies to the animals as they ask to join in the trip, including 'don't muck about' to the pig and 'don't flap' to the chickens, make an excellent starting point for talking about language with young children.

## OTHER STRATEGIES

### Spelling rules

In order to be useful spelling rules need to

- be applicable to a large number of words
- have few exceptions
- be simple to understand yet exact enough to cover only the appropriate words.

Rules have a limited value in effecting accurate spelling and so need to be treated with caution. The often used 'i before e except after c' can lead to confusion about how to spell words such as *their*, *eight*, *weight*, *height*, *receive*. Peters (1985) describes an experiment where a computer was programmed with over 200 spelling rules and then given over 17 000 words to spell. It failed to spell more than half correctly, including *bus*, *team* and *tie* which emerged as *buss*, *teem* and *ty*. As they can be unreliable spelling rules should not be stressed. It is more helpful for children to become aware of probable letter strings and develop their own awareness of words rather than using rules which may lead them to make errors that they are not aware of.

### Dictionaries

Dictionaries help writers to spell more accurately and can foster an enduring interest in words. Efficient use of dictionaries does not develop automatically; it needs to be modelled and taught so that children can use them independently and effectively.

To help children to become familiar with commercially produced dictionaries children can learn about their format and layout through making a large class dictionary. This can be used to list words that are needed for work that the class is undertaking. The words can be entered by the children, which gives them a purpose for spelling carefully and correctly. Involving children in making dictionaries familiarises them with alphabetical order and the idea of using resources to look for correct spellings.

Another way of introducing young children to alphabetical order is through involving them in the production of an alphabet poster or frieze. A good starting point for the words on a class-made alphabet frieze is the names of children in the class and the school and their friends and family members, or the words that are associated with a class theme such as food, animals or countries. In Year 1 or later children can be asked to compile a correctly ordered alphabet book for younger children. Children can also practise using alphabetical order during role play. They might make patient record cards in the doctors' surgery or hospital or write names in an address book in the home corner.

When introducing more sophisticated alphabetical ordering skills, using letters beyond the initial letter, the children's own names are again a good starting point. For example, they might be asked to sort the names Thomas, Tina and Tom into the correct order. The principle of using the second and subsequent letters of the alphabet when looking for words in a dictionary can be explained during this activity.

Once published dictionaries are introduced the teacher needs to help children to find their way around them easily and quickly. They can be can be given challenges such as finding the longest *A* word and the shortest *B* word, or to discover words with unusual beginnings such as *gn* (gnat, gnome, etc.) or *wr* (wrist, wrong, etc.).

Asking children to look up a word that is part of the theme can help them to understand how to use dictionaries and recognise the information that dictionaries contain. For example, when investigating food the children could be asked to find the word *hamburger*. The teacher might suggest that children first find the section for *H*, then look for words beginning with *HAM*; to help them do this they might use the guide words at the head of the page. Once they have found the word they should then read the meaning and any other details.

Children should also be told that dictionaries give interesting information about words. They indicate usage, pronunciation, plural forms, type of word and derivation. The abbreviations which indicate this information can be explained to children. This is one way of introducing children to the language of grammar and adding to their knowledge about language.

The following activities also help children to use dictionaries. They can be simplified or made more difficult depending on the age and needs of individuals.

- Ask the children to find a word with lots of letters, such as *kaleidoscope*, and ask them to make as many words as possible from it. To check whether they are all real words they should look in a dictionary.
- Challenge the children to find a word beginning with each of the 26 letters of the alphabet. You can make this more difficult by specifying the number of letters that the words should have.

- Many English words have been taken from other languages, for example *pyjamas* (Urdu), *hamburger* (German), *anorak* (Inuit). Ask the children to track down the origin of words such as *piano*, *canoe*, *alligator* and *zebra*.
- Ask the children to make a pack of letter cards containing all the letters of the alphabet. Vowels and the letters *c d h l m n r s t w* can be written twice. The cards should be spread out face downward. Two children can then select seven cards each, and in the time it takes for the sand to run through an egg timer try to make as many words as possible. The children can work individually or together. When time runs out they should check their spellings in a dictionary.

## Computers

### Word processing

Using word-processing programmes may help to develop children's spelling abilities. Potter and Sands (1988) have suggested that children are more able to identify incorrect spellings when they see them on the screen or on a printout than when they appear in their own handwritten texts. Words that are identified as incorrect can be checked or changed using any appropriate strategy. Deleting and inserting words is straightforward and less messy on the computer than it is on paper. This ease of correction can encourage children to experiment with spellings and unusual words.

Children may be more motivated to produce correct spellings in writing that is produced on the word processor since the printout, with its similarity to commercially published texts, emphasises the public nature of writing and the understanding that others will read what has been written. With the possibility of an audience the need for correct spelling has more significance.

### Spell checkers

These provide children with another source for finding correct spellings or checking words that may be wrong. If children are writing straight on to the computer it is best if the spell check is not used until the first draft of the writing is complete. Using it as children are writing their first drafts may encourage them to become too engrossed with correct spelling and their composition may suffer.

## Word lists

There are many commercially produced word lists and word books, or teachers can make their own. Sometimes they can be helpful if they contain a limited number of words that children use frequently in their writing. However, words that are needed regularly need to be learned and the time that is used to find words on the list might be used more profitably to teach or learn the spelling. Relying on lists does not encourage children to remember spellings and has similar drawbacks to the use of word books. More effective are dictionaries or word collections that are made by the children working with the teacher. These can be lists or books of words that will be needed for work on a theme or topic, and the act of making them familiarises children with the words that are available and introduces them to how they are spelt.

## Spelling tests

If tests incorporate the words that many children have found difficult and that have been the focus of look copy cover write check by the class or individuals they may be useful in encouraging children to make extra efforts to remember frequently needed words. They may also identify important words that need extra practice. However, using commercially produced spelling lists to give weekly tests has limited value. Because tests do not necessarily include words that are relevant to and used by all the children in the class they are unlikely to be remembered by the majority of children after completing the test. The way that lists are constructed implies that words should be known at a particular stage and that if they are not children may have a spelling problem. This is not necessarily the case. Alternatively some of the words on externally produced lists may already be known, so giving them to children to learn may not be extending their abilities. Most importantly giving children spellings to learn at home in preparation for a test does not help children to develop strategies for learning how to spell, to identify and remember spelling patterns and to use these to help them spell unknown words.

## Mnemonics

Mnemonics are memory aids. They can be useful with words that are very troublesome, and sometimes have a place as one of a number of spelling strategies. Frequently they take the form of silly sentences containing words beginning with the letters of the word that is difficult to remember. Mnemonics are inevitably idiosyncratic but they can be fun to devise. An example of a mnemonic is Big Elephants Can't Add Up Sums Easily ('because'). If they are overused or become too complicated the spelling and the mnemonic can both be forgotten.

## Handwriting

It has been suggested that introducing children to cursive script from the beginning of their school life can help them to produce correct spellings. In printing, each letter is isolated from the one before it and the one that follows. When letters in words are joined there is an increased possibility that children will memorise common letter strings such as *-ing* and *-tion* as they produce connected sequences of letters (Peters, 1985). The disadvantages of teaching cursive writing early are that it is different from the printed form children encounter in books and it can fit uneasily with a developmental approach to writing.

---

**Activity**   Using the samples of writing you have collected try to identify the spelling strategies the children are using and the spelling stage they have reached. Consider how best to extend their spelling ability.

---

## DEVELOPING SPELLING WHEN RESPONDING TO WRITING

Responding to children's writing is a valuable opportunity for teaching spelling as the help that is provided is specific to the individual child. Before commenting on the child's spelling teachers should first respond to the content, organisation and style of what the child has written and react positively to what the child has done. Then the spelling mistakes the child has made should be examined carefully in order to identify either those spellings which require the least work to make them correct, or important, frequently used words that it would be helpful for the child to know. It is useful to look for high-frequency words like *when* and *said* that children will not be able to work out through applying phonic knowledge. It is also worth asking children to identify words that they think are wrongly spelled and would like to be able to spell correctly. After analysing what the child has written select one, two or three words to work on. The exact number will depend on the age of the child and the length and sophistication of what they have written. The techniques that follow are useful for refining children's spelling skills when responding to pieces of writing.

### Positive correction
Write the correct spelling below the child's word and draw attention to the letters that are correct in the child's version by ticking these letters (Figure 6.7). Then together look at the letters that are incorrect and compare these with the correct letters. Finally follow the look copy cover write check routine to establish the correct spelling.

**Figure 6.7**

bĺĭóŃŃA
balloon

## Visual reinforcement

After writing the correct spelling it can be helpful to highlight the difficult part of a word, for example the *wh* in *when*. This could then be compared to the *wh* in *why* and *what* by writing these words and highlighting or underlining each *wh*.

## Correcting a first draft

Before the writing is shown to the teacher children can be taught to proofread their work. One aspect of proofreading is to identify any words that the author thinks are spelt incorrectly. Before asking for adult help with these children can be encouraged to consult a dictionary or write the word again. Any words that they are still unsure about can be marked with a dot or underlined. After the teacher reads the writing the misspellings that the child has identified can be worked on using the teaching strategies previously outlined. First drafts may also be read by response partners, who may help their peer to correct spelling mistakes.

To support the development of spelling without deterring children from composing the following list may serve as a helpful reminder.

**Do**

- Encourage children's interest and delight in words and their meanings.
- Play letter and word games as part of your daily programme.
- Keep spelling in perspective.
- Accept invented spellings and recognise that this is an important stage in spelling development.
- Praise children's attempts at spelling before helping with the tricky parts.
- Promote scrutiny of environmental and classroom print for words within words and letter patterns.
- Encourage children to use classroom resources to discover correct spellings for the words they want to use.
- Discuss word meanings and pronunciation when reading.

**Table 6.1**
A summary of teaching
strategies for spelling

| Spelling stage | What the child can do | Teaching strategies |
|---|---|---|
| **The pre-phonemic stage** | • pretend writing, scribbles<br>• mark-making<br>• some letter shapes | • write for the child<br>• draw attention to print<br>• introduce alphabet books<br>• introduce sound–symbol relationships |
| **The semi-phonemic stage** | • some phonic awareness<br>• uses letter names | • continue phonic work<br>• foster interest in words<br>• write for the child |
| **The phonetic stage** | • knows more letter sounds<br><br>• overuse of phonic strategies | • continue phonic work<br>• foster interest in words<br>• write for the child<br>• introduce visual analogies<br>• introduce look copy cover write check<br>• work on letter strings<br>• play word games |
| **The transitional stage** | • writes some words using visual memory<br>• begins to combine phonic and visual strategies<br>• spells some words correctly<br>• may confuse letter order | • stress look copy cover write check<br>• provide personal spelling books<br>• introduce dictionaries<br>• discuss word endings<br>• use positive correction<br>• ask children to proofread |
| **The correct stage** | • uses a combination of strategies<br>• has a body of known spellings<br>• writes confidently | • continue look copy cover write check,<br>• ensure children proofread<br>• introduce thesaurus<br>• continue dictionary skills<br>• study roots, prefixes, suffixes, word meanings |

- Help children to take responsibility for their own spelling through proofreading their own and other children's writing.
- Teach correct spellings in context.
- Emphasise look copy cover write check to develop visual memory.
- Show children how to use a dictionary to find correct spellings and word meanings.
- Ensure that children rewrite the whole word when they correct spellings.
- Encourage children to discuss their writing with each other.
- Make sure that parents and children understand how spelling is taught.

**Don't**

- Tell children they are poor spellers.
- Give lists of randomly chosen words for children to learn.
- Ask children to sound out an unknown word or sound it out yourself.
- Allow letter-by-letter copying of correct spellings.
- Let children believe that success in spelling is more important than attempting interesting words or the content of what they have written.

**Activities**

It might be possible to target your teaching of spelling so that it meets children's needs more effectively. Thinking about the following questions may suggest some alternatives to the ways in which you teach spelling.

- When is the best time to correct or give children assistance with their spelling?
- Do you use the whole range of teaching strategies that are available?
- Which teaching strategies can be used with the whole class, groups and individuals?
- Do you maintain a balance between correcting spelling and encouraging children to feel confident at expressing themselves in writing?

Try out some different practices and evaluate their impact on the children's spelling.

## MEETING THE STATUTORY REQUIREMENTS

Most children who are taught to spell using the suggestions outlined in this chapter will meet the requirements described in the Desirable

Outcomes for Children's Learning (SCAA, 1996) and the English National Curriculum (DfE, 1995). Readers will be able to make their own connections between the preceding activities and the aspects of the requirements that they are intended to develop.

By the age of five children are expected to be able to:

- associate sounds with words and letters
- associate sounds with syllables
- recognise the shape and sound of letters
- communicate meaning through pictures, symbols, familiar words and letters
- write their names.

By the age of seven children are expected to be able to:

- communicate meaning through writing
- write each letter of the alphabet
- use their knowledge of sound–symbol relationships
- produce phonetically plausible spellings
- use simple spelling patterns
- write common letter strings within familiar and common words
- spell commonly occurring simple, monosyllabic words correctly
- spell words with common prefixes and suffixes
- check the accuracy of their spelling
- use word books and dictionaries
- experiment with spelling complex words
- discuss misspellings.

## Summary

Learning to spell most words correctly takes time and so it is important that teachers do not expect too great a degree of accuracy too soon from young children. This chapter has suggested that, in order to become good spellers, teachers need to teach children how to spell and use strategies which help them to remember frequently needed words. This should be done in a way that maintains children's confidence in their abilities as writers and develops positive attitudes towards writing so that they can become independent and increasingly competent writers.

*The key points covered in this chapter were:*

- **aspects of the English spelling system and the implications for teaching spelling**

- **the way children's spelling develops as they gain experience of writing and reading**

- ways of teaching spelling
- how to match teaching to spelling ability
- the statutory requirements for spelling in the early years.

**Further reading**

Dombey, H., Moustafa, M. and the CLPE (1998) *Whole to Part Phonics*, Centre for Language in Primary Education, London
A brief yet balanced explanation of the role of letter–sound relationships in reading and spelling.

Mudd, N. (1994) *Effective Spelling: A Practical Guide for Teachers*, Hodder and Stoughton, London
As the title suggests this book contains many practical ideas that can be used to help children to become good spellers. It also contains helpful chapters on the development of spelling.

Peters, M. L. (1985) *Spelling: Caught or Taught?*, Routledge, London
A key text about spelling which has influenced ideas about how spelling is learned and best taught.

Redfern, A. (1993) *Practical Ways to Teach Spelling*, Reading and Language Information Centre, University of Reading
A short booklet with a number of suggestions for the classroom.

# 7 Handwriting

**Introduction**

We are now very conscious that teaching handwriting and the other presentation skills should not take precedence over teaching children about the use and composition of writing. We are also aware that in the past, the look of children's writing may have received more attention from adults than the content, organisation and style of what was written, and that this was detrimental to many children's understanding of the use of writing and their confidence as writers. Nevertheless, since writing is a communicative activity, the communication is helped when the author is able to write quickly and clearly and the recipient can understand the message easily. Consequently the development of clear, well-formed handwriting remains an important aspect of learning to write.

## PROGRESSION IN HANDWRITING

Children's early experiments with writing show that their handwriting passes through a number of stages as it develops. The beginnings of handwriting are seen when children first produce marks on objects in their environment without and with writing implements. Later children begin to limit their mark-making to surfaces that are intended for writing and drawing. These early explorations of pictures and writing help children to become familiar with writing implements, shapes and symbols. As children approach the age of four the majority of them can distinguish between writing and drawing and will engage in both activities knowing that they are different and have distinct characteristics. However, they may use drawings as a substitute for writing and as a means of communicating as these are often easier for them to produce (Kress, 1997). They also have a more immediate connection with objects and experiences than with letters and words. As children become more familiar with using implements for writing and gain greater experience of seeing the layout and shapes used in writing they increasingly incorporate its features into their own efforts. The way in which the features of handwriting develop can be seen in the examples which follow.

Initially children tend to make straight up–down and side-to-side lines using a stabbing motion (Figure 7.1). At this stage they may hold the writing implement awkwardly.

They may also produce scribble writing using anti-clockwise and clockwise movements (Figure 7.2).

They then begin to write more quickly across the page using more open scribble forms (Figure 7.3).

Writing produced during the first three stages may not contain any recognisable letter shapes, but at around the age of four years many children begin to include some letters and numbers in their writing. They often select letters that they are most familiar with, such as those that are present in their names. Sometimes children produce row upon row of single letter shapes (Figure 7.4).

**Figure 7.1**

**Figure 7.2**

**Figure 7.3**

Mark    has        some        playmobile        lego.

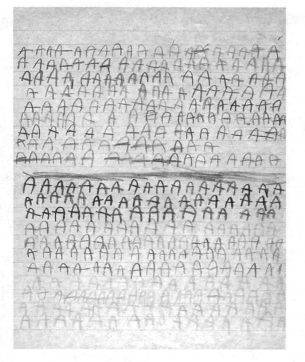

**Figure 7.4**

They may also write lists of words each of which contains up to about six characters (Figure 7.5).

Repeating a limited numbers of letter shapes over and over gives way to writing that incorporates many different letters. At this stage the letters may be formed incorrectly, for example from bottom to top, be orientated inappropriately or reversed, and the writing may go from right to left across the page (Figure 7.6).

Gradually children begin to orientate their letters correctly, exclude numbers and non-letter symbols and include letters that match some of the sounds the words contain. Realising that written letters represent spoken sounds, that there is a correspondence between **graphemes** and phonemes, is an important stage in children's writing development and is reflected in children's handwriting. At this stage children often use upper- and lower-case letters in their writing as they attempt to represent the sounds of words (Figure 7.7).

Next children begin to include spaces between words and to write in straight lines from left to right across the page. They will be able to make good use of guidelines to keep their lines of writing horizontal (Figure 7.8).

**grapheme**
the written representation of a sound, which may consist of one or more letters

**Figure 7.5**

Finally children produce writing which contains letters that are consistent in size and correctly formed. At this stage children will be able to use lined paper and to begin to join letters, if these have not previously been introduced (Figure 7.9).

Analysing children's early attempts at writing can help teachers to appreciate what children know about the shapes and strokes which

**Figure 7.6**

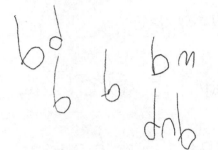

**Figure 7.7**

are used to form letters. It is important not to dismiss children's existing knowledge as this can be used as the basis for extending what children can do.

In order to develop children's handwriting skills teachers need to have realistic expectations about what can be achieved at different stages and ages. They need to have a clear picture of the sequence of handwriting development and provide activities that are appropriate to the current needs or that lead on to the next stage of handwriting. The following list shows what children need to learn about handwriting and indicates the types of experiences that they need.

**Figure 7.8**

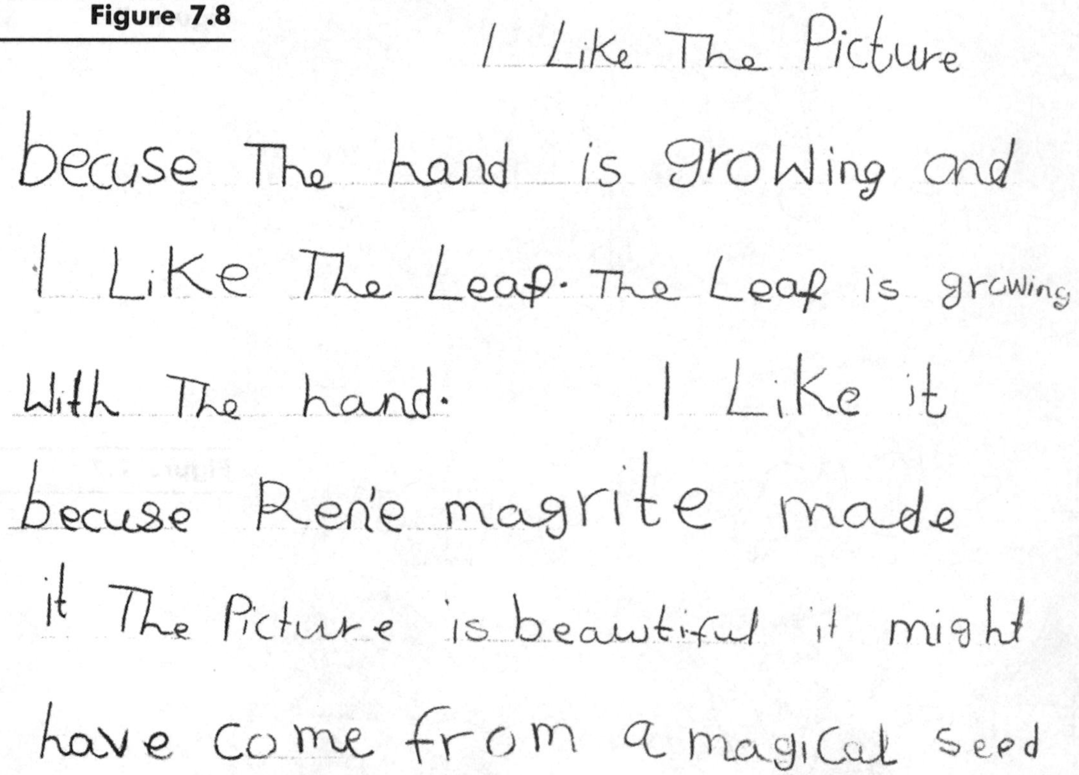

I Like The Picture becuse The hand is groWing and I Like The Leaf. The Leaf is growing With The hand. I Like it becuse Ren'e magrite made it The Picture is beawtiful it might have come from a magiCal seed

*The youngest children* need to:

- gain familiarity with the resources and materials used for writing
- become comfortable with writing implements and develop a secure and appropriate pencil grip
- experience pattern-making to develop the movements needed for correct letter formation
- look at and talk about letters
- develop an awareness of letter strokes and the vocabulary needed to understand some of the concepts about the writing system.

*Children at Key Stage 1* need to:

- develop correct letter formation, beginning and ending letters at the right points
- develop a legible script using consistent letter forms and spaces between words
- produce smaller writing
- realise that some letters have **ascenders** and some have **descenders**
- be able to produce at least some joining strokes by the end of this stage.

**ascender**
the part of a letter which extends above the height of a, o or c, e.g. the single vertical stroke in the letter *b*

**descender**
the part of the letter which goes below the line, e.g. the tail in the letter *g*

**Figure 7.9**

paul Klee

paul Klee was born in 1879 in Switzerland. His grandma made fairy tales and illustrated them. Paul Klee never drew nature he always drew fantasy His grandma died when he was five. paul Klee loved his grandma's painting. He always drew down the margins of his book instead of doing his proper work. In September 1898 aged nearly nineteen he went to munich to study art. He started playing the violin at the age of Seven and at the age of eleven he could play very well. His family wanted paul klee to be a musion but he really wanted to be an artist because he loved drawing.

> **Activity**
>
> Collect some samples of writing from children of various ages. Identify the differences that emerge over time. Can you see signs of progression in the handwriting?

## TEACHING HANDWRITING

### The principles of teaching handwriting

There are a number of key principles associated with handwriting and these can be used to guide teachers' actions and the activities they select when they are considering how to develop children's handwriting skills.

**cursive script**
handwriting in which the
letters in words are joined

Writers need to develop a clear and legible style of handwriting if their writing is to be readable and they are to communicate efficiently. Clarity and legibility involve making well-shaped letters and using spaces between words. Accurately formed letters support speed and fluency and lead to an easily formed, readable **cursive script**. Children need to be encouraged to use the correct points of entry and exit for letters when they begin to make recognisable letter shapes. Once incorrect or awkward writing habits are established it becomes increasingly difficult for children to alter them. Writing that is consistent in size is attractive and makes it easier for readers to read what has been written. Children who are at ease with the writing system, writing implements and resources and have established an automatic knowledge of correct shapes and joining strokes are likely to produce clear, fast and economical handwriting. Insisting on correct movements from the earliest days will help children to make smooth progress towards acquiring a flowing hand.

Three helpful rules about handwriting that can be used to guide children and teachers are:

- Each letter should begin and finish in the correct place.
- Letter heights should be consistent and differentiated according to letter group.
- Vertical strokes should be parallel.

If these rules are adhered to the product is likely to be legible and attractive, as the example in Figure 7.10 illustrates.

### Selecting a handwriting style
A number of models for handwriting exist. They generally have a teacher's manual which gives information about letter formation

**Figure 7.10**

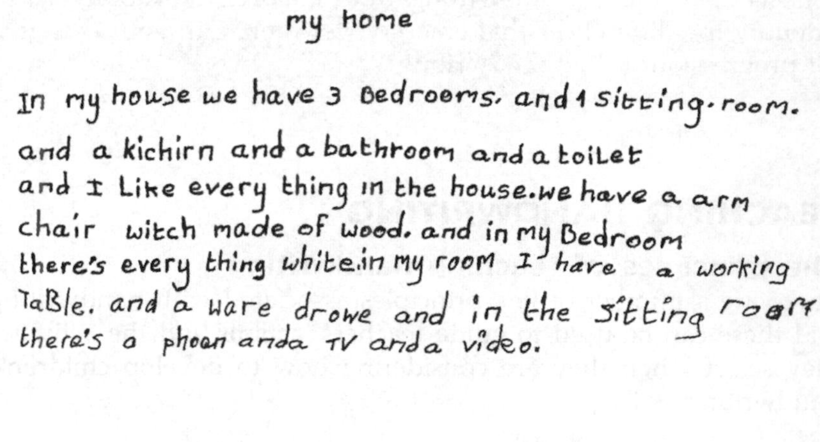

my home

In my house we have 3 Bedrooms. and 1 sitting.room.
and a kichirn and a bathroom and a toilet
and I Like every thing in the house.we have a arm
chair witch made of wood. and in my Bedroom
there's every thing white.in my room I have a working
TaBle. and a ware drowe and in the sitting roarr
there's a phoan anda TV anda video.

and cursive script. All styles have their merits and schools may have individual preferences about the one that they select. Sassoon (1995) compares a number of handwriting schemes and styles and suggests the strengths and limitations of each. Whatever style is chosen it is important that all members of staff are aware of, agree to and model the style that has been selected, that the print form leads smoothly into a joined style, that it is rational, consistent and easy to accomplish, and that as far as possible consistency of style is maintained between early and later years of primary schooling. The National Literacy Strategy *Framework for Teaching* (DfEE, 1998) expects schools to have an agreed policy on style and presentation and to ensure that teaching is consistent throughout the school.

## Cursive script

The aim of every handwriting programme is joined writing because print is rarely as quick as cursive writing. The National Curriculum description of a Level 3 writer (DfE, 1995) includes the statement 'Handwriting is joined', and the National Literacy Strategy *Framework for Teaching* introduces basic handwriting joins at the beginning of Year 2. To enable children to meet the National Curriculum target some schools may introduce children to joined writing from the age of four or five while others may wait until correct letter formation in print script has become established before encouraging joins between letters. The latter are likely to teach children a style that is easy to join later. Sassoon (1990) has suggested that in the early years schools might like to adopt a style that is part way between print and cursive script. She has proposed that from the start, children should be introduced to letters with exit strokes. Letters that are made in this way retain the print form similar to that found in books for young children, give children the opportunity to absorb and use correct letter formation and provide a model for the flowing movement needed for cursive script. With this style children will only need to extend the exit strokes to form joins as their handwriting matures and when the teacher judges that cursive script will enable the child to write more quickly. Figure 7.11 shows a teacher's demonstration of exit strokes under a child's writing.

## A variety of styles

Writers need to be able to use different forms of writing, including cursive script, if they are to be able to suit their writing to different purposes and situations where different speeds and styles are required. Just as the content, style and organisation of writing varies according to its audience and purpose, handwriting will also vary according to who is to read what has been written and what will happen to the writing once it is finished. Writing that is read

**Figure 7.11**

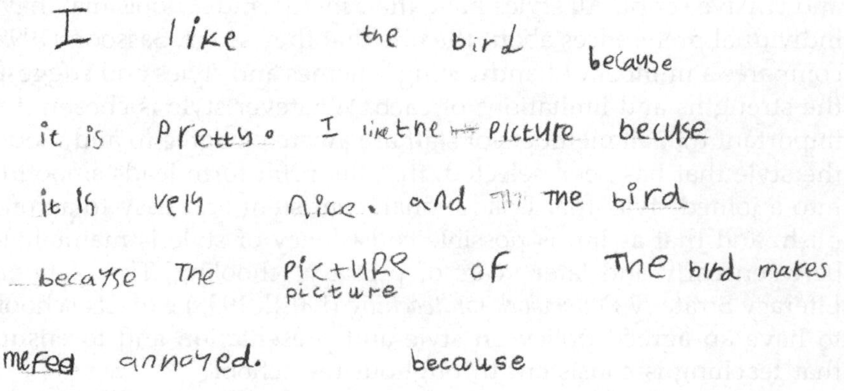

I like the bird because it is Pretty. I like the picture becuse it is very nice. and the bird because The Picture of The bird makes me feel annoyed. because

only by the author may be untidy and hardly legible to others. A first draft may contain a number of crossings-out and corrections. Writing for special occasions, such as public writing on invitations, letters and displays, always requires care and attention. Diagrams and charts may need labelling in print rather than joined script.

### Personal style

In time children begin to develop a personal style of writing. This is often a sign of the writer's growing maturity and ease with the writing system and should not necessarily be discouraged. Handwriting can be a reflection of a person's individuality and can add character to what is written. As long as the development of an individual style is guided by the principles of fluency, speed and legibility children should be allowed to develop their own style. As Jarman (1993) wrote, handwriting is one example 'of the compromise we all reach between cultural obedience and individual integrity' (p. 12).

## Organisation

### Physical arrangements

Attending to practical arrangements helps children to produce their best handwriting. Tables and chairs should be the right height and should enable children to sit comfortably. A firm surface to rest on is needed to produce good handwriting. There should be sufficient space between children for them to write easily and to position their paper and books at a suitable angle to their body. Writers need good lighting to be able to see clearly what they are writing.

Left-handed writers may experience particular difficulties with handwriting. When working with them it may help to consider the following points.

Left-handed children:

- Need the light to come over their right shoulders so that they are not writing in the shadow of their own hands.
- Need to have paper on the left side of the centre of the body. It can be helpful to tilt the paper to the right or left so that the writer can see what is being written.
- Should use pens with specially designed nibs or smooth pens because they form letters by pushing rather than pulling the pen across the page.
- Should hold the pencil or pen a little further from the point than right-handers so that the writing is not obscured. They may benefit from using a pencil grip to find the right place for their fingers.
- Should not sit too close to the right of a right-hander when writing. This will avoid their arms colliding.
- May write slowly until competence increases.
- Benefit from demonstrations given with the left hand.

### Time

Handwriting 'lessons' where children copy out rows of isolated letters, letter patterns and words do not necessarily result in good handwriting. Helping children to write clearly, legibly, accurately, consistently and fluently does not need to involve dull teaching. Copying from the board can be difficult as it is hard to transfer one's eyes from something at a distance to a book or paper near at hand and at the same time retain an exact image of what has to be reproduced. Teaching handwriting in this way seems to have little transfer to real writing situations. Identifying it as a discrete session on the timetable can overemphasise the significance of neat writing to children. Class sessions do not provide the teacher with opportunities to see when children are forming letters incorrectly or having difficulties. As Jarman wrote, 'a child will not *learn* to write from a workcard or copybook. The teacher must teach the shapes and movements personally' (Jarman, 1993, p. 37).

Teachers should seek to improve children's handwriting by working with individual children, and suiting their personal need. Their correction should relate to what the child has written, be accompanied by an explanation of the purpose of clear writing, and present children with a good model.

## Resources

Varied and high-quality resources can be used in different settings and across the curriculum in order to develop children's handwriting. As children use writing implements and practise making the strokes and shapes of letters and words their familiarity with the system will grow.

There are a number of basic resources that are needed for handwriting. The following sections give some suggestions about these.

### Writing implements

The following points may be helpful when making decisions about implements:

- Thick pencils are not necessarily helpful for small fingers.
- A selection of different sizes of pencils, fibre-tipped pens, felt tips, wax crayons and pencil crayons should be provided for all ages.
- Fibre-tipped handwriting pens can be introduced to children as soon as they start school and are excellent for writing final drafts.
- Left-handed writers should use fountain pens with specially angled nibs or pens with smooth rounded nibs.
- Children should hold pens and pencils correctly, firmly and comfortably.
- Children with awkward pen holds may be helped by placing a piece of Plasticene around a pencil and moulding a correct finger hold.
- A rubber band wound around a pen prevents fingers from getting too close to the point.
- Commercial pencil grips are available to remediate uncomfortable holds.
- Children should learn that particular implements are more suitable for different sorts of writing, for example writing pens for final drafts, and pencils for first drafts.

### Paper

- Unlined paper is best for inexperienced writers. Young children may have problems keeping to lines. They are not always sure which part of a letter rests on the line and may place the tails of letters such as *p* and *g* on the lines if given lined paper too early. Unlined paper gives children the freedom to experiment with letter formation and size as well as giving them the flexibility to incorporate drawings into or near their writing.
- As children begin to use smaller writing and to form letters correctly, they can be introduced to line guides to help them keep their writing straight. These are made from strong, pale card on which bold, dark lines are drawn at the desired width. The guides are placed beneath the child's writing paper and kept in place with paper clips. The lines show through and provide a guide for writing. Using line guides rather than lined paper

allows children to choose where to place their illustrations. The finished product is often more aesthetically pleasing, which is a significant consideration when displaying writing or making books.

- Children should be provided with notebooks, card, different sorts of paper and first draft books for writing, as well as with different shapes, sizes and colours of paper.
- Squared paper can be helpful for children who have difficulty with writing consistently sized letters or distinguishing between the different sizes of letters such as *a* and *d*.

## *Other resources*

The following may be useful:

- commercial or pupil-made alphabet friezes
- individual alphabet strips which can be placed on the table when writing
- the teacher's own writing, which provides children with a good model and gives them the opportunity to see how well-formed handwriting is produced
- examples of a range of handwriting styles, including different scripts, which can be collected in a scrapbook and used to show how handwriting varies according to the purpose and audience of the writing
- a print-rich school environment with displays of lists, greeting cards, notes, letters, name labels, books and notices showing different styles of writing
- access to typewriters and word-processing facilities as these produce good and varied writing models.
- a collection of autographs and examples of adult writing collected from staff and parents.

## Activities

These should give children practice with:

- writing implements
- the strokes and shapes of letters and joins
- skills such as hand–eye coordination, muscle control and visual sensitivity.

The skills that are needed for handwriting, including hand–eye coordination, muscle control and visual sensitivity, develop with experience and enable children to become relaxed, confident and competent writers. In nursery and reception classes children should be encouraged to play and experiment with pens, pencils, paper and card in the writing corner. They should be given opportunities to match, sort, trace and use tactile letter shapes made from plastic, foam, wood, sandpaper and other material. The class sand tray and individual trays containing small amounts of sand or damp cornflour can be used to practise making letter shapes and patterns. Children can write on the playground and the outside walls of the school using water and large paintbrushes or chalk. In art sessions children can produce patterns using letters, print with letter shapes and produce patterns when finger painting. Close observation drawing can be particularly helpful in developing children's visual discrimination and attention to detail. Role-play areas such as shops and offices can be equipped with writing resources and models, and the children can make labels for their supermarket or restaurant. They may also write labels for models that they make. Work that is to be displayed can be finished off with borders containing hand-writing patterns and letters. Children can fill large letter shapes with matching letters and these can be used as labels for display areas. These activities provide a context for handwriting practice and give children an incentive to produce well-formed letters and words.

Children's names are a good starting point for discussions about letters, and their shape and size. Routines such as children signing in when they come into class provide daily practice at writing and give the teacher a regular opportunity to observe children writing. Initially children might write their first name and later add their family name or sign in a friend. The teacher can vary the activity with older children by asking them to write their name in capital letters or cursive script. They can vary the size of their writing, use a variety of writing implements and write on paper of different textures and colours.

Although learning about handwriting should arise from what the child writes in the course of the school day, teachers from time to time may wish to work with children on particular aspects of writing, such as letter strokes or letter joins, to meet an individual, group or class need. To help to develop the correct movements for each letter and to help children remember the correct entry and exit points for letter strokes the 26 letters of the alphabet have tradi-tionally been separated into groups, although some letters fit into more than one group. Each group consists of letters that share similar initial strokes. Figure 7.12 shows the stroke-related letter groups.

Letters can also be grouped into join families as shown in Figure 7.13.

The National Literacy Strategy *Framework for Teaching* (DfEE, 1998) suggests that children in Year 2 should concentrate on the four basic handwriting joins, which it identifies as:

c a d g q o e s
r n m h b p
i l t u y f j
v w x z k

**Figure 7.12**

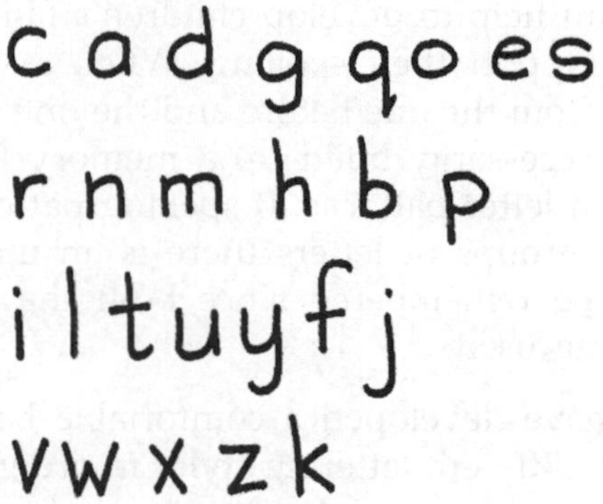

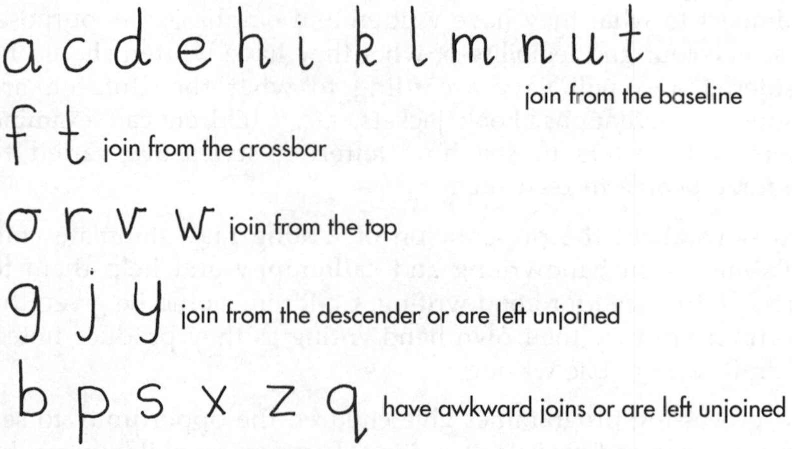

a c d e h i k l m n u t
join from the baseline

f t join from the crossbar

σ r v w join from the top

g j y join from the descender or are left unjoined

b p s x z q have awkward joins or are left unjoined

**Figure 7.13**

- diagonal joins to letters without ascenders, e.g. *ai, ar, un*
- horizontal joins to letters without ascenders, e.g. *ou, vi, wi*
- diagonal joins to letters with ascenders, e.g. *ab, il, it*
- horizontal joins to letters with ascenders, e.g. *ol, wh, ot*.

Some children benefit from practising letter and join families in order to become familiar with the set of movements needed to produce legible writing quickly and easily. Practice may help children who are experiencing particular difficulties but should not be an automatic feature of a handwriting programme for all the class as skills do not always transfer if isolated from real writing situations.

Sassoon (1995) suggests that teaching the correct formation of capital letters is less important than working on lower-case letters because they are not joined. However, it may be necessary to model efficient ways of forming capitals if children are producing poor shapes. Work on straight and curved strokes may also be helpful. Handwriting patterns and pattern-making also help children to internalise the movements needed to make correct letter shapes.

Cursive script can help to develop children's familiarity with letter strings and so support their spelling. When a writer prints, each letter is isolated from the one before and the one following, and the hand does not necessarily build up a memory for how it feels to produce common letter patterns. If spelling patterns are reinforced through joining groups of letters there is an increased possibility that these will be remembered since both the visual and motor memory are being used.

Once children have developed a comfortable basic style they can be introduced to different lettering styles in order to add interest to their handwriting and to see that it can be an art form. They can be encouraged to think about trying out writing styles that will add impact to what they have written and emphasise its purpose. The size, colour and legibility of what they have written should be considered and will vary according to what the children are designing – invitations, book jackets, etc. Children can examine leaflets and posters to see how lettering styles are varied to encourage people to read them.

**calligraphy**
handwriting as an art

Discussions about the presentation of writing may stimulate children's interest in handwriting and **calligraphy** and help them to appreciate the need for good writing. Children should be given the opportunity to vary their own handwriting as they produce notes, first drafts and public writing.

Word-processing programmes give children the opportunity to see different styles and models of writing. Very young children can be invited to play with the keyboard or to try and write their names as a way of helping them to recognise the connection between upper- and lower-case letter forms.

In order to produce good handwriting of their own, children need to see well-formed, clear handwriting as it is produced. Shared writing with the whole class or with groups of children provides a good opportunity for this. Teachers should also make sure that all their writing provides a good model for children. When they write under children's writing, work with children on spelling corrections or demonstrate writing at other times, they should provide children with high-quality examples that they can imitate.

**Activity**  This chapter may have provided you with some new ideas about the teaching of handwriting. If it has, experiment with one of them to see if it has a place in your handwriting programme.

# IMPROVING HANDWRITING

It is good practice to match the teaching of handwriting to individual children's needs as they occur in everyday writing. Comments such as 'untidy' are not helpful. Children benefit from positive and constructive help which focuses on one difficulty at a time and is given when the problem arises.

While observing writing teachers might ask themselves if the child is:

- able to write legibly, fluently and quickly
- holding the pen comfortably
- mixing lower- and upper-case letters within words
- starting in the right place, moving in the right direction and joining letters correctly when forming letters and words
- differentiating letter heights
- maintaining consistency of size, spacing and slope
- using a handwriting style appropriate to the task.

If the teacher identifies a problem she should demonstrate the handwriting behaviour that is appropriate, for example the correct formation of a letter. She can then ask the child to practise this by producing a line of correctly formed letters and rewriting the word in which the mistake occurred. An ideal time to emphasise careful presentation of written work is just before the child is making a final draft, so that earlier corrections can be included and reinforced. At this time children can see the point of making writing legible and attractive since others may read what they have written.

The teacher can help a child who is using inefficient joining strokes or producing reversals by providing an outline made with a highlighter pen on which the entry and exit points are marked with a different colour; this can be traced over by the child. Children can be asked to trace letter and word shapes in the air or on the table with their finger to help them to remember letter shapes and strokes. As they form the correct versions of letters they can be asked to verbalise the movements for the strokes that they are using by phrases such as 'round, up and down' for *a*, for example. Focusing on letter families which contain similar shapes and call for similar movements, or practising joins between letters in common letter strings and joining strokes between letters which join easily, can help to develop the automatic memorisation of letter strokes. The groups of letters shown in Figure 7.14 are often found together and could be usefully used to practise joins.

The fine motor control of some children can lead to difficulties with handwriting. Their writing can appear untidy and ill formed because

**Figure 7.14**

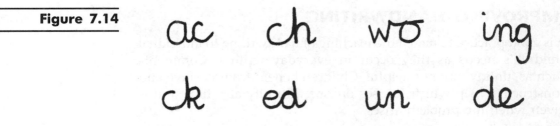

their pen hold is too tense or too loose. Help with relaxing or strengthening muscles resulting in a firm but comfortable grip can be given through pattern-making activities, or exercises such as squeezing a ball.

Letter forms in the English language contain very few strokes, so a number of letters are mirror images of each other. It is not uncommon for children to reverse letter forms when they are learning to write. Children who persist in reversing *p*, *q*, *b* and *d*, or those who demonstrate their uncertainty about orientation by including the capital forms in words, benefit from being introduced to the joined forms of these letters. The open *b* and the *q* with a tail emphasise the difference between the letters. Tracing over letter forms made with a highlighter pen and practice at pattern-making to increase awareness of visual discrimination may also help. A small number of children produce mirror writing which goes from right to left across the page. These children may need a clear visual indication of where to begin each line of writing, and extra practice at and reminders about left-to-right directionality in English writing.

## CHILDREN'S PERCEPTIONS OF HANDWRITING

Children's ideas about what is important in writing are illuminating and should prompt us to ask questions about how we teach and what we praise in relation to all aspects of writing. During the National Writing Project (1985–8) teachers found that 'Children often judge the success of their writing by its neatness, spelling and punctuation rather than the message it conveys' (National Writing Project, 1990, p. 19).

These findings have been supported by a number of other recent surveys of primary-aged children, which reveal that a disturbing number of them view the secretarial skills, including neatness and handwriting, as the most important features of good writing (Wray, 1994). Research by the Assessment of Performance Unit (Gorman *et al.*, 1989) linked children's negative attitudes towards writing with their learned preoccupation with the appearance of what they produce. Findings such as these emphasise how important it is to teach and correct handwriting sensitively and individually and to explain why it is necessary to develop well-formed handwriting.

Mixed messages about the role and importance of handwriting can be transmitted to children when explanations are being given about the writing they are asked to do. After a discussion about content and style, the teacher's final words may be an emphatic reminder to write carefully and neatly. When a child presents a piece of writing to the teacher to read, her first comment may be 'That looks nice. Well done.' Comments such as this transmit messages about the significance of presentation and the insignificance of content. If handwriting is to be kept in proportion, adults should refrain from remarking on the appearance of the writing until after they have read and commented on the content of what the child has written.

**Activity**

When giving children feedback about writing try to specify exactly what is good and what could be improved. Try to keep your comments about transcription and composition separate so that the children are clear about what is valued in writing and the place of handwriting in the writing process. Consider what impact this has on how children write. Does it slow down the progress they are making in mastering the skills of handwriting? Does it help them to pay greater attention to composition?

## PARENTAL CONCERNS

The real or assumed opinions of parents and carers about handwriting can cause some teachers to overemphasise this aspect of writing. It is true that some adults, recalling memories of their own schooldays, do believe that neatness is the criterion upon which acceptable work is judged. Greater communication between school and home about handwriting, writing and learning might help parents to understand the handwriting policy of the school and the place of handwriting in children's overall development as writers.

Some children enter school able to write their name in capital letters. Children who can use capital letters should never be criticised, nor should we give their carers the impression that they taught their children wrongly. Being able to use any letter forms means that the child has some understanding of the writing system, is familiar with the use of resources for writing and can produce letter shapes. Capitals are used in writing and it is useful to know about them.

# MEETING THE STATUTORY REQUIREMENTS

The suggestions outlined in this chapter are intended to help children meet the requirements described in the Desirable Outcomes for Children's Learning (SCAA, 1996) and the English National Curriculum (DfE, 1995). Readers should be able to select from the activities outlined in this chapter and aspects of the requirements that they will develop. These two documents state that:

By the age of five children are expected to be able to:

- recognise the shape of letters
- use symbols, familiar words and letters in their writing
- write their names with appropriate use of upper- and lower-case letters.

By the age of seven children are expected to be able to:

- hold a pencil comfortably
- use a legible style
- write from left to right and from top to bottom of the page
- start and finish letters correctly
- produce letters that are consistent in size and shape
- incorporate spaces into writing
- form lower- and upper-case letters correctly
- begin to join letters in words
- know why clear and neat presentation is important.

## Summary

Children need to be able to write legibly and quickly so that they can be independent and confident users of written language and efficient communicators of meaning. Efficient handwriting develops over time, but as handwriting is 'a taught skill with a set of conventional rules (Sassoon, 1993, p. 190) the progress children make needs to be monitored and aspects will need direct teaching. However, sensitivity is needed when helping children to develop an easily formed, legible handwriting style to ensure that they do not become over-preoccupied with handwriting at the expense of content.

*The key points covered in this chapter were:*

- **the characteristics of children's handwriting at different stages**
- **the key elements of a handwriting programme**
- **some strategies that can be used to teach handwriting**
- **ways of monitoring handwriting, diagnosing common difficulties and remediating problems.**

Sassoon, R. (1995) *The Practical Guide to Children's Handwriting* (2nd edition), Hodder and Stoughton, London
A book which covers all aspects of handwriting from selecting a handwriting style to remediating difficulties.

# 8 Punctuation

**Objectives**

*When you have read this chapter you should:*

- understand what punctuation is for and how it is used

- appreciate how the understanding and use of punctuation develops

- have appropriate expectations of young children's use of punctuation

- be able to develop children's abilities to use punctuation appropriately.

**Introduction**

As with all aspects of the writing system, it takes time for young children to understand and then use punctuation marks appropriately. Children's appreciation of the role of punctuation grows out of learning about writing. Its correct usage generally takes longer than the other transcription skills because children have to develop other writing competencies before they need to incorporate punctuation into their writing. They need to be able to write longer texts that require sentences to be demarcated and they need to be using different forms of writing such as questions and direct speech before punctuation is necessary. Children need to be given plenty of opportunities to see, discuss and experiment with punctuation before they can be expected to use it correctly.

## THE PUNCTUATION SYSTEM

Punctuation is used to mark boundaries between units of language and indicate the type of message that has been produced. The punctuation system includes marks such as full stops, commas and spaces. These conventions enable writers to express their meaning more clearly and help readers to make sense of what has been written. They can also indicate some of the writer's intentions that may not be communicated by the words alone, for example emphasis or posing a question. Correctly used, punctuation helps to decrease the possibility of ambiguity for the communicator and the recipient of a written message. Since one of the goals of teaching writing is to ensure that children can use writing to communicate clearly and effectively with others it is important that they develop an understanding of punctuation and incorporate it into their writing.

Boundaries between units of language, including words, phrases, **clauses** and **sentences**, are marked by spaces, capital letters, full stops and commas. Types of utterances including statements, questions, **imperatives**, direct speech and exclamations are indicated by other forms of punctuation. The features in Table 8.1 are the aspects of punctuation that are most likely to be used by young children.

## THE COMPLEXITY OF PUNCTUATION

When we talk we pause, use facial expressions, tone of voice, intonation and gesture to convey meaning. These have no direct parallel with the punctuation marks that are used to clarify written communications. The developmental model of writing shows that when children begin to write they draw on their knowledge of oral language. They use letters to represent the sounds of words. This

**clause**
a unit of language which contains at least a subject and a verb

**sentence**
a unit of language containing at least a subject and a verb, which makes sense on its own

**imperatives**
orders or instructions

| Marks | Used to: |
|---|---|
| Spaces | • separate words <br> • indicate the start of a new paragraph <br> • separate sections of text |
| Capital letters | • indicate the start of a sentence <br> • identify special names <br> • indicate the beginning of direct speech <br> • begin words in titles of books <br> • begin lines of poetry <br> • begin words of exclamation <br> • denote the pronoun *I* |
| Full stops | • mark the end of a sentence |
| Commas | • separate items in lists <br> • separate phrases and **simple sentences** in a **complex sentence** |
| Inverted commas | • signal the start and end of direct speech <br> • show the special use of a word |
| Question marks | • mark the end of a question |
| Exclamation marks | • denote words, phrases and sentences that express surprise or intense emotion |
| Apostrophes | • show possession <br> • identify contractions |

**Table 8.1**
*Types of punctuation marks*

**simple sentence**
a complete unit of meaning including a subject and verb and usually an object

**complex sentence**
a complete unit of meaning made by joining simple sentences using conjunctions other than *and* and *but*

support is not available with punctuation. Making a connection between pauses and commas and full stops, which are silent, is not as obvious as sound–symbol correspondences, and this makes both teaching and using them difficult. Even inserting spaces between written words is not simple. There is no parallel to a space in spoken language. It is hard to realise and recognise that the flow of speech is composed of words that are quite separate. Imagine yourself listening to a group of people speaking a language that is unfamiliar to you and you may get a sense of how difficult it is to identify where individual words begin and end. Though children seem to work out word boundaries for most words, some words that often occur together can be confusing; for example, *alot, alright* and *could-have* or *couldof* often appear in children's writing. As well as drawing on their knowledge of oral language as a starting point for writing, children have to learn the differences between speech and writing and then acquire a set of conventions that apply to text.

Even mature writers can find punctuation difficult to use and even more difficult to explain. In order to understand the correct positioning of full stops in text it is necessary to know what constitutes a sentence. Most adults and some children may have an intuitive grasp of what a sentence is, but this does not make it easy to explain to others. Smith (1982) described the sorts of conversations that must be familiar to many teachers when he wrote:

> 'Begin every sentence with a capital letter.'
> 'What is a sentence?'
> 'Something that begins with a capital letter.'
>
> (p. 84)

This type of conversation is reflected in the definition of a sentence given in the Kingman Report (DES, 1988), where it is described as 'what it is that is enclosed between a capital letter and a full stop' (p. 21), and the National Literacy Strategy (DfEE, 1998), which describes a sentence as 'a unit of written language which makes sense on its own' (p. 88). Perera (1987) has written that 'although in one sense educated adults all know what a word like sentence means, there is no denying that linguists find it exceptionally difficult to produce a watertight definition of even such a common term' (p. 11).

Explaining simply what is enclosed between a capital and a full stop is very difficult. When telling children what is meant by a sentence and where to place a full stop adults may use phrases such as 'a complete thought', 'a group of words that make sense', 'where you stop', 'where you take a breath'. Complete thoughts and groups of words could refer just as well to phrases as to sentences. Stopping and breathing places can occur anywhere, particularly when the author is composing the message and thinking pauses are frequent.

Punctuation is a way of marking meaning and supporting communication and is there to help the reader to make sense of what has been written; 'it helps the reader to identify the units of structure and meaning that the writer has constructed' (Cox, 1991 p. 148). However, until children are able to communicate meaning confidently in their own writing they will not need to clarify what they intend to express. Writers have to aware that their meaning can be misunderstood before they can knowingly apply punctuation marks to specify how what they have written should be understood. They also need a sense of audience and to understand that it is the writer not the reader who is responsible for conveying meaning. This demands a sophisticated level of awareness about grammar, one's own use of language and the requirements of an audience.

Consider your own use of punctuation. Is it always correct? Can you use your own experiences with punctuation to set realistic expectations about children's understanding and usage? **Activity**

## THE DEVELOPMENT OF PUNCTUATION

In order to discover how young children use and learn about punctuation, Cazden, Cordeiro and Giacobbe (1985) analysed samples of writing from a class of 22 six-year-old children collected over a period of nine months. They found that children begin to incorporate full stops, question marks, commas and apostrophes into their own writing when they become aware of these in the writing of others. At first children place punctuation marks in the wrong places in their writing. This shows their awareness of punctuation marks but indicates their lack of understanding of what it is for and how it should be used. They may overuse the system, which again shows their confusion. Over-generalising and misapplying rules is a common stage in all language learning and one that gives way to increasingly correct applications. As children continue to experiment, observe demonstrations and models and receive feedback about the use of punctuation, their own use of punctuation becomes increasingly correct.

Understanding sentence boundaries and correctly denoting these with capital letters and full stops is the main focus of the requirements for punctuation at Key Stage 1. It is also the most fundamental aspect of children's knowledge about written grammar (Kress, 1994). Once this is understood further learning about other aspects of punctuation is possible and will follow. On the way to identifying sentences and using the appropriate punctuation children seem to pass through six stages of experimentation with the position of full stops. They place them:

- between each syllable in words
- between each word
- at the end of each line
- at the end of a page of writing
- between phrases
- between phrases and at the end of sentences.

When children are able to place full stops between phrases they are using their intended meaning to guide their decisions about punctuation. It is at this stage that children are on the way to understanding what a sentence might be and as a result where to position full stops correctly. Ferreiro and Teberosky (1983) suggest that it is around the age of six that children begin to understand some of the uses of punctuation, although they may not be able to use the marks appropriately in their own writing.

The developmental model shows that although young children might use punctuation incorrectly they do not just use it randomly. It demonstrates that children are actively thinking about its use and in doing so are trying to build up an understanding of the rules that govern the use of punctuation. They are trying to discover how it should be incorporated into writing. Their errors do not become permanent bad habits. They are revised and amended as they learn more about the writing system. At each stage in the model children seem to be using what they know about the system to over-generalise, play with the rules and experiment before discarding and refining their guesses as they gain greater understanding of writing.

## TEACHING CHILDREN TO PUNCTUATE

Being aware of the complexity of the system and how children's knowledge and use of punctuation develops can help teachers to match their teaching to the needs and understanding of young learners and present their teaching of punctuation in a simple and logical way. In their research Cazden, Cordeiro and Giacobbe (1985) found that direct teaching about punctuation using exercises or drills did not hasten its development. It is likely that, as with other aspects

of writing, skills learned in a decontextualised setting do not transfer easily into writing that children compose themselves. Punctuation should be taught within the context of children's own writing and other encounters with print. Children should also be allowed to experiment with punctuation so that teachers can discuss this with them and help them to refine their understanding. The strategies that follow are intended to develop children's understanding and use of the conventions of punctuation in meaningful ways.

## Spaces between words

Children can be helped to see this convention in action as the teacher writes beneath the children's own writing and discusses how he writes it. Further experiences can be provided through discussions of texts in published books. As the teacher introduces children to the terminology of language, pointing out letters, words and sentences, he will be helping children to recognise that words are formed through combining letters and that each word is separated from the next by a space.

## Capital letters

Discussions about writing, as in the previous section, will help children to appreciate that some words, particularly those at the start of a story or a sentence, begin with capital letters. Children may already know that their names begin with capital letters and may incorporate these into their writing. Further discussions will build on what children already know.

## Using books

Discussion about punctuation marks after sharing a story or big book with the class enables the teacher to explain the use of punctuation in a meaningful and visible context. This form of teaching can be conducted with children of all ages. Many children's books contain a wealth of punctuation marks and they all contain full stops. It is important to use books that contain written language that is realistically rather than artificially divided into sentences as models to share with children. Books containing sentences that stop at the end of every line or that contain repeated, short, simple sentences of the type found in many reading schemes are poor models since they are unlikely to resemble the writing that children produce and need to punctuate (Kress, 1994).

## Providing models

Teaching can take many forms. The lessons provided by an adult who writes with and in front of children can be a very effective teaching method. Making a written response to children's writing which contains a full stop or a question mark and reading the sentence with the child, pointing out the punctuation, helps them to appreciate when and how punctuation marks are used. The teacher can also draw attention to his use of punctuation during shared writing sessions or as he scribes for children. This makes the processes and decisions involved in writing explicit and helps children to make sense of the complexities of the system.

## Writing activities

With older children the teacher might follow up a modelling episode or a discussion about the punctuation contained in a book by asking the children to engage in a writing activity that necessitates the use of one aspect of punctuation. For example, the children could be asked to contribute to a class book or make an individual book based on *Where's Spot?* (Hill, 1980) or *What's the Time Mr Wolf?* (Hawkins, 1983) to encourage them to use question marks, full stops and capital letters.

Writing and publishing books can encourage children to pay attention to punctuation as there is a real reason for ensuring that the meaning is clear. Other writing for public audiences, such as making posters, may also encourage children to think about and use punctuation.

After looking at an unusual object the class could be asked to compile a set of questions about it. They could then be asked to find out the answers to these questions and to write the answers as statements. The questions and the answers could be displayed around the object. Both activities could be used as opportunities for practising punctuation marks.

Giving the class some prepared answers to questions and asking the children to think up and record as many questions that result in the answers as they can is an enjoyable activity. Answers might include 'fish and chips', 'next week', '£1.00'. The questions that could lead to these answers could be very varied. Teachers might need to discuss making written questions explicit – for example, 'How much was it?' may not be a good written question – as well as reminding children to use capital letters and question marks. A collection of questions could be displayed around the answers.

## Speech bubbles

Looking at the writing contained in the illustrations and the text in books such as *Funnybones* (Ahlberg and Ahlberg, 1980) helps children to see how direct speech contained in speech bubbles can be represented in a text. Working with a familiar story, children can be asked to find examples of direct speech and represent these in speech bubbles. As a next step they might be asked to represent the speech in a book such as *Bet You Can't!* (Dale, 1987) as part of the narrative. These activities should draw attention to the use of inverted commas.

## Using other children's writing

When writing is read by a response partner he or she can comment on the use of punctuation. If, at times, the teacher identifies this as a specific focus for the response both children can learn a great deal. They will be considering and exchanging ideas about the role of punctuation in writing.

---

Make a collection of picture books written for young children to use as starting points for discussions about punctuation.          **Activity**

---

## DEVELOPING PUNCTUATION WHEN RESPONDING TO WRITING

Using children's own writing to develop their understanding and ability to use punctuation is one of the most valuable starting points for learning. Before teaching any aspect of punctuation the teacher needs to know what children know and understand, and more importantly be sure that children feel confident about writing. All children can benefit from general discussions and teacher models of punctuation, but specific teaching is probably most appropriate when children are producing an extended piece of writing that *could be improved* by demarcating sentences or when children are beginning to incorporate punctuation marks into their writing. Before talking about the use of punctuation in a piece of writing the teacher might ask himself:

- Has the child used any punctuation marks?
- If not, is the child ready to begin to incorporate punctuation into her writing?
- How has the child used punctuation?
- What has the child done well?
- What could easily and usefully be improved?

If the child has not used punctuation the teacher can demonstrate where its use would help the reader and improve the writing. He could also explain how and why punctuation is necessary. If the child has misused punctuation in her writing the teacher might begin the teaching episode by asking the child why she has used it in the way she has chosen. Then the teacher might comment on what the child has done and explain how its use might be changed to clarify meaning further. Providing guidance on punctuation is often useful after children have produced a first draft. Children then have the opportunity to incorporate their new understanding into the final version and to consolidate their learning.

The following list provides some guidelines to help adults who are working on punctuation with young children.

- Keep the teaching of punctuation in proportion. It is one of the transcription skills of writing and is competing with spelling and handwriting for children's attention.
- The function of punctuation is to clarify meaning.
- It is best explained and taught in meaningful literacy contexts.
- Children need to understand what punctuation is for before they can be expected to use it correctly.
- Children need to see how punctuation is used.
- Children benefit from teachers modelling the use of punctuation.
- Match teaching to need and understanding. Children are likely to be at different stages of understanding and not all of them will benefit from the same teaching.
- Completing decontextualised exercises and worksheets does not help children to transfer punctuation skills to their own writing.

**Activity**    Through an analysis of pieces of children's writing and discussions with the authors find out what children know about punctuation.

## MEETING THE STATUTORY REQUIREMENTS

Young children are only expected to show a growing awareness of how punctuation is used in writing. Some facility with capital letters, full stops and question marks will be the normal achievement by the age of seven, and this expectation is expressed in the National Literacy Strategy *Framework for Teaching* (DfEE, 1998). The suggestions outlined in this chapter will help most children meet the requirements for punctuation described in the Desirable Outcomes for Children's Learning (SCAA, 1996) and the English National Curriculum (DfE, 1995). These documents specify that:

By the age of five children should be able to:

- use upper-case letters appropriately when writing their names.

By the age of seven children should be able to:

- understand the purpose of punctuation
- show awareness of how full stops are used
- demarcate sequences of sentences with capital letters and full stops
- use question marks
- begin to use commas.

## Summary

This chapter has examined the punctuation system as it relates to what young children need to learn. It has shown that the appropriate use of punctuation is probably the last writing skill to emerge and is likely to be last technical aspect of writing to be mastered. Children need a great deal of experience of print and some competence at writing extended pieces of text before they need or are able to incorporate many elements of punctuation into their writing. While teachers need to have realistic expectations about what children will be able to achieve they can begin to introduce them to aspects of punctuation even in the earliest stages of schooling.

*The key points covered in this chapter were:*

- **an introduction to the English punctuation system**

- **the role and use of punctuation in texts**

- **the way children's understanding and use of punctuation develops**

- **some strategies that can be used when teaching children about punctuation**

- **the statutory requirements for punctuation in the early years.**

## Further reading

Bunting, R. (1997) *Teaching about Language in the Primary Years*, David Fulton Publishers, London
This book contains some useful ideas about teaching children about punctuation whilst heightening their awareness of language.

Hall, N. and Robinson, A. (eds) (1996) *Learning about Punctuation*, Multilingual Matters, Clevedon
A comprehensive account of learning about and teaching punctuation. The book contains a number of useful accounts of classroom practice.

# 9 Writing in context

## Objectives

*When you have read this chapter you should:*

- be aware of the connections for learning between oral language, reading and writing

- recognise how role play can contribute to writing development

- appreciate the cross-curricular use and application of writing

- understand the statutory requirement to teach standard English and language study when teaching writing at Key Stage 1.

## Introduction

**standard English**
a dialect of English commonly used in formal communications

Although writing is taught in English sessions it can also be developed in other areas of the curriculum when children use their ability to write to record and consolidate their learning. Children also need to discover the out-of-school uses of writing and these can be demonstrated and explored in school, particularly in role-play activities. The National Curriculum requirement to teach children about **standard English** and language study provides opportunities for children to learn more about writing and about how to write with greater skill. These opportunities to develop writing outside writing sessions provide a wider context for writing in school.

## SPEECH AND WRITING

### The similarities between speech and writing

Language is a way of communicating and receiving meaning. Sharing meanings through language depends on the use and interpretation of an agreed set of symbols. In oral English these symbols are the 44 sounds or phonemes that make up the English language and in writing they are the 26 letters of the alphabet or graphemes. Listeners and readers perceive and interpret the oral and written symbols in order to understand, and speakers and writers use the symbols to communicate their meaning. As English is partially an alphabetic language there is a relationship between the individual sounds of the language and the shapes that represent them. There is also a structural relationship between oral and written language since words within utterances are ordered in similar ways. These similarities are exploited by adults and used by children when spelling and formulating written sentences in school.

## The differences between speech and writing

Over-relying on the similarities between oral and written language and ignoring some significant differences between them can be misleading. If these differences are not acknowledged and if teaching does not take account of them, learning to write can become a major challenge for some children. Some of these differences are represented in essence in Table 9.1.

The reasons for the differences between spoken and written language are, for the most part, to do with the purposes for which each is used. Writing evolved long after speech and did so in order to fulfil needs which the spoken mode could not satisfy. It developed in response to the need to keep records of belongings, financial transactions and important agreements. Because speech is impermanent it is more suited to communicating information that does not need to be stored and to establishing and maintaining informal relationships. At times both speech and writing can be used formally and informally and there is no absolute boundary between them,

| Speaking | Writing |
|---|---|
| a continuous stream of phonemes | words separated by spaces and punctuation |
| fragmented utterances | complete sentences |
| intonation and stress | spelling, punctuation and layout |
| the listener is present and may add to the text | the reader is absent when the text is constructed |
| context helps the listener to understand | no necessary shared context |
| the listener can seek immediate clarification | no immediate response from the reader |
| often informal and repetitive | formal, condensed, clear |
| immediate, often unplanned | planned and revised |
| often emotional and trivial | often serious |
| transitory | permanent |
| quick and requiring little physical effort | tiring and demanding |

**Table 9.1**
*The differences between speaking and writing*

but in the main, speech and writing were and continue to be used for different purposes and in different contexts.

Whilst the connections between oracy and literacy, which link what is unknown with what is familiar, are helpful as a basis for introducing children to the writing system, relying too much on the similarities and having an oversimplified view of the links between spoken and written language can create difficulties in teaching and learning. Knowledge and experience of oral language can provide children with a basis for and a way into writing. When children first begin to write they know that writing is a way of expressing meaning and they often use writing to communicate their experiences. At this stage what children write is similar to their spoken utterances. However, writing as they speak soon begins to let children down in content, structure and transcription. The spoken comment 'It's a picture of my dog' is likely to become 'This is my dog' when written down. The absence of a shared context means the writing has to be explicit. The word 'is' can only be written as *i* and *s*, not *ez* or *es* which are other possible representations of the word based on pronunciation.

Children need to learn about the differences between oral and written language if they are to make progress in writing. They need to be taught about what writing offers and what it is used for. They can then be given reasons for learning about a different system of communication and taught about the structure of different written genres, the need to sequence events and ideas, to organise information and to transcribe clearly. When children realise that writing is different from speech they should recognise that it has something new to offer them and they may be more willing to invest the effort that learning about the conventions of writing demands.

## READING AND WRITING

There is an important and beneficial relationship between learning to read and learning to write, although the ability to write generally develops more slowly than the ability to read. Children are often able to recognise words before they can write them accurately.

### How reading supports writing

*Learning about the uses of writing*

An important part of the classroom writing environment is provided by books. This includes books that are in the library or book corner, books that are taken home by the children, books that are read to children, books that are made by children, books that are made by the teacher, and big books that are shared with the class. Familiarity with books provides children with important lessons about how writing works, what it can do and how they can use it.

When stories are shared teachers are familiarising children with the notion of authorship. As children realise that books are written by people they can be introduced to the idea that they too can be authors and produce texts for others to read. Lessons about writing for an audience are given an immediate and significant context when children write books that become part of the classroom resources for reading, make charts, lists and diagrams that will be consulted by others or produce labels for displays.

### Learning about texts

When reading children learn that symbols used in writing are not arbitrary: writers use a set of symbols with a particular form. They can see that writing is arranged in a particular way. In the English language it moves from left to right and top to bottom on a page. Spaces separate words and punctuation is used to separate ideas.

Written language is used in particular ways that have to be experienced and understood before they can be produced. Experience with reading introduces children to the pattern, style and explicit nature of written language. It also introduces children to a wide range of written genres and styles. Through reading and their experience with texts children also learn about how to structure their own writing; this is helped when children are encouraged to reflect on the ways in which different sorts of texts are organised.

Books and other forms of text provide ideas for writing; as Smith (1982) wrote, 'composition is stimulated by reading'. For reading to benefit writing development as much as possible, it is essential that children have access to a wide range of good-quality books which present a range of ideas, styles and organisational structures.

### Learning to spell

When children are encouraged to write independently from the start they are faced with the problem of how to represent spoken language in written form, how to represent the sounds of the language and how to spell words. Initially children represent words through what they can hear. They are applying their phonological awareness to writing as they try and match letters to sounds. In order to spell accurately children need to use visual and memory strategies in addition to phonic strategies. Sharing books with others and practising reading in the early stages encourages children to attend closely to words and sequences and letters in order to discriminate between words that look similar, such as *where* and *when*. This has three benefits. It helps to develop visual awareness, helps children to remember what frequently used words look like and helps children to internalise letter strings or spelling patterns in words, all of which help to develop spelling.

**Activity** Look back at Chapters 5, 6 and 7. Try to identify how the connections between speaking, reading and writing are helpful and misleading to beginning writers. Can you eliminate the confusion imprecise teaching, which relies on these connections, causes in your own work?

## ROLE PLAY AND WRITING

It is not easy for teachers to devise authentic activities which provide children with opportunities to explore the full range of writing purposes, audiences and formats that exist. Role play is one way of making a variety of writing available to children in the classroom. It is also a means of demonstrating the variety and purpose of writing. Indoor role-play areas are a common feature in early years classrooms. Outdoor role-play areas can also be set up and resourced with literacy materials. For example, a garage could make reading and writing an integral part of bike riding. The children could carry out MOT checks and pay and receive bills for repairs to their vehicles.

During play activities children are given opportunities to experiment with writing in a relaxed environment. The writing they produce need not be assessed, improved or redrafted, but by observing children writing in play situations the teacher can gain insights into their understanding of the writing process and may plan to extend this in the more formal writing sessions that take place in the classroom.

### The role of the adult in play

Play is not only a time when children learn; it can be a time when adults teach. Direct teaching where adults take control of children's actions would be inappropriate, but there are other ways in which support can be given when adults participate in children's play. Godwin and Perkins (1998) identify these as:

- modelling
- sustaining
- extending
- collaborating
- supporting.

### Modelling

When participating in play that involves using literacy materials adults can model their use as they work alongside children. They can read magazines and newspapers and complete crosswords or word games as they wait, in role, as a patient in the doctor's surgery, write in the appointment book, give a written appointment card, or consult records and make notes in the diary when acting as the doctor's receptionist. Modelling helps children to realise the potential of the literacy resources that are supplied, presents them with a clear demonstration of their use and can give them the requisite skills to benefit from the resources and experiences that are provided.

### Sustaining

If children's play becomes repetitive adults can change some of the resources that are available in order to rekindle or stimulate the children's interest. For example, greeting cards, wrapping paper and labels can be added to the home-corner resources at times of celebration. The children can be asked for their ideas about the sorts of writing activities they have seen in different locations, and resources to support these can be provided or made.

### Extending

When playing alongside children adults can model extensions to the play. They may make a trip to the library area to borrow books to read to the dolls at bedtime or write invitations to a few members of the class asking them to come to a birthday party for one of the toys. Adults can also extend children's play by introducing a new dimension to the activity. The clothes shop may hold a sale necessitating the writing of posters and labels. The home-corner family might decide to plan a holiday. Sometimes a timely question such as 'Are you going to . . . ?' might be sufficient to move the children's play into a new area.

### Collaborating

In the role-play area adults and children can work together to solve problems and set up more productive imaginary situations. They can discuss how to transform the area into Princess Gloriana's palace (McGough, 1996), produce the resources and cooperate on the initial re-enactments of the story.

### Supporting

During role play adults can help children to stay in role and help a group to stay within their story. This can help with children's storying abilities, which is beneficial when they are planning and

159

writing stories of their own. Adults can also support children's independent work by monitoring turn-taking and the equitable use of resources.

Teaching during play is not just opportunistic, although at times it might be. Play provides a real opportunity for observing children's abilities in writing, and intervention based on assessment can be planned and undertaken during role play or provided through other writing activities.

## Resourcing the role-play area for literacy

Role-play areas often arise from the theme that is being undertaken by the class. For example, a travel agency, an airport or a train station might be set up if the children are working on the theme of Journeys.

When establishing the area it is useful to involve the children in writing the signs, notices, menus and price lists that will become part of the play setting. This gives them practice at writing and also provides them with the knowledge and experience of the context, which supports them as they engage in the writing activities that may arise. They are then more likely to understand the purpose, style and audience of the writing that accompanies their play and to take advantage of the opportunities in the way the adults intended.

Below are some suggestions about how to give the role-play area a literacy focus.

### A railway station

Include timetables, posters, notices, a cash till, receipts, cheque books, tickets, a computer screen, notepads and envelopes in the booking office. Next to this a newsagent's and a snack bar could be set up, to provide further writing opportunities, as they are often found in railway stations.

### A newspaper shop

Newspapers, magazines, comics, local maps and travel guides, sweets, chocolate and crisps provide a variety of reading material in this role-play area. It could also stock a range of stationery including greeting cards and postcards as well as pens, pencils and stamps. Some of these items could be made by the children and they could be encouraged to examine the writing on the real examples before making and writing them for themselves.

### An airport

An imaginative play area set up as an airport offers similar literacy opportunities to those available in a railway station. Check-in areas where tickets, passports and boarding cards are needed, shops and cafes are all found in airports. To extend the opportunities for story-making, reading and writing there could also be a plane and spaces to represent holiday destinations. On the plane there are instructions, pamphlets, magazines and guidebooks to read, and hotels and beach areas provide further opportunities for literate role play which could usefully inform children's own imaginative writing.

### The home corner

Whilst it is always worth setting up unusual and imaginative role-play areas, sometimes it can be productive to set up the role-play area as a literate home corner. Many children will have some experience of reading and writing activities at home, and the models they have seen will enable them to make good use of the resources that are provided. The familiarity of the home corner and the way in which it reflects all children's experiences outside school means that children may practise some of the writing they try out in the imaginary home corner in their own homes.

In the home corner children can write books to read to the dolls, invitations for a dolls' party and greeting cards, take telephone messages, make shopping lists, leave notes for the milk deliverer, enter items in a diary and fill in forms. The area should have resources for writing such as pens, paper, postcards and notepads. It is useful to use the home corner to illustrate the different sorts of writing that are found in most real homes. To this end it might contain magazines, local and national newspapers, letters, greeting cards, postcards, recipe books, a calendar and a telephone directory, as well as packets and containers with writing on them. These resources give children ideas about how writing is represented and about different types of writing.

---

**Activity**

Observe the children as they use the role-play area. Did you notice any times when adult support might have introduced the children to different and productive ways of using the literacy resources in the area?

---

## WRITING ACROSS THE CURRICULUM

### Integrating writing with other subject areas

Writing is both part of a distinct curriculum area, English, and a part of every other area of the curriculum. It is easy to identify writing as a part of the English curriculum when children are writing stories, poems or letters. However, the starting point for writing may well be science, technology, geography or history. Children may write a recipe as part of a science investigation into the ways in which materials change. They may describe and evaluate how they made a musical instrument as part of a technology session The focus may be on geography if children are planning a route from the school to a local park in preparation for a class picnic. Writing can arise from history if the children are arranging data collected from older people in the locality or gathered from their own reading.

Earlier chapters have indicated how writing can accompany many of the activities in the nursery to provide opportunities for writing and to encourage children to explore the range of purposes for writing. Genre theory has indicated the importance of teaching children to craft their writing in different ways to make it appropriate for its purpose. When the writing demands of particular tasks are analysed much of the teaching about format and style can take place within curriculum areas other than English. Children can certainly practise and apply their knowledge of genre across the curriculum. Because writing arises from every part of the curriculum it does not need to be a distinct part of the curriculum only taking place with status during 'creative writing lessons' or within the literacy hour.

## ICT and writing

The role of ICT (information and communications technology) is largely to support children's learning across the curriculum. The National Curriculum suggests that ICT capability and skills are best learned in appropriate contexts, many of which relate to work in other curriculum areas (SCAA, 1995b). Writing provides a particularly rich context for the development and use of ICT skills using hardware and software. The introduction of the word 'communications' into IT signalled its importance as a tool for transmitting, recording and retrieving information. ICT can also be used to give children help with forming letters, spelling and punctuation. Although the use of software to practise transcription has a place in the writing curriculum it should not be overused or given to children who would not benefit from it. In many cases content-free software is of most benefit and can be used more productively with greater numbers of children. Used creatively the computer can widen the writing curriculum.

### ICT and transcription

A great deal of software, developed to help children with writing, concentrates on ways of helping children to practise letter formation, learn spellings or place punctuation marks in the correct places in pre-written sentences. However, the possibilities of computers for learning about transcription are greater than this. At the simplest level children can be shown how to use spell checks to resolve spelling queries. This encourages children to re-read their writing critically and spend time on self-correction. It also helps them to look more carefully at words and develop their visual strategies for spelling. A more creative use of the computer to help with spelling might be to work with the class to make a database of words that are needed when writing. This could be an alphabetically ordered collection of words that are often misspelled by the class or a set of words needed for work on the theme being studied by the class. The advantage of using the computer in this way is that the words that the children are entering and looking up have been created to meet the specific needs of the children in the class.

## ICT and composition

Composing directly on the computer can help children to become confident with writing. The appearance of recognisable letters on the screen can encourage children to try out writing for themselves, to take risks and to take more responsibility for their own learning. Young children who have difficulty holding and manipulating writing implements for long periods often find the computer keyboard easier to use. This can help children to concentrate on the content of what they are writing and enables children to write fluently. Concept keyboard overlays are often useful for young beginning writers. They provide children with the words and phrases they need to compose without having to think too much about how to represent them through letters. Pre-prepared concept keyboard overlays can be made to suit individual, group or class requirements. Overlays can also accommodate children's home languages and provide opportunities for children to write in their first language and to gain experience of languages other than English.

Communication in any media is concerned with choosing the best way to get a message across to a particular audience. Using ICT for writing enables children to produce and revise their work easily as they explore alternative ways of composing a message that is suited to its audience or consider how best to arrange information so that it is accessible at a later date.

Desktop publishing can give children the chance to discover how audience, purpose and content affect writing style. Producing items for a school or class newsletter allows children to see how texts can be transformed. For example, items about future topics to be studied by classes can take the form of a news item, an advert appealing for artefacts, or a personal recollection by children who studied the same topic in previous years. Putting the computer in the role-play area also encourages children to write using different genres such as letters or records (Minns, 1991).

Computers can bring different and authentic writing activities into the classroom. Outside the classroom ICT is used to produce posters and many publications. As in real life children could use the computer to create suitable messages for a range of greeting cards or combine text and graphics to produce professionally finished notices and posters for the school. Databases can be used to collect, record, analyse and present information in charts, graphs and reports. Information that needs to be retrieved in different ways, such as reviews of books containing details about types of books, authors, illustrators and quality, could be compiled in this way. Databases and graphics programmes also help children to learn about writing and organising information texts. Now that e-mail is becoming more available in school children will be able to experiment with this new genre of writing. It will allow children to correspond with known and unknown others outside the classroom in a way that is immediate and often more casual than traditional letters.

### ICT and review

Word-processing facilities on the computer make it possible for writers to plan, draft, reorganise and amend their writing without writing anew at each stage. This can make what sometimes seems a time-consuming and laborious process more easily available to young children. The use of the computer can also make shared work easier. Two children working together can make choices and decisions about their writing as they type and amend their text.

### ICT and special needs

Using ICT with children with special educational needs can be beneficial as it can provide support with some of the aspects of writing that they might find difficult. It can be used to develop or make transcription easier for children with some forms of physical impairment. Children with less developed handwriting and presentational skills can benefit from seeing their writing presented clearly and attractively. They are often more motivated to write when they produce an aesthetically pleasing, professional piece of work or when they realise that the computer gives them the opportunity to redraft and edit their writing easily. Computers can also successfully hold the attention of children with behavioural or concentration difficulties.

*Planning*

If ICT is to be used productively to support writing its use needs to be considered carefully and planned for. Time needs to be made available to introduce and teach the skills that are required. Time also needs to be allocated for children to develop and practise skills such as drafting, and for children to become familiar with unfamiliar software. There are many possibilities for the appropriate and productive use of ICT in English sessions and writing activities if we are alert to them and plan carefully.

**Activities**

1  Do you plan opportunities for children to apply and consolidate skills acquired in literacy sessions in work in other subjects? If you do not already do this include opportunities for children to use their knowledge of different genres to write in sessions other than literacy. For example, children could use their knowledge of report writing in humanities sessions.

2  Consider how you might develop work begun in other subjects in literacy sessions. For example, the write-up of a science investigation could be left until a writing session when there might be more time to prepare the children to write in an appropriate form. When the opportunity arises incorporate teaching children how to write reports or recounts needed for their work in other curriculum areas into your planning for literacy.

## STANDARD ENGLISH AND LANGUAGE STUDY

All three National Curriculum programmes of study for English – Speaking and listening, Reading and Writing – include a section entitled 'Standard English and Language Study'. This part of the requirements is concerned with developing children's understanding of language and their communicative competence. Learning about language enables users to judge and question the language they encounter and select the language needed to match their meanings and intentions. It is not envisaged that this section of the programme of study is taught as a separate unit. It should be taught in meaningful curriculum contexts and integrated with other teaching that takes place in the classroom (DES, 1990). As you read this book you will see that much of what is expected at Key Stage 1 and before is covered by teachers as they teach children about the processes, functions, forms and transcription skills of writing. Through discussions about writing adults provide children with the vocabulary used to describe and talk about language and draw children's attention to specific aspects of language including standard English. They will also be helping children to communicate clearly by showing them how to make their writing increasingly suited to its purpose and clear to its audience.

## Standard English

**dialect**
a variety of language with a distinct vocabulary and grammar

Standard English is a systematic **dialect** of language that has accepted rules and conventions. This is true of all dialects. The difference between standard English and other dialect forms is that standard English is the form of language used for 'non-regional public communication' (Whitehead, 1990), and because of its public and official use is often thought of as the most socially prestigious dialect form of English.

The National Curriculum Council Consultation Report on English in the National Curriculum stated that:

**grammar**
the way in which words are organised to produce meaningful combinations. It also includes word agreements, such as plurals, and tenses.

> Standard English comprises *vocabulary* as found in dictionaries, and agreed conventions of *spelling* and *grammar*.
>
> ... Core grammatical features of Standard English include subject verb agreement, correct and consistent use of verb tenses, correct use of pronouns, adverbs and adjectives.
>
> ... The aim should be to equip young people with the ability to use Standard English when circumstances require it.

(NCC, 1993, p. 16)

Standard English is appropriate in formal communicative situations and when meaning has to be precise. It is the dialect most commonly found in books and the one that is often needed when writing for others. The language used in books provides a model of complete and grammatically exact language for children. As children begin to write for audiences beyond themselves they will begin to appreciate the need for extended and clear communication which draws on a vocabulary and grammar that is shared by all potential readers. Sensitive intervention in children's writing can lead to the discussion of the different varieties of English that exist and the reasons for their existence, and provide opportunities for children to learn about and use standard English purposefully and appropriately. Children who can use and manipulate writing according to context are developing the confidence and competence necessary to communicate with a range of people and in a variety of circumstances, which is one of the aims of learning to write.

While children should be given the opportunity to express themselves in standard English when it is appropriate, it is not necessary to use standard written English all the time. When communicating informally in notes written to friends or colleagues jargon and incomplete or irregularly constructed sentences are often used. Reminders and notes for oneself may not pay attention to the standard forms of language. Dialogue in stories and plays may be written in dialects other than standard English. In jokes, rhymes and poetry, where language is manipulated for effect, English may not be used in a standard fashion. Children need opportunities to hear, read and discuss language variations in order to learn when and how to use different varieties of English in their own writing. In particular they need to know that notes and plans can be informal and abbreviated in order to save expending unnecessary time and effort on this type of writing.

## Developing language awareness in the early years

The rationale for developing children's understanding of language is that it will extend their ability to communicate appropriately in a range of circumstances. We do know that very young children already have a great deal of communicative competence in oral language.

> Most children, by the time they are ready to begin school, know the full contents of an introductory book in transformational grammar. One such text is a bit more than 400 pages long and it covers declaratives and interrogatives, affirmatives and negatives, actives and passives, simple sentences, conjoined sentences and some kinds of embedded sentences. The pre-school child knows all this.
>
> (Brown, 1968, p. v)

Wells (1986), in a long-term research project into language development, found that young children know a great deal about language and are able to use it for a variety of purposes to suit the many communicative situations in which they participate. Their early encounters with books will already have alerted most children to the words and linguistic structures that are appropriate to stories and rhymes. They expect that written language, like oral language, contains meaning and is structured and organised. While children's explicit knowledge of language and their ability to transfer their knowledge about language to their own writing is initially limited, the understanding that they bring to school provides a firm base which the teacher can build upon when developing their conscious awareness of language.

Building on young children's oral language competence teachers widen their ability to manipulate language in the written form by:

- helping children to express themselves clearly in writing
- developing grammatical correctness, spelling and punctuation
- introducing children to specialist vocabulary used in subjects across the curriculum
- ensuring that they use different written forms appropriately
- helping them to become aware of audience and style.

Children's explicit understanding of language and their ability to use it in different ways to suit the demands of particular contexts, purposes and audiences will grow as they use language in a range of situations, as they reflect on language, and through planned opportunities for language study.

## Use and experience

Children are interested in language from an early age. They play with its sounds as they babble and explore its construction when they produce their early two- and three-word utterances. They also learn about the conventions of language, including how to formulate conversational exchanges to suit different audiences. They ask about word meanings, what people are saying and what they mean. They very quickly realise that some words, such as *bottom*, have the power to shock. All this occurs without being explicitly taught. By the time children start school they have a great deal of implicit knowledge about language and its appropriateness. At school, the planned play and teaching opportunities in the early years classroom require children to use and become explicitly aware of the language system and its conventions. Joining in with refrains in stories and rhymes develops children's interest in the sounds of words and the patterns they make. Shared and individual reading of a variety of texts and the discussions that accompany these events introduce children to the **metalanguage** of language. Adults ask children to look at *words*, to re-read *sentences*, to find *letters*, to compare similar *words* and to identify differences between *words*. Oral language and board games provide similar experiences. The writing opportunities provided through play that is resourced with literacy materials, and the demands that are placed on children to practise their writing as they write their names, contribute to big books and produce their own stories, enable them to use language in different ways and introduce them to the different forms that written language can take. All these almost incidental activities develop children's understanding and use of English in authentic situations.

## Reflection and discussion

Opportunities to reflect on language and how it can be used can arise out of most aspects of the school curriculum and at many times

**metalanguage**
the terminology for discussing and describing aspects of language

during the school day. These will generally be related to children's interests and needs and take place in a meaningful context such as the reading and writing that the children are doing and that may not have been planned in advance by the teacher.

English activities are rich sources for discussion. New words, names and phrases are introduced during shared reading times and these can be explored by the children. As children compose, plan and re-read their writing and respond to that produced by their peers they may be thinking about appropriateness and clarity. Writing demonstrations, conferences and discussions about spelling provide rich opportunities for language study and examining the variety of English dialects. These activities will involve discussions, using the appropriate terminology, about how language works. There might be opportunities to discuss ways of joining sentences using words such as *but*, *so* or *because* in addition to *and*. This is the first step in introducing children to the idea of simple, compound and complex sentences. Alternatively there might be opportunities to discuss what a sentence is and the use of punctuation associated with sentences. Consulting the dictionary for correct spellings or to find alternative words for a piece of reading will involve discovering word meanings and noticing connections between words.

The language demands of subjects across the curriculum are varied and mean that children need to be aware of and use language in different ways. Each subject has its own specialist vocabulary which children will draw upon in their writing. Presenting information for history projects, undertaking research into aspects of geography or recording findings in mathematics necessitate using different formats for writing.

## Planned opportunities for language study

Language study means developing linguistic awareness and understanding that language is composed of different components which fit together to produce coherent and extended texts. Morphemes, letters and words can be arranged in varying ways to signify meaning. As language is a rule-governed system, the way in which the component parts can be arranged follows a set of established conventions. Letters in words, words in sentences and sentences in extended text follow expected patterns. For example, it is unlikely that a word in English would contain a *u* followed by a *q*. It would also be unusual to produce a sentence such as *Bike can a ride I.* Knowledge of textual conventions means that it would be surprising to see an account of an experiment written in sonnet form. The National Literacy Strategy *Framework for Teaching* (DfEE, 1998) suggests that the parts of language and the way in which they combine to produce meaning result in three organisational layers in writing. It identifies these as the word level, the sentence level and the text level.

## Words

**graphology**
the symbols of written language

**phonology**
the sounds of language

**morphology**
the identification of the elements of a word which carry meaning

When working with young children to develop their writing abilities, teachers are extending their awareness of **graphology**, the writing system and the alphabet, and helping children to make connections between the sounds of speech and their relationship with the alphabet. They are developing children's understanding of the relationship between **phonology** and graphology. As they introduce children to correctly spelled words and teach them strategies for remembering conventional spellings they will be discussing word structures and the derivations of words, or **morphology**.

Sharing books with children and discussing classroom routines and activities will introduce children to previously unknown words or familiar words used in unfamiliar ways. Schools employ many vocabulary items that are used in special ways, for example words such as *break time, register, ruler, assembly, special person*, even *home corner*. Exploring word meanings and ensuring that children develop a wide-ranging vocabulary are two further aspects of knowledge about words that teachers need to make explicit to children.

## Sentences

Sentence-level work is sometimes known as grammar or syntax. It is concerned with the different function words fulfil in sentences, how the words agree with each other and how they may be ordered. Introducing children to nouns and verbs alerts them to the different functions of words. Discussing the dialectical use of *I were* or *I says* raises the issue of agreement. Proofreading written work often reveals words that have been omitted or duplicated, which results in sentences that contain incorrectly ordered words. Sentence-level knowledge is also concerned with different types of sentences, such as statements and questions, and how word order and punctuation denote these. When children make notes and plans they may only write phrases or key words rather than complete sentences. Suggesting that children use words other than *and* to connect sentences, or full stops rather than a series of *ands* in their writing, is drawing attention to grammar.

## Texts

Text-level knowledge is concerned with an awareness of the forms that writing can take. It develops as children are introduced to writing narrative and non-fiction for different audiences and for different purposes. When teachers show children how to organise their writing, when to include connectives such as *first*, *then* and *because* and how to consider the different elements of writing such as plot and characterisation, they are teaching children about textual conventions. All these activities help children to use written language more effectively and with increasing precision.

## Planned activities

As teachers plan the English scheme for the term and the year they will endeavour to cover the content suggested in the National Literacy Strategy. For example, in Year 1 children are expected to write stories, rhymes, poems, signs, labels, captions, lists, descriptions, observations, messages, letters, notices, invitations, instructions and information texts. These forms of writing will be introduced through teacher demonstrations of the structure and characteristics of different text types. Teachers will also explain how context, audience and purpose affect the way language is presented and the register that is used. Writing invitations and an information text for the class library are likely to require children to use standard English, whilst writing a poem based on a rhyme in *No Hickory No Dickory No Dock* (Agard and Nicholls, 1991) will involve them using a Caribbean dialect with a different grammar and rhyming system. This will encourage children to compare and investigate varieties of language and language systems.

## Using names

Themes such as *Ourselves* or *All about Us* are common in early years settings. As part of these teachers can use children's names to examine words, their derivations, the writing system and the links between spoken and written language. Collections of names can be sorted and matched according to initial letters, number of syllables and length. They can be arranged in alphabetical order and may be used to make an alphabet frieze or poster or incorporated into a large book for the class. Children can experiment with writing their names in various colours and sizes using a variety of tools and materials. The sounds, names, shapes and formation of all the letters contained in the names and the use of capital letters can be discussed and compared during the activities and later when the poster or the frieze is referred to. Children can discuss how the spellings of names can vary, how names can be shortened, nicknames and name changes. They can investigate the popularity of names at different times, make a survey of names and present their findings in chart form. Similar activities may also arise from an examination of food packaging and labels, environmental print in and around the school, slang words, subject-specific words and words associated with TV programmes or computer games.

## A writing project

Setting up a project which looks at writing can be a very beneficial way of extending children's understanding of language. It is a way of helping children to:

- know about the structure of the language
- know about varieties of language including standard English
- use language with greater awareness
- develop an interest in language
- learn and use the formal terminology associated with language
- gain insights into the meaningful use of language beyond the classroom
- improve children's composition and transcription skills.

The project could begin with the children looking at their own writing and themselves as writers. They could consider:

- when they write at school
- when they write at home
- when they like writing
- when they don't like writing
- what they can do with writing.

They could then investigate when, how and why others write. The others could be children in different classes, adults in school, family members, those who work in the locality. This might lead to looking at all the writing in the school and writing in the environment. From this it would be easy to examine different sorts of writing, different ways of presenting writing and writing scripts. Looking at the relationship between content and presentation might lead to experiments with resources, layout and writing styles and could result in improved standards of presentation in writing. Slightly older children might undertake some research into the history of writing. Very young children might limit their investigations to examining the letters, words and arrangement of text on food or toy packaging.

Other possibilities for activities which encourage children to investigate language include:

- finding out about the origins of words
- oral word play including jokes and riddles
- exchanging writing with other classes
- exchanging writing with children in different regions and countries using e-mail
- making a timeline of their own writing development
- making collections of subject words, words with similar meanings, opposites, words with more than one meaning

- writing a book of word games
- investigating typefaces and styles in books, newspapers, comics, magazines and catalogues
- identifying important words in advertisements
- writing advertisements for a book or for a toy
- making a collection of different types of sentences such as statements and questions.

## Summary

This chapter has looked at the many ways in which writing development can be supported across the early years curriculum. It has identified how speaking and listening, role play, cross-curricular work and work on standard English and language study can be used to develop writing competence and understanding of the purposes of writing. It has also examined how writing itself can add to learning across and beyond the school curriculum. Placing writing in a wider context provides us with insights into its structure and use. It can also help us to recognise ways in which the writing curriculum can be extended and enhanced.

*The key points covered in this chapter were:*

- **the similarities and differences between oral and written language**

- **the way in which learning to read supports learning to write**

- **the benefits of providing writing opportunities in role play**

- **ways in which writing can be developed across the curriculum**

- **ways of teaching children about standard English and language through writing.**

## Further reading

Bunting, R. (1997) *Teaching about Language in the Primary Years*, David Fulton Publishers, London
This book contains some useful ideas about introducing children to language study in ways which develop their oral and written language skills.

Hall, N. and Robinson, A. (1995) *Exploring Writing and Play in the Early Years*, David Fulton Publishers, London
A book which amply illustrates the possibilities for writing during play.

Inner London Education Authority (1990) *Language and Power*, Harcourt Brace Jovanovitch, London
This is an excellent source of ideas for work on language study and standard English.

Minns, H. (1991) *Primary Language: Extending the Curriculum with Computers*, National Council for Educational Technology, Coventry
This booklet contains a number of illuminating case studies about the use of ICT to develop speaking, listening, reading and writing.

Moyles, J. (ed.) (1994) *The Excellence of Play*, Open University Press, Buckingham
This book contains a host of ideas about setting up and supporting play activities which extend young children's learning.

SCAA (1997) *Use of Language: A Common Approach*, SCAA Publications, Middlesex
A booklet containing suggestions about planning for developing aspects of language in all curriculum areas.

Sealey, A. (1996) *Learning about Language*, Open University Press, Buckingham
A book about incorporating work on standard English and language awareness across the curriculum.
The **National Council for Educational Technology** has produced a book of reviews of educational discs. This is available from NCET, Milburn Hill Road, Science Park, Coventry CV4 7JJ, telephone 01203 416994.

# Individual differences 10

*When you have read this chapter you should:*

- be aware of the contribution that parents do and can make to writing development

- understand how gender differences affect writing

- be able to plan some writing activities that cater for bilingual learners

- have some understanding of the difficulties some children experience with writing.

## Introduction

All children do not learn in the same way or at the same time nor does all their learning take place at school. Some children learn to write easily and enthusiastically; others learn more slowly and more cautiously. Most children learn a great deal about writing before they start school and, once they have started, outside the classroom walls. Personality and experiences affect what and how children learn. These factors should influence the teaching that is provided so that individual differences are catered for and individual learning needs are met.

## PARENTS AND WRITING

### Writing before school

Significant adults and home and community environments make an important impact on young children's literacy learning. They provide many examples of writing in use and models of writers. At the very least homes contain junk mail, post, packaging and newspapers. The majority of homes will contain many more examples of a variety of written texts, some of which, such as letters or bills, will be responded to in writing. Many adults will involve young children in writing greeting cards and letters and comment on the writing that children produce. They also help children to write their personal and family names. Others buy teaching resources such as pencils and felt-tip pens, plastic letters, alphabet books and workbooks produced for parents. At home most writing is placed in a context and is undertaken with a purpose. It is an integral part of everyday life and the instruction that children receive generally takes place in an enjoyable context or is provided within meaningful situations.

Research studies repeatedly show that learning about writing and learning to write before school is widespread. In one of the more recent the author wrote:

> Virtually all children born into a print culture have a great deal of experience with the written word at home and in their communities, often mediated by their parents, before they formally start school.

> (Weinberger, 1996, p. 15)

She found that 'virtually all parents help their child in some way with literacy' (p. 114), a finding she considers generalisable beyond her own research. The experience of living in a print-laden society and the findings from studies which have investigated literacy practices in the home suggest that the majority of children enter nursery and reception classes with an awareness of what writing is for and how it is produced.

This is helpful to schools and teachers. They have a foundation on which to build their teaching. For most children their development as writers will have begun. They may know what writing is for, how it looks and what writers do in order to produce writing. When children start school teachers can assess what children can do where they are on the developmental sequence, described in Chapters 2 and 4, and begin their teaching at a point that matches the child's abilities. They will rarely have to begin with first principles.

Judgements about what children know and can do when they enter school can be made if they are given opportunities to write in a variety of contexts and time is made to discuss writing with them. Parents need to be asked about the writing children do at home and the opportunities and resources they have access to. Not only does this give the teacher valuable information about children's writing development, it is also a first step towards developing mutual respect and understanding between home and school.

## Writing outside school

Although they confidently and successfully support their child before school, many parents are not sure about how to support their child's learning once they start school. They are not sure about what is expected of them, whether what they are doing is 'right', and may not understand the way writing is taught at school. Weinberger (1996) has suggested that schools should plan to involve parents in the continued development of literacy and has devised a checklist of procedures which will help. She suggests that schools should:

- have a school policy on parents and literacy
- include parents in record-keeping and assessments of literacy
- provide written documentation for parents on literacy
- have formal contact with parents about literacy
- have informal contact with parents about literacy
- accumulate detailed knowledge of children's home literacy experiences.

These practices should ensure that parents understand the school's approach to writing, feel that they can make a contribution and continue to help their child to learn to write in the advantageous one-to-one and contextualised writing situations that the home can provide.

## Providing parents with information

Teachers and schools can provide parents with three types of information:

- about the approach the school employs
- about their child's progress
- about the support they can provide.

### The school's approach to writing

Most schools have a school booklet or prospectus which contains information about the curriculum. This may contain details about how writing is taught. It is helpful if parents are aware of the way the school arranges the teaching of writing. This is particularly true if the school has a developmental approach. Many parents will not be familiar with this as it is likely to be different from the way in which they were taught to write. They may also be anxious about how their children will learn to spell. Schools need to take every opportunity to explain what they do. They can hold a writing evening, make an informative display and include explanations in a home–school writing booklet. When parents are clear about what the school is doing they are in a better position to support what the school does.

### Information about progress

Reports and parents' evenings are times when parents learn about their child's progress. However, if parents wish to help their child with writing it can be useful for them to know which aspects of their child's writing need attention. The National Literacy Strategy

(DfEE, 1998) suggests that the teacher's targets for children's literacy development should be shared regularly with parents so that home and school can work together to support progress.

*Providing support at home*

All parents can support children's development. Schools can provide parents with a great many suggestions about activities suitable for young children that can be undertaken at home. These do not need special equipment and do not need to take up a great deal of time. The most beneficial experiences are when adults involve children in everyday writing events at home. Other simple activities might include:

- looking at words on the packaging that comes with toys, on birthday cards, on postcards
- providing children with old diaries or calendars to write on
- giving children envelopes and forms that come in the junk mail to play with
- pointing out letters in words from time to time
- playing with magnetic fridge letters and making words that are important to children, such as their names
- playing with plastic letters and letters that stick on the sides of the bath.

When parents and teachers are working together on literacy targets specific activities which will help the child will need to be discussed. Teachers may need to take account of what can realistically be done at home and make suggestions which suit particular home circumstances. Whatever work parents do at home with their child it is worth mentioning that if children are forced to write this can have a detrimental effect on their interest and confidence.

**Activity**  Reflect on how much you know about the home literacy experiences of the children you teach. Do you know about them in a general way or do you know about the children's out-of-school writing experiences in detail? Can you think of ways to find out what and when children write at home? Try out some of your ideas.

## GENDER DIFFERENCES IN WRITING

In recent years the different ways in which boys and girls tackle and succeed at literacy has attracted considerable attention. Whilst much of this has drawn attention to boys' underachievement it is important to remember that not all boys do badly. The problem is largely associated with white working-class and black Afro-Caribbean boys, who seem to be the ones most vulnerable to underachievement. However, it is also fair to say that girls too can experience problems with writing. These are not as obvious as those manifested by boys but they can lead them to underperform in different ways.

## Achieving differently

Children learn about what they should be interested in and what they should aspire to from the role models they are presented with. At home it is very often women who read fiction and who write letters to friends and family members. Men are more likely to read for information purposes and to write more formal communications. Many men may write at work but not at home and so are not available as models for the children to see. Even when this is not the case at home, the images of readers and writers that children are presented with in the media suggest that different sorts of literacy are associated with each sex. This is often reinforced at school, where in the primary years the majority of teachers who are promoting literacy are women and the sorts of books they most often recommend are stories. From these experiences boys can come to believe that writing, particularly literary writing, is a female subject and as result give it less attention than is needed.

The models and expectations about literacy that children witness can result in boys and girls having different attitudes towards writing and demonstrating different strengths and weaknesses in written work. Girls enjoy writing narrative and poetry and receive support for this from the fiction they read. Boys tend to produce shorter stories. They often contain fantasy, and the plot and characters may be based on cartoons or comic books. As they prefer reading non-fiction and annuals, they do not benefit from the models of stories which girls may benefit from. Girls can find it difficult to write non-fiction texts, whilst this style of structured and often shorter writing may suit boys' capabilities. In school, narrative writing dominates the curriculum. This can leave all pupils poorly equipped to cope with the writing demands they will face in the world outside the classroom.

Adults can make initial judgements about children's writing based on length and presentation regardless of content. On both these criteria girls do better than boys. Adults may expect girls' writing to be neater and for them to find story writing easier than boys. These sorts of expectations can reinforce stereotypical writing. Boys, who are expected to be and who often are more assertive than girls, are more likely to reject activities when they do not see their purpose. Girls, who are expected to be more passive, are generally more accommodating and tolerant of teachers' sometimes ambiguous and long-term aims. This too has a direct effect on achievement in writing.

The common characteristics of girls' and boys' behaviour which impinge on literacy and of their writing are compared in Table 10.1. When tabulated in this way it is possible to identify areas where boys and girls may underachieve in writing and to see why this happens.

## What can be done

When the achievements and inclinations of boys and girls are recognised as different, teachers can take action to create a more gender-fair curriculum. The list which follows contains some suggestions which can be used from the nursery onwards.

- Integrate writing activities and literacy materials into indoor and outdoor activities so that writing is associated with getting things done.
- Challenge girls and boys to do better and to extend themselves in all aspects of writing.
- Organise some writing activities in a more active way to include collaborative writing with peers, shared writing and response partners to help boys become more involved.
- Include learning about a broad range of genres in the writing curriculum.

**Table 10.1**

*Comparison of the literacy characteristics of boys and girls*

| Boys | Girls |
|---|---|
| drawn to non-fiction | prefer story writing |
| writing is more concise | produce longer narratives |
| untidy handwriting, inaccurate presentation | spend a great deal of time on presentation |
| include more fantasy and action in their stories | include more domestic or everyday activities in their writing |
| read non-fiction, read less than girls | read story and poetry |
| engage in active play involving single words and noises | develop stories in play |
| more likely to have initial difficulties with literacy | achieve more highly in literacy |
| ideas, plots and character often underdeveloped | make more use of dedicated writing areas |

- Ensure that all children read widely to give them models for their own writing.
- Teach the features of different text types and strategies for reading and writing them explicitly.
- Use assessment to identify gender-related strengths and weaknesses and to arrange group teaching which targets areas of need.
- Use the computer for planning, drafting and writing.
- Give writing activities a clear purpose and explain how best to shape writing in order to achieve this.
- Plan for a range of writing formats including captions, lists, maps, charts, graphs and other visual representations.
- Use environmental print as a starting point for literacy activities.
- Display and use resources which show men and women, boys and girls using writing.
- Intervene in children's play to support story making.
- Use resources and props such as puppets in order to rehearse and draft stories.
- Make sure that book provision in the classroom includes non-fiction, fiction and poetry.
- Curtail the praise given to girls for neat writing, and praise those boys who present their writing well.

**Activity**

Observe the writing behaviour of the children in your class and ask yourself the following questions:

- How does the length of girls' and boys' written work compare?
- Are there differences in action, plot and characterisation?
- Are there differences in the way informative writing is organised?
- How does the amount of time boys and girls spend on and off task when writing compare?
- Do girls spend more time on presentation than on planning and organising the content of what they write?
- Do boys spend too little time on presentation, even when there is an outside audience for their writing?
- Can you use any of the suggestions in this chapter to address any gender-related aspects of underachievement which you have identified?

## DEVELOPING BILITERACY

Young bilingual learners will almost always benefit from additional help when they are learning to write in English. Those who appear to find writing quite straightforward may be capable of achieving more and benefit from more attention, and those who are finding it difficult obviously merit support.

Children who begin school fluent in languages and aware of scripts other than English are not in the best position to benefit from the correspondences between oral and written English that their peers can draw upon. This is one of the supports that children use as they attempt to represent words that they say in writing. They may also miss out on the praise and comments that English-speaking children get when they include some letter shapes in their early writing since the features of their home script may go unrecognised. Such comments are a particularly important teaching device in the early years since they introduce children to the relationship between spoken and written language, identify and name letter shapes for the child and include references to other letters and words. The majority of teachers, who are unlikely to be biliterate in the child's language, will not be able to make these connections for most bilingual learners.

Native English speakers do not always find writing easy. Having something to say, knowing how to say it, knowing how to organise it and using the appropriate secretarial skills to record it are demanding when operating in a known language. Having to do all these things and think about how to translate one's thoughts into writing using an unfamiliar language and script places additional demands on developing bilinguals.

Although bilingual children will benefit from being able to speak English when they write they should not be deterred from writing until their oral English has developed. Experimenting with writing and participating in writing activities helps children to understand the system and the uses of writing. Focused writing activities introduced through adult demonstrations and accompanied by clear explanations are times when children learn important lessons about their new language. They are able to see and hear language together and are given important lessons about the relationship between speech and print.

Children who are learning to become biliterate will benefit from some of the strategies suggested in the section on children with difficulties in this chapter, not because they have learning difficulties but because they will need extra support. They need to be given tasks where the outcome is clear and where the visual support is high. They need writing activities that enable them to feel successful. Learning to write in a class where independent writing is the norm and where all the writing that children produce is treated with respect will encourage them to write and show the teacher what they can do.

When working with bilingual children it is helpful for the teacher to know about the languages the child is able to speak and his experiences with print outside school. This may enable her to recognise elements of other scripts that appear in the child's writing and to acknowledge this positively. It is also helpful to know how the child's name is written in the first language. The teacher may then be able to recognise when the child incorporates elements of this into his writing. When the teacher is aware of the child's home language she is in a better position to look for and measure progress using the sequence of developmental stages described in Chapter 2.

To help children develop their English writing abilities teachers can employ the following strategies when planning writing activities:

- devise visually explicit activities such as picture planning followed by writing
- use visual supports such as pictures and puppets as starting points for writing
- choose activities which emphasise and reuse certain words and phrases
- arrange collaborative writing activities
- provide models for writing through shared writing
- emphasise the importance of writing as communication rather than stressing correctness
- use structured written tasks which rely on using written or picture prompts
- allow children to respond to some activities through pictures rather than always having to write
- scribe for the child
- use multilingual word-processing packages
- obtain translations of some words to help children make connections between writing in a known script and writing in English.

**Activity**

Devise a writing activity where the content, presentation and outcome can be explained and demonstrated visually rather than orally. Try it out with an English-speaking peer. Were they clear about what you wanted them to do and why?

## DIFFICULTIES WITH WRITING

Children who have difficulties with writing find it hard to transcribe or compose or do both. However, for the majority of children who are identified as needing additional help with writing the difficulties are most likely to originate in transcription rather than composition. Most children, unless they have severe all-round language impairments, can compose adequately when they are speaking, and it is likely to be their problems with the tools of writing that deter them from recording. Spelling, handwriting and punctuation are skills that can be hard to learn and they can take up a great deal of children's attention as they write, leaving them little time to compose well or to write at length. Difficulties with these aspects of writing are also very visible to the child and can become a source of embarrassment. They can act as a constant reminder of failure. They also attract adult attention and disapproval, which can reinforce the child's feelings of inadequacy as a writer.

## Transcription

Difficulties with transcription can be found in spelling, handwriting or punctuation. For children at Key Stage 1 or younger it is probably too early to say that they need extra help with punctuation as the ability to use punctuation accurately would normally be developing towards the end of this period.

### *Spelling*

Poor spelling is probably the most frequently identified as the problem that children have, and can lead to children being identified as poor writers. Spelling errors are often attributed to one or more of the following causes:

- defective eyesight
- laziness
- poor memory
- poor visual perception
- bad habits
- not reading enough
- not speaking properly
- dyslexia
- over-reliance on phonics
- too little phonics
- the English spelling system.

Attributing the source of the difficulty in this way is not particularly helpful. Many of the reasons are located in the child and the language system, and they show confusion about the place of phonics as an aid to spelling. If children are to learn how to spell well teachers need to take responsibility for teaching children how to spell in the best possible ways. They need to understand something about the English language and about the nature of spelling, and give children strategies which will help them to learn how to spell, how to make good attempts at unfamiliar words, and to remember frequently needed words. The strategies described in Chapter 6 are useful for all children, including those who find accurate spelling difficult.

Rather than concentrating on the deficiency, unless this can easily be corrected by, for example, a pair of spectacles, it is more productive to begin a programme of remediation by identifying what the child can do. Most children employ some phonic strategies when they spell, and indeed rather than being the solution they may be contributing to the problem if they are overused. Careful analysis of samples of a child's writing will reveal the spelling strategies they are using and the problems which require the most urgent action (see Figure 10.1).

This piece of writing shows that Grant is using the sounds of the language to help his spelling. He is able to analyse words into parts and to match these to letters. He now needs to develop a visual memory for words and letter strings and to learn that writers see words as well as sound them. For Grant, the teacher's aims in the long term would be to develop his visual spelling strategies and to encourage him to become aware of the way words look. To do this she might use some of the activities described in Chapter 6. Grant would probably benefit from being given a spelling notebook, being introduced to the look copy cover write check strategy and being encouraged to try out and compare versions of words before opting for a particular spelling. He could also be encouraged to read his writing through to identify incorrect words and to either have another go at these or try to find the correct versions using the resources in the class.

**Figure 10.1**

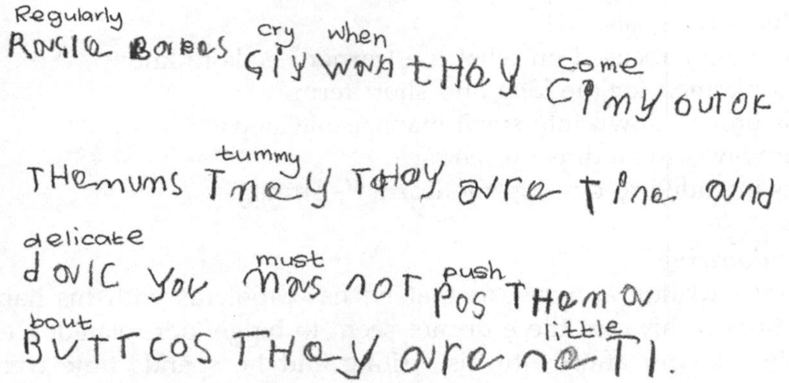

> Regularly
> RnGle Barbes cry when Giy wnh tHey come ciny ouror
>
> THemums tummy Tney Tney arre tine ond
>
> delicate dovic you must nns nor push pos THem av
> bout BUTT cos THey are little neTl.
>
> Grant

In the shorter term the teacher might consider that Grant should learn to spell frequently used words such as *when* and *come*. She might begin to do this using positive correction methods where the child's spelling and the correct word are compared and the difficult parts located and worked on. This builds on what the child knows about the word and extends his success. If this piece of writing was typical of Grant's work, the teacher might want to consider working on commonly occurring letter combinations such as *sh, st* and *ou*. It is likely that there would be other children in the class who were also unsure of these letter strings. If so they might become the subject of a sequence of activities for a group or for the class.

As a general rule, when teaching spelling as an immediate response to children's writing the teacher should select one or two words to correct and teach. Her choice should be guided by considering:

- which the child has most nearly got right
- which the child uses most frequently.

The remainder of the misspellings can be left as it is unlikely that children will remember how to spell more than two words correctly during one teaching session. However, if the child learns how to spell one or two words each week in individual spelling sessions, is taught to use visual strategies and is introduced to letter strings through group and class spelling his spelling will improve over the long term.

The description of the teaching programme for Grant embodies some of the principles of teaching that are useful when working with children who are experiencing difficulties. It

- has clear goals
- is clearly focused on what the learner needs to know
- is planned for the long and short term
- is broken down into small manageable steps
- involves some direct teaching
- is intended to develop the learner's strategies.

### Handwriting

Grant's writing also reveals that he has problems with his handwriting. In his case these do not seem to be gender related. He is willing to put effort into his writing and he spends time trying to get it to look right. His *y* formations, although incorrect, were not hastily produced. Grant's handwriting is inefficient and is probably taking up a great deal of his concentration as he writes, leaving him less able to focus on spelling and composition. Grant needs to be helped to form his letters more efficiently. He needs to internalise the movements that will reduce the amount of time he spends forming each letter and lead to the production of consistent letter shapes that end in a place best suited to making the next letter.

Grant would probably benefit from activities that help him to make flowing movements. He might practise handwriting patterns using paint, crayons and felt-tip pens. He could decorate his writing with borders containing patterns or letter shapes. In the shorter term the teacher might want to show Grant how to form the letter *a* correctly. Some of these are well made while others appear to be made from left to right rather than from right to left. Once he has improved his formation of *a* the next letter to work on would be *e*, which is also inconsistent and inefficient. The third goal might be to reduce the number of capital letters Grant includes in his writing by introducing him to the lower-case forms. He may be incorporating these into his writing because he is unsure about how to make the print versions. After becoming confident with the lower-case versions of *a* and *e* he might be more receptive to the suggestion to use lower-case letters and be willing to experiment with these.

Grant would probably need support for half a term or longer to improve his handwriting capabilities. However, the long-term benefits could be immense. Not only would the appearance of his work improve but more importantly once the letter forms became automatic Grant could give more attention to spelling and composition, although the latter is not a particular difficulty for Grant at the moment. In this example of his work he is writing appropriately and making adventurous choices about vocabulary. This makes intervention with transcription all the more necessary, because if Grant were to become frustrated with writing through his difficulties with transcription he might become less motivated and lose interest in writing.

## Composition

Difficulties with composition can manifest themselves when children are reluctant to write and demonstrate little interest in writing. They then

- write very little
- rarely finish a piece of writing
- produce writing that does not fulfil the requirements of the task.

To tackle problems with composition the teacher needs to find out whether the child does not know what to write or how to organise the writing, or whether the child dislikes writing. She needs to know whether she is remediating a knowledge or an attitude problem. To discover this she may need to observe the child as he writes and to discuss writing with the child during a writing conference.

### Motivation

Very young children enjoy experimenting with writing, so much so that at times parents may have to confiscate pencils and crayons to preserve their wallpaper and furniture. Young children also want to imitate adult behaviour and join in with others as they write. In the early years most children want to write. However, some children lose their initial interest in writing as they progress through the school system. Some of the most common causes of this are:

- not seeing the point of writing
- being expected to write too much or too frequently
- finding writing too difficult.

Children do not automatically know about the uses of writing and cannot always see the immediate benefits of becoming a writer. When learners are unable to recognise the significance of what they are being taught they might pay little attention to the teaching they are receiving and engage in learning activities in a desultory way. If this is the reason for some children's difficulties the solution is likely to be in the teacher's hands. The starting point will be to examine the writing programme for the class. Teachers might want to ask themselves whether the writing activities children undertake are framed in ways that make the uses of writing clear. They may ask themselves whether they have an audience, a purpose and an outcome that children can recognise as relevant.

They might also want to consider whether writing is given status through being planned to take place over a number of days. Do children have the opportunity to:

- plan their writing?
- draft it?
- revise what they have written?
- discuss their writing with others?
- make decisions about how to present it?
- share it permanently through a display, in a book or by giving it to others to read?

Increasing the number of writing tasks that are planned in this way and including opportunities for children to choose what they want to write about can improve children's motivation.

For some children the solution to their difficulties with composition may lie in reducing the number of writing tasks and the amount of writing involved in each activity that they are being asked to undertake. Limiting their writing to a few lines may help them to see that writing is manageable and help them to concentrate on the essential information they wish to include. Responses to some tasks could take the form of a picture, a sequence of illustrations, illustrations with captions, diagrams, charts or on tape. Some writing might be undertaken collaboratively with a partner or with an adult.

## Knowledge

Extending children's knowledge about how to write may also be straightforward. Problems with structure, organisation and sequence in children's writing can be helped when they are taught about the characteristics and forms of different types of writing and when they are given clear structural guidelines to follow. Planning using sequences of pictures, individual words or captions helps to order children's writing. Brainstorming for ideas and recording these provides a support for children when they are thinking about what to include in their writing. Teacher-devised prompt sheets which remind children about the sort of information that needs to be written and provides them with guidance about the order in which it is written may also give children the knowledge they need in order to write effectively. Using familiar stories or regular and repeated sentence structures such as *I like . . .* or *Blue reminds me of . . .* provides children with a framework that can be used temporarily in order to give them a feeling of success with writing. Giving children opportunities to rehearse orally what they are going to write helps them to organise and order their thoughts. This can be done with a peer partner or with an adult who can make suggestions about alterations that will result in better writing. Play and role play may also be times when children rehearse stories and ideas that can later become part of their writing, and they are potentially times when children can write in their own ways at their own speeds and when they wish to.

Modelling, teaching, supporting and limiting written responses to those that are important and manageable are probably the essential elements of a teaching programme for children who experience difficulties with composition. Decisions about the strategies that are used will depend on the child's needs, and the support that is given will be differentiated to suit the child's interests.

**Activity** Identify a child who would benefit from extra help with writing. Over the course of a week observe them as they write, examine samples of their writing and hold a writing conference with them. Using the information you have identify three important targets for them. Devise a sequence of activities which address these learning aims. If you have the opportunity, try these out over a period of a few weeks and evaluate them and the child's progress towards the targets you set.

## Summary

The degree of support for literacy that children receive outside school, their gender and their fluency in oral English can affect the ease with which children learn to write. This chapter has looked at some of the causes for differences in achievement in writing between children. It has also included suggestions about how some individuals and groups of children can be given the support that will help them to succeed at writing.

*The key points covered in this chapter were:*

- **the contribution that parents do and can make to writing development**
- **the way in which gender may affect attainment in writing**
- **the sort of provision that will support bilingual children as they learn to write**
- **the difficulties some individuals manifest when learning to write**
- **strategies for dealing with differences and difficulties.**

## Further reading

Buxton, C. (ed.) (no date) *Language Activities for Bi-lingual Learners*, Language Support Services, London Borough of Tower Hamlets
A short booklet outlining a number of activities which are particularly suited to the needs of young children who are acquiring English.

QCA (1998) Can Do Better, Qualifications and Curriculum Authority, London
The results of a survey into practitioner research concerned with improving boys' achievement in English. The booklet contains a number of examples of good practice and practical suggestions for teachers.

Weinberger, J. (1996) *Literacy Goes to School*, Paul Chapman Publishing, London
This book is the result of the author's research into parental involvement in nursery children's literacy development. It suggests ways of creating real partnerships between school and home.

# Assessing writing 11

**Objectives**

*When you have read this chapter you should:*

- understand why assessment is important
- know how to plan for assessment using a range of methods
- understand the statutory requirements for assessment
- be able to use the results of assessment to inform teaching and learning.

**Introduction**

**assessment**
all the ways used to measure learning in all its forms. It uses many sources of evidence about learning.

**Assessment** identifies the progress that children have made and enables teachers to make provision for the learning that needs to follow. It has three broad functions:

- to keep track of children's progress and development
- to inform evaluations of teaching and curriculum provision
- to demonstrate accountability to parents, governors, the local authority and other interested parties.

Writing can be appraised almost continuously because so many activities throughout the school day are accompanied deliberately or incidentally by written outcomes that are read and responded to by adults. Each piece of writing that children produce provides tangible evidence of what they are able to do. However, assessment needs to be focused rather than merely reactive. Planned assessments allow the teacher to study children's writing in depth, help teachers to plan their future teaching for the class, groups of children and individuals, and prevent overwhelming learners with instant feedback, correction and teaching.

This chapter considers different ways of organising and planning for assessment as well as how to make the most of unplanned opportunities when responding to what children have written.

## WHAT ASSESSMENT IS FOR

Assessment is a way of establishing what children know and can do. It consists of collecting and analysing information and evidence about children's achievements. It provides teachers with insights into what children have learned and enables them to understand more about children's learning needs.

There should be very close links between assessment, learning and teaching. The information gathered from assessment should prompt teachers to reflect on classroom practices and consider whether their curriculum provision and organisation is enabling the children to learn what they intend. As a result teachers may modify their future plans and alter some aspects of their teaching in order to help children learn more effectively. HMI (1996) noted that one of the characteristics of good teachers of literacy was their use of assessment to inform their short- and medium-term planning.

## ASSESSING WRITING

### What should be assessed

It is obvious that assessing writing will involve appraising what children can do in composition and transcription. Teachers will also want to find out what children know about these two aspects of writing and to monitor what children know about the uses of writing. In addition they will want to discover children's attitudes towards writing as these can have an effect on how they compose and transcribe.

Assessing composition involves examining:

- planning
- drafting
- content
- structure
- appropriateness for audience and purpose
- language
- style.

Assessing transcription involves examining:

- spelling
- handwriting
- punctuation
- grammatical conventions.

Assessing attitudes involves examining:

- motivation
- interest
- concentration
- effort.

The following questions might be helpful when teachers are trying to establish children's capabilities in these three aspects of writing.

## Composition
- Does the child write independently?
- Does the child intend the writing to carry meaning?
- Is the child able to talk about and read back what they have written?
- Does the child think about or plan what they are to communicate before writing?
- Does the writing achieve its purpose?
- Does the writing take account of its audience?
- Are the ideas expressed in writing equivalent or nearly equivalent to those expressed orally?
- Is the language vivid, imaginative and appropriate?
- Is the writing well organised?
- Can the child write for a variety of purposes?
- Can the child use a range of genres?

## Transcription
- Does the child have an awareness of writing conventions?
- Does the child use phonic strategies when spelling?
- Does the child use visual strategies when spelling?
- Is the child demonstrating an ability to form some letters?
- Is the child's writing clear, legible and correctly formed?
- Does the child make use of capital letters, full stops and speech marks?
- Does the child use grammatically appropriate structures?
- Does the child use simple, compound or complex sentences?
- Does the child use a range of connectives?
- Does the child proofread what is written?
- Can the child use strategies for planning, drafting, revising and publishing?

## Attitudes
- Does the child choose to write freely?
- In which contexts does the child choose to write?
- Does the child become involved when writing and sustain this involvement over time?
- Does the child have specific writing interests?
- Can the child identify personal reasons for writing?

## Examining errors
Errors are an important source of information about how children are understanding and progressing and it is right that they are given

attention. They can reveal the strategies the child is using and those that have not been fully grasped. Knowing this helps teachers to decide what children should be taught next and how. The errors the child makes may indicate that only a small amount of guidance and practice are necessary for the child to master one aspect of writing or they may indicate that the child has completely misunderstood something that they have been taught.

Errors are also significant because they are likely to be a reflection of what has been taught. Generally children learn the skills that are emphasised by the teacher and take longer to master those that are not given priority. This is particularly true for children who experience difficulties with learning to write. Very often they are only able to do what they have been taught, whereas more able writers seem to have the ability to integrate and go beyond what they have been shown (Smith and Elley, 1998). Children's mistakes or the gaps in their learning may indicate that something has not yet been taught or that it has not been given sufficient attention by the teacher. Viewed in this way errors can provide teachers with useful food for thought.

Because errors are revealing, the classroom climate needs to be one where mistakes are permitted and there is no expectation that children's writing will look perfect. Errors need to be seen as natural and beneficial. When children are given too much adult help with their writing and encouraged to erase their mistakes the information that teachers need to make accurate judgements about what children can and cannot do is lost and the data that they need in order to match future teaching to learning needs is obscured. If assessments are to be accurate and beneficial it is essential that teachers create an environment where errors are tolerated and risk-taking is encouraged so that they can see what children genuinely can and cannot do.

**Activities**

1 Examine the recent writing of six children in your class and identify writing errors that are common to some or all of them. Analyse the possible reasons for these difficulties and formulate some ways in which you and the children can address one or two of the most significant ones.
2 Look again at the writing samples you have collected and the errors or omissions these contain. Identify two aspects of writing that could be attended to in the short term and two aspects that could be developed in the longer term. For the long-term goals plan a sequence of activities and experiences that will result in the children's success.

# FORMATIVE ASSESSMENT

The term formative assessment refers to the monitoring which takes place every day when teachers respond to the writing that children are doing or have completed. It also refers to regular, planned assessment opportunities. The information that is gathered from informal and planned assessments helps the teacher to build up an increasingly detailed picture of each child as a learner, the progress they are making and their learning needs. The purpose of formative assessment is to discover what children have learned, how it was learned, and to note the children's attitudes to their learning. It helps teachers to diagnose problems, identify areas that need more attention and modify practice. Data from the teacher's formative assessments is amplified by contributions from parents, children and other adults in school. Records of formative assessments can be kept in cumulative pupil records which can be referred to at a later date.

## Conferences

Teachers respond to children's writing during roving, individual, group and whole-class conferences. At these times teachers are able both to assess and to provide immediate teaching. The quality of the teaching depends on the teacher's skill in making a fairly swift appraisal of what the child has done and what help is needed. During roving conferences and individual conferences, when the agenda is generally not planned, the teacher has to respond swiftly to the child's writing. If the time spent on conferences is to be used productively it is important that at these times the teaching that is provided accurately addresses the child's needs.

Before commenting on what the child has done the teacher needs to ask the child to talk about the writing and to read back what they have produced. The teacher can ask questions, draw out ideas and check understanding. This gives the teacher time to see what has been done well and what might be given attention, and will help him to focus his response on what the child needs to know. Initial feedback should focus on the positive aspects of what the child has written before the teaching points are made. It is good practice to focus first on what has been written (the composition) and then on how it has been written (the transcription), and, if possible, to make one positive comment and one teaching point about each of these. The help that is given should focus on what the child can almost do and be related to immediate need. It should be helpful and informative. It is not sufficient to say or write 'That's really good' or 'Well done'. The teacher needs to explain why the writing is good so that the child can incorporate the good features into the next piece of writing; similarly if the writing could be improved the teacher needs to explain how this could be achieved. Ticks, crosses and general comments do not give children information or advice that they can act on.

When making an immediate response to children's writing the teacher needs to act as a supportive partner, not merely as an inspector of deficiencies. In order to develop as writers children need opportunities to write often in a climate that encourages confidence, celebrates achievements and is tolerant of errors. Young children will always make some mistakes with punctuation, spelling and handwriting. Concentrating disproportionately on these can easily create an over-critical atmosphere and may inhibit future efforts at writing. No one enjoys making their mistakes public, particularly if they are always received negatively. When giving feedback the teacher should be guided by the importance of the errors. He also needs to consider how typical they are of the child and of other children at this stage. Apparently careless errors can arise because of the writer's lack of involvement, lack of interest or lack of knowledge, and each of these conditions will require a different response. The teacher's understanding of writing development and his knowledge of individual children and the circumstances in which the writing took place should guide his assessments and his teaching.

As a result of the assessments made during a conference the teacher may decide he needs more time to explore an aspect of the child's writing behaviour more thoroughly. This could lead to his arranging a planned assessment opportunity. Alternatively if the difficulties he identifies are common to a number of children in the class the teacher might note this and plan for a group teaching activity or group conference.

The information that the teacher gleans from his interactions with children about their writing during conferences helps him to make up-to-date judgements about their developing abilities. Some of this information and the conclusions he draws can be incorporated into the records that he keeps and can be used when discussing the children's progress with parents, carers or other interested parties.

## Planned assessment opportunities

Regular opportunities to monitor writing should be identified in weekly and half-termly plans. Planning for assessment means that time is allocated to assessment, assessments are systematic and regular and all children are monitored. If assessment is not planned it can be easy to overlook quiet children and to give attention to those who have difficulties or frequently seek help. Over time planned assessments should cover different aspects of composition and transcription. They may be undertaken because the teacher feels he needs more information about particular children or about specific features of their writing. Often they will be planned to assess how well children have understood and are able to incorporate new ideas into their independent writing. Although assessment opportunities are specially planned they should take place during authentic literacy activities. They do not need to interrupt the normal flow of writing activities.

Planned assessment opportunities can include observing groups or individuals as they write, questioning children, teacher-led discussions and analysing samples of writing. Teachers may plan to observe one writing activity that will be completed by all the children over the course of a few days. The teacher will focus on each group of children as they undertake the same writing activity. Alternatively the teacher may identify two or three children to observe each day until all the class have been assessed.

The method of assessment that is selected will depend on what the teacher wishes to discover and the way writing is organised in his class. The following questions may help readers to choose the situations and activities that are most likely to reveal the information that they want to discover.

*Do I want to find out:*
- What children already know?
- What they have learned after a period of teaching?
- What they need to know next?

*Can I discover this:*
- As they write?
- After the writing is completed?
- As they play?
- By talking to children about writing?

For example, if the teacher wants to see if children are familiar with a number of different text types he may observe them as they play and use literacy materials in the role-play area as well as when they record their findings after an investigation. He may then collect the pieces of writing that were produced and look at them more carefully when the children are not present.

Teachers will not want to assess every aspect of writing when examining a single text or observing one writing activity. They will have decided beforehand what they want to look at closely. This should coincide with the task that has been set and with the explanation that the children have been given. For example, children will not necessarily show all they know about spelling strategies if they are writing a first draft. When setting the task teachers will have identified their own aims for the activity and made clear to the children their expectations about what they should concentrate on. Teachers' aims for the activity and their expectations about how it should be tackled will affect what can fairly be assessed and guide the judgements that are made.

The findings from planned assessment opportunities enable teachers to monitor progress, diagnose problems, set individual pupil targets, provide data for the evaluation of teaching and inform future planning.

### Literacy interviews

The National Literacy Strategy (Literacy Task Force, 1997) advises teachers to conduct individual discussions with children about their literacy development at least once every half term. Literacy interviews involve children in the assessment process and help them to reflect on and understand what they have learned. They can take place when teachers are reviewing the children's writing profiles. The child can be asked to select a recent piece of writing to be included in the **portfolio**. This can be brought to the interview and discussed. Or the adult can ask the child to comment on one or all of the pieces of writing that have already been selected. Children can be asked about:

**portfolio**
a collection of work gathered over a period of time

- how they think they can improve their writing
- what they would like to be able to do better
- their attitude towards writing
- their out-of-school writing.

As the child talks the teacher notes down what is said and includes these comments in the profile. The child's comments may provide additional evidence for the teacher's assessment of the child's writing ability and give him information that will influence planning for writing. During the literacy interview the child and the teacher can discuss and agree on a target that will improve the child's writing. This should be clear and attainable. The target should be recorded so that progress can be assessed during the next interview.

### Observation

Observation involves listening to and watching children as they undertake an activity in order to gain information to make assessments about learning. Some observations should be planned and have a specific focus, while others may occur spontaneously. When teachers make observations about children's work and progress in the course of daily classroom activities they can gain insights into the strategies children are using and their individual learning style. They may notice important moments of literacy learning which represent a significant step in the learning development of a particular child. For example, observations of children in the role-play area may show that some children are aware of the uses of writing in everyday life. Others, who seem to lack confidence in writing, may show that they are prepared to write independently.

In the nursery, where other assessment methods may not be appropriate, observations are a particularly important assessment tool and will take place much more frequently than at Key Stage 1, where it is probably sufficient to plan for one or two observations each term. Observations should be recorded briefly. When a number of people work with the children observations should be shared so that assessment information can be acted upon by all the staff.

### Analysing samples

Collecting samples of children's writing and examining them carefully gives the teacher an opportunity to gain insights into children's progress as writers. It is useful to collect one piece of writing from the beginning of the school year as this provides a baseline from which teaching can proceed and a reference point when assessing how much progress children have made over a term or a year. Over the course of a year samples should be drawn from a variety of starting points and curriculum areas and represent a variety of genres. First drafts as well as fair copies should be included to show how the child revises and corrects writing and how suggestions from the teacher or peers are acted on. On some occasions children can select the pieces of writing to be analysed.

Samples should be dated and the teacher's analysis of what they reveal should be written in note form and included with the child's writing. The writing can be assessed using the National Curriculum level descriptions and the results can be recorded The child's comments can be included as part of the accompanying annotation. The teacher may add samples to the children's portfolios and use them later as a starting point for discussions with children and carers. Samples can provide useful information for the teacher when he is compiling the end-of-year summaries and reports for the children's next teacher and parents.

The purpose of analysing samples of writing is to establish:

- what the child can do
- what the child needs to be able to do
- the activities which will enable the child to move on.

It is helpful when examining samples, and particularly when anno-
tating them, for records or portfolios to have a framework for
analysis. This can be provided by a series of headings such as those
which follow.

*Context*
This section might include notes about how the work arose, the
purpose of the writing and the intended audience, the length of
time the child spent on the writing, how it relates to other activities such as conferences, discussions or practical work, and whether
it is a first draft or intended for publication. Information about the
child's previous knowledge or experience of writing in this genre
or style should also be recorded.

*Commentary*
This section is concerned with the strengths and weaknesses
displayed by the child as a writer. Making entries under two headings, composition and transcription, can be a useful reminder to
look beyond the surface features of the writing. It is always useful
to look for positive points in children's writing and to ask oneself
at the beginning of the analysis what the child has attempted and
achieved. If earlier samples have been collected the progress that
has been made should be noted. The comments might refer to
attitude, content and writing conventions as displayed in the piece
of work. The child's attention to audience, realisation of purpose
and the choice of format might also be considered. If plans and
drafts are collected the teacher might note the differences between
the drafts and refer to the learning processes that the child has
gone through between the first and final copy.

*Ways forward*
Under this heading are listed the targets that are to be set for the
child and the activities, experiences and work that might extend
the child as a learner and enable them to meet the targets. To ensure
that these are provided individual targets should be referred to
when the teacher is planning work for the short and medium term.

*National Curriculum requirements*
A note can be made here of the baseline assessment targets met,
programme of study requirements covered and the level descriptions reached, in this piece of work.

## Other sources of information

*Pupil self-assessment*
Children can be involved in assessing their own development as
writers through:

- talking about writing
- selecting pieces of writing to be included in their personal portfolios
- identifying the aspects of writing that they would like help with
- making a contribution to the written analysis of samples
- deciding on the targets to be set during writing interviews
- writing an end-of-term report on their own progress.

Involving children in parts of the assessment process can be of tremendous benefit to them. When children have to articulate what they find difficult and where they need help they are reflecting on the writing process and their understanding and knowledge about writing. Contributing to discussions about targets helps children to understand what they need to learn and what they are aiming for.

When writing reports on their own progress children can be asked to address a set of questions such as:

- What can I do easily?
- What do I find difficult?
- What do I want to be able to do?
- What would help me to do this?

Their reports, which they can write termly or yearly, can be taken home to share with parents and a photocopy can be kept in the pupil record.

### Contributions from others

Most assessment is carried out by the class teacher but other significant adults can also make a contribution. Parents, carers and all the adults who work with the children may be able to offer information about children's writing development. Parents have a unique knowledge of their own children and they can often provide teachers with insights into children's abilities and interests that are not apparent in the classroom.

Initial discussions with the parents of nursery children may take place during home visits before children start school, when parents can tell staff about the child's out-of-school experiences with print. Later some of the evidence in the child's record can be used to structure a discussion about the child's development and parents' comments can be added to the record. Some examples of children's writing can also be sent home. Cairney (1995) suggests that if this is done parents can be asked to comment on what they think about their children's progress, strengths and needs. This could be a good way of involving those parents who find it difficult to get into school for open days or parents' meetings in the assessment process.

Discussions with parents can lead to shared understandings and expectations about writing which make it easier for school and home to work together to support children's learning.

All the staff who work with young children can make an active and important contribution to the assessment process. Support staff who often work closely with individual children are in a good position to notice a great deal about children's learning. They can also be included in the planned assessment opportunities.

### Checklists

Checklists for writing can help teachers to keep track of what children can do. Checklists can list common behaviours seen as children's writing develops or objectives that have been achieved. As children demonstrate the behaviours that are listed or incorporate the strategies into their writing, the relevant box is marked. Some teachers make one mark when the child is beginning to use a strategy and a different sort of mark when it is being used confidently and consistently. The Literacy Project draft documents (NLP, 1996) recommended that teachers keep a record of what has been covered by the class each term using the headings 'satisfactorily covered', 'covered but needs more attention' and 'not covered'.

## KEEPING RECORDS

### Pupil records

Teachers store the information they collect about pupil learning because they need to refer to it at the end of a key stage of learning to make their summary judgements about progress. These are needed to fulfil the statutory requirement for teacher assessment at the end of Key Stage 1. Records also help when teachers are writing reports to parents and when the school is calculating the **value added** during a period of learning. The information teachers collect about pupils each year is the evidence which supports their judgements. It is also helpful to have written records and examples of work to support a request for a statement of special educational need and to show to OFSTED inspectors, although there is no statutory requirement to retain the observations, notes of writing interviews or samples of work which have been collected.

**value added**
a measure of progress made by children over time that can be attributed to the school

Individual pupil records for writing can include:

- annotated samples of writing covering a range of genres and writing purposes
- a record of all the significant pieces of writing attempted over a school year

- examples of drafts, revisions and final versions
- personal spelling books
- teacher observations
- the results of planned assessment opportunities
- checklists
- pupil assessments
- information gained from parents or carers
- information from other adults who work with the child
- a record of targets set during writing interviews.

## School portfolios

School portfolios generally contain annotated pieces of writing selected from different year groups. The samples included cover different forms and different stages of the writing process. Plans, drafts and final outcomes can all be included. The work that is included should be accompanied by a brief commentary about the context, what the work shows the writer can and cannot do, the action that was taken and the level of attainment that has been ascribed. School collections provide evidence of the school's agreed interpretations of the National Curriculum levels and can serve as exemplars for new members of staff and supply teachers. They also record examples of good practice in teaching and assessment that can be referred to by all staff.

**Activities**

1 Suggest some ways in which you might involve children in making assessments of their own capabilities and progress in writing. Try to build in opportunities for children's self assessment into your medium term plans.
2 Think about how you can plan to obtain reliable information about the achievements and progress of all the children in the class over one half term.
3 Collect two or three samples of writing from one child. Use these to make an assessment of the child's strengths and future needs. Identify two or three developmentally appropriate priorities. How might you cater for these needs in your future teaching plans?

## SUMMATIVE ASSESSMENT

Summative assessment records the achievements of children after the completion of a phase of learning, such as at the age of five or at the end of a key stage. It is a summary of what each child can do, knows and understands at a transition point such as entry to school, when children change classes and at the end of a key stage. Making summative assessments in English at the start of compulsory schooling and again at the end of each key stage is a statutory requirement.

## Baseline assessment

In September 1998 it became a statutory requirement for primary schools to undertake formal assessments of children when they enter school. The purpose of this assessment (SCAA, 1997a, p. 3) is to:

- provide information to help teachers to plan effectively to meet children's individual learning needs
- measure children's attainment, using one or more numerical outcomes which can be used in later value added analyses of children's progress.

**baseline assessment**
an assessment of children's capabilities on entry to school

**Baseline assessments** are intended to inform reception teachers about children's pre-school experience and their early achievements so that they can accommodate individual needs into their planning. They may also lead to the early identification of special educational needs and more able children. By referring to the results of these early assessments, when later assessments are made, schools and teachers will be able to measure the progress that children make in school and identify the contribution they have made to learning.

In the guidance produced by SCAA (1997a) about baseline assessment it is suggested that writing should be assessed by finding out whether children can:

- distinguish between print and pictures in their own work
- write some recognisable letter-like shapes
- write their first name independently, using upper- and lower-case letters and spelling it correctly
- write words including at least six three-letter words correctly.

The guidance states that most children in their first weeks in reception classes will be able to achieve the first three of these items and about 20 per cent of children will be able to fulfil the requirements for the fourth item.

## National Curriculum tests

Towards the end of Key Stage 1 the writing abilities of all children are assessed by a set of standard attainment tasks and tests and teacher assessment. Although the exact format of the formal tasks and tests changes each year, the general arrangements remain similar. The writing task involves children undertaking a piece of writing derived from a starting point introduced by the teacher. It is suggested that teachers present the writing task in the same way as they would present other writing activities. As far as possible the writing task is intended to resemble the writing activities that normally take place in the class. The processes that the children go through and the organisation of the children can be the same. The piece of writing can be connected to other classroom activities and given a purpose and an audience. Children can be encouraged to plan, consider the format for their writing, think about story features and appropriate vocabulary before they write, although as the writing has to be completed in an hour children would not have the time to write and revise first drafts. The children are not to be given help with their writing, which must be completed independently. The writing that is produced is examined to see whether children can communicate meaning in writing, use some aspects of punctuation appropriately, spell some words correctly and write legibly. Specific criteria are provided to help make these judgements. Children who attain Level 2 or above are given an additional spelling test.

## Formal teacher assessment

This refers to the statutory requirement for teachers to make an assessment of the levels of attainment towards the end of each key stage. Teacher assessment is an essential part of the National Curriculum assessment requirements and has equal status with the tasks and tests. The results of teacher assessments are reported alongside the test results. Teacher assessment should be based on a summary of teachers' formative assessments. As formative assessments occur continuously throughout each key stage of learning, the formal teacher assessment can take account of progress as well as achievement in a range of situations and can represent a broad picture of the child's strengths and weaknesses. When making teacher assessments, 'best fit' judgements about the level of attainment reached by each child are made by matching the evidence contained in class records and pupil portfolios to the National Curriculum level descriptions. These judgements can be moderated by referring to the school assessment portfolio, the Exemplification of Standards (SCAA, 1995a) and discussion and comparison of standards with other staff.

## Reports

Teachers prepare a formal summary of progress at the end of each school year which is passed on to the child's next teacher and shared with parents in the child's written report. It may also be discussed with children. Reports draw on all the assessment data that has been collected during the year. In many schools reports are discussed with parents and carers, when reference can be made to samples of writing and pupil portfolios.

---

**Activity**   In school find out how teacher assessment is continued between the nursery and reception classes and between reception and Key Stage 1. How do teachers make use of the information gathered in earlier classes or phases of education?

---

**Summary**   Assessment plays an important part in the planning, teaching and learning cycle as the assessment of learning influences what is planned and how it is taught. This chapter has looked at the uses of assessments in general and the assessment of writing in particular. What should be assessed, how to assess and when to assess writing have been examined in some detail.

*The key points covered in this chapter were:*

- **the role of assessment in teaching**
- **the aspects of writing which should be assessed**
- **ways of monitoring progress in writing**
- **the statutory requirements for assessment in the early years.**

---

**Further reading**

Bearne, E. (1998) *Making Progress in English*, Routledge, London
A photocopiable resource to help with the assessment of all aspects of English at Key Stages 1 and 2.

Sainsbury, M. (1996) *Tracking Significant Achievement in Primary English*, Hodder and Stoughton, London
A book which contains a number of suggestions about how best to undertake assessment in the early years.

SCAA (1995) *Consistency in Teacher Assessment: Exemplification of Standards*, SCAA, London
This booklet contains a number of examples of how to make and record judgements about progress in writing.

# Planning for writing 12

**Objectives**

*When you have read this chapter you should:*

- be aware of the importance of long-term plans and goals for learning

- know how to construct medium-term plans

- be able to write short-term plans to develop children's writing abilities.

**Introduction**

Effective teaching, meaning that which results in learning gains commensurate with and sometimes beyond children's abilities, is founded upon clear planning for the long, medium and short term. This chapter explains the part each type of plan plays in developing learning. It also contains suggestions about how to plan.

Planning brings together all that teachers know about a subject, learning, organisation and children. Good plans depend on teachers having a secure understanding of what they are teaching, of whom they are teaching and of how to teach. These topics were explored in the earlier chapters of this book: Chapters 1, 2, 6, 7, 8 and 9, which looked at subject knowledge; Chapter 3, teaching methods; and Chapters 4, 5, 10 and 11, children as learners.

When planning, teachers have to address the following questions:

- Where am I going?
- How am I going to get there?
- Where will I start?

If they can do this they will have produced a coherent learning programme for children that develops their learning.

## LONG-TERM PLANS

The National Literacy Strategy *Framework for Teaching* (DfEE, 1998, p. 3) includes a list of statements describing and defining literate pupils which could be used as the long-term aims for children's

> **long-term plan**
> a school document which states the intended aims for learning at the end of a phase of schooling, such as the end of a key stage

literacy development. Those pertinent to writing suggest that by the end of primary schooling children should be able to:

- write with fluency, confidence and understanding
- understand the sound and spelling system and use this to spell accurately
- have fluent and legible handwriting
- have an interest in words and their meanings and a growing vocabulary
- know, understand and be able to write in a range of genres in fiction and poetry, and understand and be familiar with some of the ways in which narratives are structured through basic literary ideas of setting, character and plot
- understand, use and be able to write a range of non-fiction texts
- plan, draft, revise and edit their own writing
- have a suitable technical vocabulary through which to understand and discuss their writing
- through writing, develop their powers of imagination, inventiveness and critical awareness.

All long-term plans are likely to specify these or similar intentions as the aims for their teaching of writing. Some schools may include other aims, perhaps concerned with attitudes and confidence, such as:

*Children should:*
- see writing as a relevant and important activity
- be well motivated towards writing.

The aims that schools identify for children's writing development are the answer to the question 'Where am I going?'

Schools' aims and long-term plans for learning are often contained in their policy documents for English, which may also describe some of the key experiences which will be offered to pupils in each year group. The purpose of long-term plans is to indicate progression in learning and continuity in teaching during each school year and between year groups.

The National Literacy Strategy *Framework for Teaching*, with its clearly listed objectives arranged to show progression and continuity in learning from reception to Year 6, might replace the detailed language policies that some schools have at present. Some schools might want to list their own aims for children's learning but indicate that these will be achieved by following the objectives in the Framework.

Read the writing policy or long-term plans for the school you are working in. Is the work you plan in keeping with the aims and ethos of this document? Consider whether the work you set for your class will help them to achieve the long-term aims that are specified in the school documents or in the earlier part of this chapter.

## MEDIUM-TERM PLANS

**Medium-term plans** add detail to long-term plans. They take the aims listed in long-term plans and begin to address the question 'How will I achieve the aims specified in the school policy document?' or 'How will I get there?' In many schools, medium-term plans take the form of schemes of work which often cover one half-term's learning. They list, in a general way, the sorts of activities and experiences that children will need if they are to achieve the objectives for that period of learning. The details of each activity, the specific learning it is intended to promote and the exact way it will be organised are not given at this stage.

**medium-term plan**
a scheme of work which usually covers a minimum of half a term's learning

Based on the guidance provided by SCAA (1995a) some schools may identify:

- blocked work
- linked work
- continuous work

in the medium-term plan. Blocked work is a discrete unit of work on a particular topic. For example, there might be a block of three weeks in Year 1 when children are introduced to planning their writing using lists. Linked work involves work in one curriculum area being linked to work in another area. In writing this might be learning to write lists, plans and instructions during work on a theme for which the children will be designing and making toys and games. So writing may be linked to work in art, technology and science. Continuous work is concerned with skills which need regular practice and attention throughout each school year. Developing a fluent and legible handwriting style might be an example of this.

When planning your schemes of work do you consider all the opportunities for writing that work across the curriculum will provide? In your medium-term planning for English try to take account of the demands of writing in other subject areas and consider how to prepare children for these in literacy sessions.

## SHORT-TERM PLANS

**short-term plan**
usually a weekly list of learning objectives and activities

**Short-term plans** expand on the notes and headings in the medium-term plans and are usually produced weekly. Unlike medium-term plans, which are prepared well in advance of teaching, short-term plans are written almost immediately before they will be used. This means that they can accommodate the teacher's recent assessments of children's learning and that the intended activities outlined in the medium-term plan can be modified to suit the learning needs of the children.

Short-term plans should contain a brief list of objectives for learning that the teacher intends to cover in the week, a list of activities which are linked to each objective, and notes about resources or special arrangements that will be needed. They should also specify how each activity will be organised. They will indicate which activities will be undertaken by the whole class, groups and individuals, how the children will be grouped and the support that will be given. This allows the teacher to think about differentiation and the realistic use of her time. When the short-term plan for the week is complete the teacher should be clear about what the children are going to learn, what they will do in order to learn and where they are going to begin.

Even when the National Literacy Strategy *Framework for Teaching* is taken as a starting point for planning, the teacher has the freedom and the responsibility to devise the activities she will use to enable the children to meet the objectives. These should be appropriate to the needs, age and interests of the particular children she teaches.

## DAILY PLANNING

### The literacy hour

As a result of the National Literacy Strategy *Framework for Teaching*, which was distributed to schools in the summer of 1998, some schools have chosen to adopt a dedicated literacy hour as a means of organising the teaching of reading and writing each day.

The general organisational pattern for the hour is a period of whole-class teaching followed by group work and ending with a whole-class session. During the hour children are expected to undertake text-, sentence- and word-level work. The activities that the children undertake are devised by the teacher and should address the objectives, appropriate to the age of the children, listed in the Framework.

Planning for the literacy hour has to include:

- clearly specified learning objectives
- a balance of text-, sentence- and word-level work
- a balance of whole-class and group work.

The planning will cover reading and writing but the examples which follow describe how the hour can be used to teach writing.

## Learning objectives

The objectives in the *Framework for Teaching* are very clear but they indicate what should be learned over a period of a term rather than in a week or a session. To make them manageable and realisable it may be necessary to break them down even further when planning for the short term. This should also help when differentiating work to meet the various needs of the children in the class. For example, in Year 1, term 1 the objective 'to recognise the critical features of words, eg length, common spelling patterns and words within words' (DfEE, 1998 p. 20) might produce the following short-term learning objectives:

- to compare the length of words using a set of known words
- to explore the concept of a spelling pattern
- to identify spelling patterns common to a number of familiar words
- to find and list words which all contain the same spelling pattern
- to list words within words that can be found in a set of familiar words.

## Text-, sentence- and word-level work

To ensure that there is a balance between these three aspects of writing the teacher will want to make sure that over the course of a week and if possible in the hour itself children will explore or use:

- a particular written genre – text-level work
- an aspect of punctuation or grammar – sentence-level work
- ways of spelling unknown words and correctly forming handwriting – word-level work.

## Whole-class and group work

During the hour whole-class work may be used to teach children about text-, sentence- or word-level aspects of writing. Shared writing could be used to demonstrate a format for their writing, a writing strategy such as planning or editing, the use of a full stop, the formation of a letter, a spelling strategy such as look copy cover write check, or how to locate and use spelling patterns.

Group work could be used to follow up a new concept introduced in the whole-class period, continue writing a text, work with a response partner and edit ongoing work, undertake a guided writing activity, or practise text structures using sequencing cards, play equipment or the role-play area. One of these activities will be guided by the teacher and used to teach a new aspect of writing or rectify a difficulty shared by a number of children.

The strategies involved in the process approach to writing, which include a variety of group and individual activities, shared writing and writing workshops, as described in Chapter 3, are all suitable for the organisational patterns advocated for the literacy hour. Play activities which have been resourced with particular learning objectives in mind and which are monitored by adults are also particularly suited to the group-work part of the literacy hour.

The final part of the hour, when the class meet to review their learning, is a time when children can reflect on and assess their learning, decide what they need to work on next and teach one another through exchanging ideas, successes and difficulties.

## Planning for writing throughout the day

Even when teachers choose to use a dedicated literacy hour there will be other times during the day when children write and learn about writing. However, some teachers will choose not to use the literacy hour and they will plan for writing throughout the day. They too will have clear objectives, cover in a balanced way what needs to be learned about writing, employ a range of class and group organisational methods and make use of cross-curricular opportunities for using and learning about writing.

Whether teachers choose to use the literacy hour or to plan for writing activities which continue throughout the day the planning they engage in will be the same. Their plans will show:

- clear learning aims for the children
- differentiated group and individual activities
- judicious use of whole-class work
- well-chosen and developmentally appropriate activities
- their understanding of the long-term goals for children's learning in writing.

**Activity**    Plan a week's worth of writing activities using the planning guides provided in the National Literacy Strategy Framework for Teaching. Working with the same learning objectives plan a week's worth of writing activities which need not take place in a dedicated literacy hour. How similar are your two sets of plans?

Clear planning underpins effective teaching and learning. It depends on teachers knowing about the subject they are teaching, knowing about children and learning and knowing about a range of pedagogical strategies. When they have this knowledge they can focus their teaching and make learning accessible to children. This chapter has emphasised the importance of putting teaching knowledge to use and described how it can be used when designing a writing curriculum for young children.

**Summary**

*The key points covered in this chapter were:*

- **the long-term goals for a writing programme**
- **ways of designing medium-term plans**
- **daily planning for writing**
- **planning for writing in the literacy hour**
- **planning for writing across the curriculum.**

DfEE (1998) *The National Literacy Strategy Framework for Teaching*, DfEE, London
This is an essential reference tool when planning for writing.

Medwell, J., Wray, D., Poulson, L. and Fox, R. (1998) *Effective Teachers of Literacy*, School of Education, University of Exeter
A study containing examples and case studies of effective literacy teaching. It reveals that the characteristics of effective literacy teachers include knowledge of the subject, good organisation and careful planning.

**Further reading**

# Glossary

| | |
|---|---|
| ascender | the part of a letter which extends above the height of *a*, *o* or *c*, e.g. the single vertical stroke in the letter *b* |
| assessment | all the ways used to measure learning in all its forms. It uses many sources of evidence about learning. |
| audience | the recipient of a piece of writing |
| baseline assessment | an assessment of children's capabilities on entry to school |
| blend | the sound produced when two or more phonemes are combined. In a blend each phoneme can still be heard, as in *cl* or *ng*. This contrasts with a digraph, where the combination of phonemes produces a new sound such as *ch*. |
| blocked work | a discrete unit of work on a particular aspect of writing |
| calligraphy | handwriting as an art |
| clause | a unit of language which contains at least a subject and a verb |
| complex sentence | a complete unit of meaning made by joining simple sentences using conjunctions other than *and* and *but* |
| composition | the act of making decisions about content, style and organisation |
| continuous work | work on aspects of a subject which need regular practice |
| cursive script | handwriting in which the letters in words are joined |
| descender | the part of the letter which goes below the line, e.g. the tail in the letter *g* |
| developmental approach | teaching children to write by first analysing what they can do alone and then working with them on their independently produced writing |
| dialect | a variety of language with a distinct vocabulary and grammar |
| discussion | a genre used to compare and contrast points of view |
| explanation | a genre used to describe a process |
| expressive writing | informal writing in the first person |
| formative assessment | the constant monitoring of progress. The information that is gathered helps the teacher to build up an increasingly complete picture of each child as a learner and is used to identify difficulties and how they have arisen in order that help can be given. |
| generative principle | understanding that writing contains different combinations of a limited number of symbols |
| genre | a type of writing with its own specific characteristics which are related to purpose |
| grammar | the way in which words are organised to produce meaningful combinations. It also includes word agreements, such as plurals, and tenses. |
| grapheme | the written representation of a sound, which may consist of one or more letters |
| graphology | the symbols of written language |
| imperatives | orders or instructions |
| lexical | pertaining to words |
| linked work | work that is clearly linked and planned for across different curriculum areas |

| | |
|---|---|
| **long-term plan** | a school document which states the intended aims for learning at the end of a phase of schooling, such as the end of a key stage. It generally indicates the time to be allocated to a curriculum area and to different parts of a curriculum area. Constant features of the school's approach to teaching, such as the use of particular resources or a method of teaching, may also be referred to. |
| **medium-term plan** | a scheme of work which usually covers a minimum of half a term's learning |
| **metalanguage** | the terminology for discussing and describing aspects of language |
| **mnemonic** | an aid to memory, which frequently takes the form of a sentence containing words beginning with the letters of the word that is difficult to remember, e.g. Big Elephants Can't Add Up Sums Easily ('because') |
| **morpheme** | the smallest unit of meaning. For example, *boy* is one morpheme, *boy/s* contains two morphemes. Prefixes and suffixes are morphemes. |
| **morphology** | the identification of the elements of a word which carry meaning |
| **narrative** | a text which relates a series of events, often in chronological order |
| **onset** | the opening unit of a syllable or word, e.g. *b*oy, *sw*ing |
| **orthography** | the writing system |
| **persuasion** | a genre which presents a point of view with the intention of influencing others |
| **phoneme** | the smallest unit of sound in a word, which includes single-letter sounds and sounds that are formed by combining different sets of letters, e.g. the phoneme *ei* as found in the words *pain* and *day* |
| **phonological awareness** | awareness of the sound system of the language and of sounds within words |
| **phonology** | the sounds of language |
| **poetic writing** | carefully crafted writing often intended to interest, stimulate or entertain others |
| **portfolio** | a collection of work gathered over a period of time |
| **prefix** | an addition at the beginning of a word, which changes its meaning, e.g. *dis*appear |
| **procedural writing** | a factual genre which describes how to do something |
| **process approach** | a way of organising the teaching of writing so that children are introduced to and use all the stages involved in producing a piece of written text |
| **purpose** | the author's reason for undertaking a piece of writing |
| **recount** | a factual genre which retells events |
| **recurring principle** | understanding that writing contains repeated shapes |
| **register** | the vocabulary and grammar appropriate to a particular genre |
| **report** | a factual genre which describes an object |
| **review** | the act of reflecting on what has been written, often resulting in changes to aspects of composition and transcription |
| **rime** | the end unit of a word, e.g. b*oy*, sw*ing* |
| **root** | the simplest form of a word |
| **scribing** | the process whereby a more experienced writer transcribes the composition dictated by a less competent writer |
| **sentence** | a unit of language containing at least a subject and a verb, which makes sense on its own |
| **setting** | the context in which a narrative is located |
| **short-term plan** | usually a weekly list of learning objectives and activities |
| **sign concept** | understanding that writing is a symbol system which can be used to represent meaning |
| **simple sentence** | a complete unit of meaning including a subject and verb and usually an object |

## Glossary

| | |
|---|---|
| **standard English** | a dialect of English commonly used in formal communications |
| **suffix** | an addition at the end of a word which changes its meaning, e.g. paint*er* |
| **summative assessment** | a summary of what a child can do, knows and understands that is usually made at a transition point such as entry to school, change of class and at the end of a key stage |
| **transactional writing** | writing used to convey or record facts |
| **transcription** | the secretarial aspects of writing, including spelling, handwriting and punctuation, which are used to record what is composed |
| **value added** | a measure of progress made by children over time that can be attributed to the school |

# Bibliography

## ACADEMIC TEXTS

Adams, M. J. (1990) *Beginning to Read: Thinking and Learning about Print*, MIT Press, Cambridge, Massachusetts

Applebee, A. (1978) *The Child's Concept of Story: Ages 2 to 7*, University of Chicago Press, Chicago

Beard, R. (1984) *Children's Writing in the Primary School*, Hodder and Stoughton, Sevenoaks

Bearne, E. (1998) *Making Progress in English*, Routledge, London

Bereiter, C. and Scardamalia, M. (1985) 'Children's difficulties in learning to compose', in G. Wells and J. Nicholls, *Language and Learning: An Interactional Perspective*, Falmer Press, Lewes

Bissex, G. (1980) *GNXS at Work: A Child Learns to Read and Write*, Harvard University Press, Cambridge, Massachusetts

Britton, J. (1972) *Language and Learning*, Penguin, Harmondsworth

Britton, J., Burgess, T., Martin, N., McLeod, A. and Rosen, H. (1975) *The Development of Writing Abilities (11–18)*, Macmillan, London

Brown, R. (1968) Introduction, in J. Moffett, *Teaching the Universe of Discourse*, Houghton Mifflin, Boston, Massachusetts

Bunting, R. (1997) *Teaching about Language in the Primary Years*, David Fulton Publishers, London

Buxton, C. (ed.) (no date) *Language Activities for Bi-lingual Learners*, Language Support Services, London Borough of Tower Hamlets

Cairney, T. H. (1995) *Pathways to Literacy*, Cassell, London

Calkins, L. (1986) *The Art of Teaching Writing*, Heinemann Educational Books, Portsmouth, New Hampshire

Campbell, R. (1996) *Literacy in Nursery Education*, Trentham Books, Stoke-on-Trent

Cazdan, C. B., Cordeiro, P. and Giacobbe, M. E. (1985) 'Young children's learning of punctuation', in G. Wells and J. Nicholls (eds) *Language and Learning; An Interactional Perspective*, Falmer Press, London

Clay, M. (1975) *What Did I Write?*, Heinemann, Auckland

Clegg, A. (ed.) (1964) *The Excitement of Writing*, Chatto and Windus, London

CLPE (1990) *Shared Reading Shared Writing*, Centre for Language in Primary Education, London

Cowie, H. (ed.) (1984) *The Development of Children's Imaginative Writing*, Croom Helm, London

Cox, B. (1991) *Cox on Cox: An English Curriculum for the 1990s*, Hodder and Stoughton, London

Czerniewska, P. (1992) *Learning about Writing*, Blackwell, Oxford.

Dawes, L. (1995) *Writing: The Drafting Process*, National Association for the Teaching of English, Sheffield

DES (1975) *A Language for Life* (The Bullock Report), HMSO, London

DES (1988) *Report of the Inquiry into the Teaching of the English Language* (The Kingman Report), HMSO, London

DES (1990) *English in the National Curriculum* (No. 2), HMSO, London

DfE (1995) *Key Stages 1 and 2 of the National Curriculum*, HMSO, London

DfEE (1997) *Teaching: High Status, High Standards. Requirements for Courses of Initial Teacher Training* (Circular 10/97), DfEE, London

DfEE (1998) *The National Literacy Strategy Framework for Teaching*, HMSO, London

Dombey, H., Mustafa, M. and the CLPE (1998) *Whole to Part Phonics*, Centre for Language in Primary Education, London

# Bibliography

Dyson, A. H. (1983) 'The role of oral language in early writing processes', *Research in the Teaching of English*, 17 (1), 1–29

Ferreiro, E. and Teberosky, A. (1983) *Literacy before Schooling*, Heinemann Educational, Portsmouth, New Hampshire

Godwin, D. and Perkins, M. (1998) *Teaching Language and Literacy in the Early Years*, David Fulton Publishers, London

Goodman, Y. (1990) 'The development of initial literacy', in R. Carter (ed.) *Knowledge about Language and the Curriculum: The LINC Reader*, Hodder and Stoughton, London

Gorman, T., White, J., Brooks, G. and English, F. (1989) *Language for Learning: A Summary Report on the 1988 APU Surveys of Language Performance*, HMSO, London

Goswami, U. C. and Bryant, P. (1990) *Phonological Skills and Learning to Read*, Lawrence Erlbaum Associates, Hove

Graves, D. H. (1983) *Writing: Teachers and Children at Work*, Heinemann Educational Books, Portsmouth, New Hampshire

Hall, N. (1987) *The Emergence of Literacy*, Hodder and Stoughton, London

Hall, N. and Robinson, A. (1995) *Exploring Play and Writing in the Early Years*, David Fulton Publishers, London

Hall, N. and Robinson, A. (eds) (1996) *Learning about Punctuation*, Multilingual Matters, Clevedon

Hills, T. (1986) *Classroom Motivation: Helping Students Want to Learn and Achieve in School*, New Jersey Department of Education

HMI (1993) *First Class: The Standards and Quality of Education in Reception Classes*, HMSO, London

HMI (1996) *The Teaching of Reading in 45 Inner London Primary Schools*, OFSTED Publications, London

Inner London Education Authority (1990) *Language and Power*, Harcourt Brace Jovanovitch, London

Jarman, C. (1993) *The Development of Handwriting Skills*, Simon and Schuster Education, Hemel Hempstead

Kinneavy, J. (1971) *A Theory of Discourse*, Prentice Hall, Englewood Cliffs, New Jersey

Kress, G. (1994) *Learning to Write* (2nd edition), Routledge, London

Kress, G. (1997) *Before Writing*, Routledge, London

Lally, M. (1991) *The Nursery Teacher in Action*, Paul Chapman Publishing, London

Literacy Task Force (1997) *The Implementation of the National Literacy Strategy*, DfEE, London

Littlefair, A. B. (1992) *Genres in the Classroom*, United Kingdom Reading Association, Widnes

Littlefair, A. (1993) 'The "good book": non-narrative aspects', in R. Beard (ed.) *Teaching Literacy: Balancing Perspectives*, Hodder and Stoughton, London

Martin, J. (1989) *Factual Writing: Exploring and Challenging Social Reality*, Oxford University Press, Oxford

Martin, J. R. and Rothery, J. (1986) *Writing Report Project: Working Papers in Linguistics No. 4*, Linguistics Department, University of Sydney, New South Wales

Martin, T., Waters, M. and Bloom, W. (1989) *Managing Writing: Practical Issues in the Classroom*, Mary Glasgow Publications, London

Medwell, J., Wray, D., Poulson, L. and Fox, R. (1998) *Effective Teachers of Literacy*, School of Education, University of Exeter

Meek, M. (1988) *How Texts Teach What Readers Learn*, Thimble Press, London

Minns, H. (1991) *Primary Language: Extending the Curriculum with Computers*, National Council for Educational Technology, Coventry

Moseley, D. V. (1990) 'Suggestions for helping children with spelling problems', in P. D. Pumphrey and C. D. Elliott (eds) *Children's Difficulties in Reading, Spelling and Writing*, Falmer Press, London

Moyles, J. (ed.) (1994) *The Excellence of Play*, Open University Press, Buckingham

Mudd, N. (1994) *Effective Spelling: A Practical Guide for Teachers*, Hodder and Stoughton, London

National Writing Project (1989) *Responding to and Assessing Writing*, Thomas Nelson, Walton-on-Thames

National Writing Project (1990) *Perceptions of Writing*, Thomas Nelson, Walton-on-Thames

NCC (1993) *National Curriculum Council Consultation Report: English in the National Curriculum*, NCC, York

Newman, J. (1984) *The Craft of Children's Writing*, Scholastic, Ontario

NLP (1996) *The National Literacy Project Framework for Teaching* (unpublished draft document), National Project for Literacy and Numeracy, Reading

Palmer, S. (1991) *Spelling: A Teacher's Survival Kit*, Oliver and Boyd, Harlow

Perera, K. (1987) *Understanding Language*, National Association of Advisers in English, University of Manchester

Peters, M. L. (1985) *Spelling: Caught or Taught?*, Routledge, London

Peters, M. L. and Cripps, C. (1980) *Catchwords: Ideas for Teaching Spelling*, Harcourt Brace Jovanovich, London

Potter, F. and Sands, H. (1988) 'Writing and the new technologies in developing children's writing', in D. Wray (ed.) *Bright Ideas Teacher Handbook*, Scholastic, Leamington Spa

Protherough, R. (1983) *Developing Response to Fiction*, Open University Press, Milton Keynes

QCA (1998) *Can Do Better*, Qualifications and Curriculum Authority, London

QCA (1999) *The Review of the Desirable Outcomes*, Qualifications and Curriculum Authority, London

Read, C. (1986) *Children's Creative Spelling*, Routledge and Kegan Paul, London

Redfern, A. (1993) *Practical Ways to Teach Spelling*, Reading and Language Information Centre, University of Reading.

Sainsbury, M. (1996) *Tracking Significant Achievement in Primary English*, Hodder and Stoughton, London

Sassoon, R. (1990) *Handwriting: The Way to Teach It*, Stanley Thornes, Cheltenham

Sassoon, R. (1993) 'Handwriting', in R. Beard (ed.) *Teaching Literacy: Balancing Perspectives*, Hodder and Stoughton, London

Sassoon, R. (1995) *The Practical Guide to Children's Handwriting* (2nd edition), Hodder and Stoughton, London

SCAA (1995a) *Consistency in Teacher Assessment: Exemplification of Standards*, SCAA Publications, London

SCAA (1995b) *Information Technology: The New Requirements*, SCAA, London

SCAA (1995c) *Planning the Curriculum at Key Stages 1 and 2*, HMSO, London

SCAA (1996) *Desirable Outcomes for Children's Learning*, HMSO, London

SCAA (1997a) *Baseline Assessment*, SCAA Publications, Middlesex

SCAA (1997b) *Baseline Assessment Scales*, SCAA Publications, Middlesex

SCAA (1997c) *Looking at Children's Learning*, SCAA Publications, Middlesex

SCAA (1997d) *Use of Language: A Common Approach*, SCAA Publications, Middlesex

Sealey, A. (1996) *Learning about Language*, Open University Press, Buckingham

Smith, B. (1994) *Through Writing to Reading*, Routledge, London

Smith, F. (1982) *Writing and the Writer*, Heinemann Educational, London

Smith, J. and Elley, W. (1998) *How Children Learn to Write*, Paul Chapman Publishing, London

Stauffer, R. G. (1980) *The Language-Experience Approach to the Teaching of Reading* (2nd edition), Harper and Row, London

Sylva, K. (1997) 'The early years curriculum: evidence based proposals', in SCAA, *Developing the Primary School Curriculum*, SCAA, London

Tann, S. (1991) *Developing Language in the Primary Classroom*, Cassell, London

Temple, C., Nathan, R., Burris, N. and Temple, F. (1993) *The Beginnings of Writing* (3rd edition), Allyn and Bacon, London

Weinberger, J. (1996) *Literacy Goes to School*, Paul Chapman Publishing, London

Wells, G. (1986) *The Meaning Makers*, Heinemann Educational, Portsmouth, New Hampshire

Whitehead, M. (1990) *Language and Literacy in the Early Years*, Paul Chapman Publishing, London

Whitehead, M. (1996) *The Development of Language and Literacy*, Hodder and Stoughton, London

Wing Jan, Lesley (1991) *Write Ways: Modelling Writing Forms*, Oxford University Press, Australia

Wray, D. (1994) *Literacy and Awareness*, Hodder and Stoughton, London

Wray, D. and Lewis, M. (1995) *Developing Children's Non-Fiction Writing*, Scholastic, Leamington Spa

Wyse, D. (1998) *Primary Writing*, Open University Press, Buckingham

## LITERARY TEXTS

Agard, J. and Nicholls, G. (1991) *No Hickory No Dickory No Dock*, Viking, London

Ahlberg, A. (1981) *Mrs Lather's Laundry*, Penguin, Harmondsworth

Ahlberg, J. and A. (1980) *Funnybones*, Heinemann, London

Ahlberg, J. and A. (1985) *The Baby's Catalogue*, Picture Puffin, Harmondsworth

Ahlberg, J. and A. (1986) *The Jolly Postman*, Heinemann, London

Ahlberg, J. and A. (1991) *The Jolly Christmas Postman*, Heinemann, London

Alborough, J. (1994) *It's the Bear*, Walker, London

Armitage, R. and D. (1977) *The Lighthousekeeper's Lunch*, Deutsch, London

Blake, Q. (1968) *Patrick*, Jonathan Cape, London

Bradman, T. (1986) *Through My Window*, Mammoth, London

Bradman, T. (1988) *Wait and See*, Mammoth, London

Browne, A. (1991) *I Like Books*, Walker, London

Burningham, J. (1970) *Mr Gumpy's Outing*, Puffin Books, Harmondsworth

Burningham, J. (1980) *The Shopping Basket*, Jonathan Cape, London

Butterworth, N. and Inkpen, M. (1992) *Jaspar's Beanstalk*, Hodder and Stoughton, London

Carle, E. (1969) *The Very Hungry Caterpillar*, Hamish Hamilton, London

Cole, B. (1986) *Princess Smartypants*, Hamish Hamilton, London

Cowley, J. (1988) *Birthdays*, Heinemannn Educational Books, Oxford

Dale, P. (1987) *Bet You Can't!*, Walker, London

Dupiasquier, P. (1986) *Dear Daddy*, Picture Puffin, Harmondsworth

Hawkins, C. J. (1983) *What's the Time Mr Wolf?*, Heinemann, London

Hill, E. (1980) *Where's Spot?*, Puffin Books, Harmondsworth

Hoffman, M (1991) *Amazing Grace*, Frances Lincoln, London

Hutchins, P. (1974) *Titch*, Puffin Books, Harmondsworth

Hutchins, P. (1976) *Don't Forget the Bacon!*, Bodley Head, London

McGough, R. (1996) *The Magic Fountain*, Red Fox, London

Sciesza, J. (1989) *The True Story of the Three Little Pigs*, Viking Kestral, London

Seuss, Dr (1960) *Green Eggs and Ham*, Collins, Glasgow

Snow, A. (1996) *The Truth about Cats*, Picture Lions, London

Thompson, P. (1993) *Messages*, Harper Collins, London

# Index